Sent Forth

American Society of Missiology Series, No. 51

Sent Forth
African Missionary Work in the West

Harvey C. Kwiyani

ORBIS BOOKS
Maryknoll, New York 10545

ORBIS BOOKS
Maryknoll, New York 10545

Founded in 1970, Orbis Books endeavors to publish works that enlighten the mind, nourish the spirit, and challenge the conscience. The publishing arm of the Maryknoll Fathers and Brothers, Orbis seeks to explore the global dimensions of the Christian faith and mission, to invite dialogue with diverse cultures and religious traditions, and to serve the cause of reconciliation and peace. The books published reflect the views of their authors and do not represent the official position of the Maryknoll Society. To learn more about Maryknoll and Orbis Books, please visit our website at www.maryknollsociety.org.

Copyright © 2014 by Harvey C. Kwiyani

Published by Orbis Books, Box 302, Maryknoll, NY 10545-0302.

Manufactured in the United States of America

Library of Congress Cataloging-in-Publication Data

Kwiyani, Harvey C.
  Sent forth : African missionary work in the west / by Harvey C. Kwiyani.
    pages cm. — (American Society of Missiology series; No. 51)
  Includes bibliographical references and index.
  ISBN 978-1-62698-101-0 (pbk.)
    1. Missionaries—Africa. 2. Christianity—Africa. 3. Missions—Africa.
I. Title.
BV2063.K95 2014
266'.0236—dc23

Contents

Preface to the American Society of Missiology Series

The purpose of the ASM (American Society of Missiology) Series is to publish—without regard for disciplinary, national, or denominational boundaries—scholarly works of high quality and wide interest on missiological themes from the entire spectrum of scholarly pursuits relevant to Christian mission, which is always the focus of books in the Series.

By *mission* is meant the effort to effect passage over the boundary between faith in Jesus Christ and its absence. In this understanding of mission, the basic functions of Christian proclamation, dialogue, witness, service, worship, liberation, and nurture are of special concern. And in that context questions arise, including, How does the transition from one cultural context to another influence the shape and interaction between these dynamic functions, especially in regard to the cultural and religious plurality that constitute the global context of Christian life and mission?

The promotion of scholarly dialogue among missiologists, and among missiologists and scholars in other fields of inquiry, may involve the publication of views that some missiologists cannot accept, and with which members of the Editorial Committee themselves do not agree. Manuscripts published in the Series, accordingly, reflect the opinions of their authors and are not understood to represent the position of the American Society of Missiology or of the Editorial Committee. Selection is guided by such criteria as intrinsic worth, readability, coherence, and accessibility to a range of interested persons and not merely to experts or specialists.

The ASM Series, in collaboration with Orbis Books, seeks to publish scholarly works of high merit and wide interest on numerous aspects of missiology—the scholarly study of mission. Able presentations on new and creative approaches to the practice and understanding of mission will receive close attention.

The ASM Series Committee
JONATHAN J. BONK
WILLIAM R. BURROWS
SCOTT W. SUNQUIST

Acknowledgments

It has taken a large village to bring this book to print. I will mention here just a few of the names, even though I am sure that I may have forgotten some of the most important contributors. Although the honor of bringing together the material that I have discussed in this book must be shared by many, I assume total responsibility for the shortcomings.

First, I am deeply grateful to my wife, Nancy. I have been so blessed to have her with me during the entire writing process. Her unwavering support made the writing of this book much easier. The support that we received from our families in Malawi, especially from my sisters-in-law, Bettie Nyirenda, Mary Ching'oma, and Martha Mkandawire, will forever be appreciated.

I am forever indebted to Jack and Ann Fecht of Mendota Heights, Minnesota, for providing me with writing space in their home. In addition to the many conversations that helped me understand a great deal about American life, I will never forget the good food that Ann made for us all. I wish also to thank the Hosanna Lutheran Church family in Forest Lake, Minnesota, for opening their hearts and their doors to Nancy and me when I needed to finish this book. The caring hospitality extended to us by Tim Hackbarth, Salim Kaderbhai, and Wendy Hazzard was beyond anything we could ever dream of. The entire Hosanna family showed us what it means to be a part of the global loving Body of Christ. A special thank-you to Jon and Kathryn Nordstrom for making us feel at home in their house, and also helping with earlier edits on the manuscript. Nancy and I are privileged to have them as our American parents. They carried all our burdens on our behalf. We did not have to be anxious about anything.

I am also deeply grateful to Charity Erickson for taking time to proofread my manuscript.

This book crowns many years of hard work, both in the mission field and in theological scholarship. Throughout, I have been privileged to have many mentors; Drs. Andrew and Queen Dube, Dr. Chris and Chipi Daza, Drs. Harvey and Gertrude Sindima, Dr. Martin and Linda Robinson, and Drs. Patrick and Jeanette Keifert, just to mention a few. Both my parents and parents-in-law deserve to be in this list too: Revs. Jonathan and Hilda Kwiyani, and Obed and Joyce Ching'oma. Many years of ministry, study, and reflection with all these great leaders, ministers, and scholars have given me the confidence to have a voice with which I speak in this book—as an African in the West—in a globalized world. A million thanks to each of them.

Introduction

I wrote this book while living and working in Saint Paul, Minnesota, a place that I have called home for the past six years. I came to Minnesota after an exciting seven-year journey working in Christian missions in Germany, Switzerland, Austria, and England. However, my life journey started long ago in Malawi, Central Africa, where I was born in a small town called Namadzi, just two miles north of the once-famous village of Magomero. Yes, this is the Magomero that is permanently engraved in Malawian history as the place of the first Christian missionary work in the country, and possibly in the entire region of Central Africa, the place where the renowned Scottish missionary-explorer David Livingstone brought Bishop Charles McKenzie and the first Universities' Mission to Central Africa (UMCA) missionaries to Africa in 1861.[1] From Magomero, my life has taken me to several Western countries where I have worked with missionary organizations and church bodies around issues of missions in the West, usually speaking and teaching on the rise of the non-Western missionary movement. In particular, I have focused on the African missionary movement, where descendants of the Africans who were converted by the nineteenth- and twentieth-century missionaries are now taking the gospel back to Europe and North America to convert those missionaries' descendants.

My father was born at Magomero, where his family still resides today. He has called it home all his life, and his family has been in the Magomero area for several generations. Naturally,

---

[1] For the history of the village, see Landeg White, *Magomero: Portrait of an African Village* (New York: Cambridge University Press, 1987).

then, his family takes great pride in their geographical connection to the work of the first missionaries in Malawi and the subsequent rise of Christianity in the country. I am lucky to have been born into such a history.

I became aware of the significance of the village at a very young age, and growing up in this historically important place kept me curious about the mission of God and the role of the missionary in the spread of Christianity. More than anything else, this Magomero historical heritage has influenced my life. Incidentally, the UMCA missionaries stayed at Magomero for only two years. Malaria was a huge problem that continually threatened their lives and livelihood and killed Charles McKenzie within months of his arrival. In addition, since Magomero was located on a slave-trade route, the mission station suffered constant disruptions from slave raids. The missionaries were not happy with their progress. In 1863, they moved to Zanzibar. The Anglican missionaries under the UMCA came back to Malawi in the 1870s, when several other European missionary groups also came to Malawi.[2]

After the UMCA moved to Zanzibar in 1863, Magomero became a piece of colonial property that belonged to the Livingstone family. As a young boy, I was always curious about the two graves that lay just outside the village soccer field, marked "William Jervis Livingstone" and "Duncan McCormick" (buried in 1915). I later learned that by 1891, when Nyasaland (the older name for Malawi) was declared a British Protectorate, the Livingstone family had acquired hundreds of acres around the Magomero Mission area, and efforts were under way to establish a coffee estate. Following Livingstone's wishes, the Free Church of Scotland's Livingstonia Mission had set up the Livingstonia Central Africa Company (1877), which later became the African Lakes Company (1878), and finally the African Lakes Corpora-

---

[2] For a detailed history of the work of the UMCA in Malawi, see James Tengatenga, *The UMCA in Malawi: A History of the Anglican Church, 1861–2010* (Zomba, Malawi: Kachere Series, 2010). See also George Herbert Wilson, *The History of the Universities' Mission to Central Africa* (Freeport, NY: Books for Libraries Press, 1971).

tion in 1894.[3] Its purpose was to encourage trade in Africa as an alternative to slave trade, but it also intended to hold property in Africa whose commercial proceeds would be used to support missionaries. It had always been Livingstone's desire for Britain to colonize Central Africa. Mission, in his opinion, had to go hand in hand with the colonization of Africa. He had said, "It is the mission of England to colonize and to plant her Christianity with her sons on the broad earth which the Lord has given to the children of men."[4] Later, Livingstone would write to a friend:

> I am becoming everyday more convinced that we must have an English colony in the cotton-producing districts of Africa. . . . Colonization from a country such as ours ought to be one of hope, and not despair . . . the performance of an imperative duty to our blood, our country, our religion, and to humankind.[5]

So by 1900 Livingstone's son-in-law Alexander Low Bruce had acquired thousands of acres around Magomero and Likulezi.[6] In 1912, Alexander Low Bruce's son, Alexander Livingstone Bruce, was managing the estate at Likulezi while his nephew William Jervis Livingstone was running the coffee estate at Magomero— a coffee estate that is still notorious for its brutal treatment of the local Africans. William J. Livingstone was brutal in his lordship over the Africans, often involving physically beating his local employees who were also his tenants. He banned schools at the estate and burned down two churches built by the Malawians in

---

3 This too is a piece of history that is not too closely connected to the immediate interests of this book; as such, I will only refer the readers to the original work of James Jack and Robert Laws, *Daybreak in Livingstonia: The Story of the Livingstonia-Mission, British Central Africa* (New York: Negro Universities Press, 1969), 24–27. Also William P. Livingstone, *The Life of Robert Laws of Livingstonia: A Narrative of Missionary Adventure and Achievement* (New York: George H. Doran, 1923), 352–53.

4 Oliver Ransford, *David Livingstone: The Dark Interior* (London: J. Murray, 1978), 159.

5 Ibid., 160.

6 White, *Portrait*, 78.

the area. Consequently, a local uprising against the three-pronged
evils of colonialism, forced free labor, and the involvement of
local Malawians in World War I—all of which were closely connected to Magomero—saw several white farmers including, William Livingstone and Duncan McCormick, killed in 1915.[7]

My grandparents made sure to pass on as much history as
possible. I grew up listening to stories about local missionaries
and colonial agents. The oral history that still informs most Africans taught me about the days when the missionaries who had
come from Europe and North America had gone from village to
village, preaching about a forgiving God who loved the world so
much that God's own son had to die to save the world. Often,
they would digress to tell us of the colonialists, but we were more
interested in the missionaries.

Needless to say, I grew up with a romantic image of the missionary. My high school and college days were occupied with
reading missionary biographies. Naturally, David Livingstone was
of special interest. However, I also found Adoniram Judson, James
Hudson Taylor, William Carey, and many others very exciting.
The romanticism in some of their biographies read more like
hagiographies, but I did not mind. All I knew was that these were
Western missionaries—great men and women—who had left the
comfortable life in Europe and North America to convert those
in need of the gospel around the world. The general identity of
the missionary in the biographies that I read was that of a nineteenth-century Western college/seminary-educated male. Female
missionary biographies were rare. Whenever women were mentioned in general missionary biographies, they were usually in the
shadows of a male missionary whose ministries they were helping. I have now realized that the world has changed greatly, such
that when the future generation reads missionary biographies, a
possible majority of them will be about Latin American, African, and Asian missionaries. In addition, a rising number of these
non-Western missionaries are serving in the West—lands that sent
missionaries to the rest of the world only one hundred years ago.
Missionaries in our generation will be men and women from all
parts of the world serving in any other part of the same.

[7] Ibid.

A New Missional Era

Strictly speaking, mission in this twenty-first century will be totally different from what it has been in the past two centuries. I say this for three reasons. First, Christianity is now a worldwide religion that reaches all corners of the world. It is no longer a "white man's religion," as it had been for the larger part of the past millennium. Now Christians come from various people groups and countries around the world, as will twenty-first-century missionaries.

Second, the great migration of Westerners that spread Europeans and North Americans—and Christianity—to the rest of the world in the nineteenth century has come to an end. Now, the postimperial world in which we live sees migrations of all peoples moving in many directions. Many are moving from the rest of the world to the West. Travel technologies, migration policies, and several other factors make this possible. Global economic realities in the twenty-first century will force some Western countries to import foreign labor just to keep their economies going. As Samuel Huntington has suggested in *The Clash of Civilizations*, the supposed dominance of the West over the rest of the world has waned with the rise of non-Western civilizations.[8] Western imperialism is quickly becoming a thing of the past, at least politically speaking, as non-Western civilizations rise.

Third, Western Christianity has been on the decline for several decades now. As a result of this decline, some Western denominations are struggling to recruit their own ministers, and they are finding it even harder to recruit missionaries that can make the sacrifices involved in serving overseas. The Roman Catholic Church in the United States, for instance, must now import priests from other countries to meet the demand for priests in its parishes. Non-Western Christians, to the contrary, are willing and able to serve as missionaries anywhere in the world, including the West. Since the rise of non-Western Christianity has coincided with the global rise of Pentecostalism—a branch of Christianity that still stands at the margins of Western Christianity—a greater

---

[8] Samuel P. Huntington, *The Clash of Civilizations and the Remaking of World Order* (New York: Touchstone, 1997), 90–91.

percentage of non-Western missionaries are influenced by the movement, which is usually characterized by its emphasis on mission. The twenty-first-century missionary movement may, therefore, involve more non-Western than Western Christians. Having many non-Western Christians on the mission field will create a very new identity for both mission and the missionary. The typical identity of a missionary in this century will no longer be that of a Westerner serving in some remote areas of Africa, but probably that of a Mexican, a Nigerian, or perhaps a Korean serving practically anywhere in the world.

I agree with Darrell Guder that despite all the controversy and debate around the impact of the great missionary movement, it has been a truly successful enterprise.[9] This great Western missionary movement that transformed Christianity into a worldwide religion took place roughly between 1800 and 1950, reaching its climax somewhere between 1900 and 1910—only a few years into the European colonization of Africa and right before the start of the First World War. At first, colonialism seemed to help the cause of mission. The spread of Christianity had to work hand in hand with the spread of civilization. However, it eventually became the very force that brought the Western missionary movement to an end. Political decolonization would not be complete without religious decolonization.

At the peak of the Western missionary movement, in the first decade of the twentieth century—a period characterized by the energetic buildup to the Edinburgh World Missionary Conference of 1910—mission was a white man's territory. Case in point, the delegates at this great missionary conference in Edinburgh—1,215 of them in total—were overwhelmingly white, male, and Western: to be precise, 1,009 men and 207 women.[10] Only 18 non-Westerners (all male) came from what were termed the "younger churches" in the mission lands: 8 Indians, 4 Japa-

---

[9] Darrell Guder, *Missional Church: A Vision for the Sending of the Church in North America*, The Gospel and Our Culture Series (Grand Rapids, MI: Eerdmans, 1998), 1.

[10] Brian Stanley, *The World Missionary Conference, Edinburgh 1910* (Grand Rapids, MI: Eerdmans, 2009), 73.

nese, 3 Chinese, 1 Korean, 1 Burmese, and 1 Turk.[11] These 18
non-Western Christians did not attend as delegates of their own
churches, but only as guests of Western missionary societies or the
organizing committee. Apart from these 18, nearly everyone else
came from Europe and North America: 510 British, 490 North
American, 171 from continental Europe, and 28 from the British
colonies of South Africa, Australia, and New Zealand. Africans
were not represented at all, except by expatriate missionaries and
8 white South Africans.[12] Not even one Christian from black
Africa was present.[13] No indigenous black African was apparently
deemed worthy of an invitation to Edinburgh, as Brian Stanley
sadly notes:

> If African churches were deemed to be insufficiently
> "advanced" to merit their own representatives, it was not
> simply because these churches were young in years, but
> also because their members were thought to be starting
> from much further back in the process of human develop-
> ment than were Christian converts in Asia. *The inhabitants
> of Africa were still in 1910 regarded as primitive, childlike, and
> at the bottom of the evolutionary hierarchy, relatively unimportant
> for the future of the world church.*[14]

Thus, the World Missionary Conference of 1910 was essentially
a Western affair. South America—being a Roman Catholic territory—was not represented, and not even discussed.[15] English
was the means of communication. The conference motto, "To

---

[11] Ibid., 92.
[12] Ibid., 97. However, Stanley mentions one Mark Christian Hayford
as the only African Christian in attendance at the conference. One wonders how Hayford's name has so far gone unnoticed, with Stanley himself
admitting that he only became aware of Hayford in the final stages of the
preparation of his book.
[13] Lamin O. Sanneh, *Disciples of All Nations: Pillars of World Christianity*,
Oxford Studies in World Christianity (New York: Oxford University Press,
2008), 272.
[14] Stanley, *World Missionary Conference*, 99 (emphasis mine).
[15] Ibid., 66.

Evangelize the World in Our Generation," seemed very achievable in their eyes.[16] Only four years after 1910, the First World War, which essentially began as a European war, dashed all their hopes of evangelizing the world in their generation. Missionaries who had worked together in the mission field were interning one another as enemies—a piece of mission history with lasting ramifications, for instance, by shaping the Lutheran relations in East Africa in ways that still affect the church there today.[17]

Aside from gender, as there were more female missionaries in the mission field than male, the makeup of the 1910 Edinburgh Conference fairly represented Christianity and missions of the time. Missionaries came from the West, especially from the Anglo-Saxon world, and were sent out from the evangelized and developed countries in Europe and North America to evangelize the masses in what they deemed the *Dark Continent* of Africa and the rest of the world.[18] There was an unstated belief that the prosperity of Western civilization had been achieved because of the gospel, which when shared with the needy uncivilized heathens abroad would also bring similar prosperity.[19] Until then, Christianity could easily pass for a Western religion that spread from Rome into Western Europe, as far north as the Scandinavian countries, and west to Ireland and, later, North America.[20]

---

[16] See John R. Mott, *The Evangelization of the World in This Generation* (New York: Student Volunteer Movement for Foreign Missions, 1900), 2. The confidence behind such a declaration led to the establishing of a magazine by the name "Christian Century" in 1902, which enjoys great circulation, even now, after over a hundred years since its inception.

[17] Bengt Sundkler and Christopher Steed, *A History of the Church in Africa*, Studia Missionalia Upsaliensia 74 (New York: Cambridge University Press, 2000), 618.

[18] A title made popular by Henry Morton Stanley in his Henry M. Stanley, *Through the Dark Continent; or, The Sources of the Nile around the Great Lakes of Equatorial Africa, and Down the Livingstone River to the Atlantic Ocean*, 2 vols. (New York: Harper, 1878).

[19] See David J. Bosch, *Transforming Mission: Paradigm Shifts in Theology of Mission*, American Society of Missiology Series (Maryknoll, NY: Orbis Books, 1991), 292–313.

[20] Of course, any balanced history of Christianity mentions that Christianity spread in all direction from Jerusalem, and therefore, from its early

Today a World Missionary Conference like that of Edinburgh 1910 would have probably as many Latin Americans, Africans, and Asians as it would have Westerners. Both Edinburgh 2010 and Cape Town 2010 brought together thousands of Christian and missionary leaders from all over the world, and in both cases, more non-Westerners than Westerners attended.[21] The world of missions is no longer dominated by the Western world, just as Christianity is no longer predominantly a Western religion. In the second half of the twentieth century, the world witnessed a significant shift in Christianity's center of gravity from Europe to Africa. Eighty percent of the world's Christians lived in the western quadrant of the northern hemisphere in 1950; that number has gone down to less than 40 percent now.[22] Over 60 percent of global Christians now live in the three non-Western quadrants of the world.[23] The twentieth century has seen the spread of Christianity at a rate that was not imaginable even at the beginning of the century—and its explosion has occurred after the great Western missionary movement came to an end.

Implications for Mission

The twentieth century has seen Christianity spread into every country in the world. Lamin Sanneh has called Christianity the world's most diverse and pluralistic religion.[24] It is the only religion that is accessible in almost every major language on earth. The implications of this worldwide spread of Christianity on Christianity itself and on the world as a whole will be manifest.

days, Christianity was never an exclusively Western religion.

[21] For Edinburgh 2010, see Daryl M. Balia and Kirsteen Kim, *Edinburgh 2010: Witnessing to Christ Today* (Eugene, OR: Wipf & Stock, 2010). Cape Town 2010 was the Third Lausanne Conference on World Evangelism, and it took place in Cape Town, South Africa, from October 16 to 25, 2010. See http://www.lausanne.org.

[22] Sanneh, *Disciples*, xx.

[23] Todd M. Johnson, Kenneth R. Ross, and Sandra S. K. Lee, *Atlas of Global Christianity, 1910–2010* (Edinburgh: Edinburgh University Press, 2009), 50–59.

[24] Sanneh, *Disciples*, xx.

We are only beginning to see a few of them emerging, and by the look of things, they may foretell the end of Christianity as we know it. The growing pains will be difficult to negotiate. The rise of world theologies will create a "clash" of Christianities—or theologies. For example, contextualized theology for Latin America, Africa, or Asia usually has generated localized theologies that are radically different from that of the West. Failure to contextualize Christianity results in situations like a Latin Mass in an awkward out-of-place Gothic building in the African desert, served by an African priest whose Africanness remains only in the color of his skin. Proper attention to contextualization, however, has produced Christianities like the African Initiated Churches and other types of independent Christian communities that interpret Christianity for the African context and are therefore able to minimize the impact of foreign culture on their Christianity. Of course, in the eyes of Western Christianity, most of these *independent* Christianities are syncretic and therefore not fully acceptable as Christianity.

In this age of globalization and migration, especially in a world where migration trends are moving people in every direction imaginable, these contextual Christianities are coming into frequent contact with one another and with Western Christianity. As we go deeper into the century, we will see these world Christianities engage one another more and more often. For the first time in several centuries, Christianity is facing a significant amount of diversity within its own base: cultural, racial, and theological. Christian leaders in this century will have to work hard to help their followers process this diversity. Before the churches can effectively engage the cultural diversity of the world in which they are located, they have to negotiate the cultural diversity within Christianity itself.

In this book, I explore one such encounter: that of African Christianity and Western Christianity *in the West*. My story constitutes only one example of what is quickly becoming the story of world Christianity. However, there are many other Africans who share my story, some glorious beyond belief. For instance, I met one Kenyan Methodist minister in London who told me, "My family was the first to be converted in the Meruland. When

I was born, my parents dedicated me to missionary service to return the kindness of the missionaries." Furthermore, in my conversations with African Christians in Germany, England, and the United States, I have heard people tell me countless times, "My great-grandfather was converted by the missionaries, and now Christianity runs in the family." I have met several German Evangelical Christians who, bursting with excitement, told me, "We gave you Africans our Reinhardt Bonnke, and you gave us your John Mulinde. What a glorious exchange!"[25] Of course, in addition to the African Christians who identify themselves as missionaries and ministers in the West, there are millions of African Christians who are living their Christianity in the West even though they have very little contact with Western Christians.

This century's missionary movement must, of necessity, reflect the worldwide nature of Christianity. An honest reflection of the contemporary missionary statistics ought also to recognize the work of Korean missionaries who have been sent around the world for the past few decades. South Korea now sends more missionaries around the world than any other country except the United States. It must also take into account the many Latinos and Latinas who have left Latin America to serve God in North America, Europe, Africa, and Asia. While this book focuses on those African Christians who are living and serving in the West, I also recognize the presence of African missionaries all over the world.

Long ago, when the Western missionary movement was just picking up in the early 1800s, missionaries looked forward to the day when Christians from the then-unevangelized lands would come to the West to reinvigorate Western Christianity. They called this "the blessed reflex." Fast-forward two hundred years, and we are witnessing the blessed reflex taking place, with many non-Western Christians now making up a significant percentage of the Christian population of the West. In this book, I have attempted

---

[25] Reinhardt Bonnke is a German evangelist who holds big crusades in Africa. John Mulinde is a Ugandan minister who runs the World Trumpet Mission in Kampala, Uganda. His ministry is well accepted among some German-speaking Christians from Germany, Switzerland, and Austria. See World Trumpet Mission, "A Brief History of World Trumpet Mission," Kampala, Uganda.

to discuss the African portion of the blessed reflex. I believe that the movement of non-Western Christians to the West is inevitable. In most cases, it is just a result of people migrating for other reasons; very few people migrate with the express intention of spreading their religion. Many of them have migrated for a better living standard, but as they migrate, they bring their faith along. This is normal for the spread of Christianity of other religions. For many various reasons, thousands of non-Westerners will keep migrating to the West for the next few decades, and they will keep on bringing their religions with them.

While arguing for the role of migration in God's mission in the world, I suggest that African missionary work in the West is not necessarily a new phenomenon. Church history gives us names of many African Christians who worked in the West in the first five hundred years of the church. However, this postcolonial African missionary movement is unique both in its context and its identity. Its general expressions and its theology are different from most of Western Christianity, and this can make it rather difficult for the two Christianities to work together. This book intends to initiate a conversation to change this—to encourage a multicultural missionary movement that will be able to proclaim the gospel in the culturally pluralistic Western context.

This book is not autobiographical in any way. It is not intended for such a purpose. However, after working with Western Christians for thirteen years (seven years in Europe and six in North America), I have been a firsthand witness to the experiences that African Christians go through when they migrate to the West. Numerous times have I been called upon to help African immigrant congregations and their leaders negotiate their culture shock. In the same way, I have worked with some Western congregations and Christian bodies to help them understand the Africans who have begun to show up in their neighborhoods and worship services. Both in Europe and North America, I have been involved in missionary work both as a practitioner and as an academic. I have had countless conversations about the multicultural missionary movement that is developing. Many of the stories that shape this book come from such conversations. I have seen the hurt, the confusion, and sometimes the indifference that characterizes the relationship between Africans and Westerners. It is my prayer that this book will help us get over these negative experiences and start down a path that leads to life-giving relationships and missional collaborations that will enable us to partner better with God in God's mission in the Western world in the twenty-first century.

Chapter One

Out of Africa
I Called My Child

There is a somewhat obscure prophecy in the Book of Hosea that says, "Out of Egypt, I called my son."[1] This prophetic word was delivered amid several other prophecies in which God reminded Israel of God's own faithfulness in caring for the wayward nation that God loved so dearly. As such, it is very likely that when Hosea made this prophecy, he was talking about how God had brought Israel out of Egypt—*in the past*.[2] It was a piece of history that had taken place hundreds of years before Hosea appeared on the scene, in the event of the Exodus, when God called God's son out of Egypt—*out of Africa*. Like many other prophecies in the Old Testament, this prophecy had the possibility of being fulfilled multiple times. Certainly, this prophecy also had some future significance, for when Matthew tells of how the baby Jesus was taken to Egypt as an infant, he tells of the fulfillment of this same prophecy.[3]

> Now after they had left, an angel appeared to Joseph in a dream and said, "Get up, take the child and his mother, and flee to Egypt, and remain there until I tell you; for Herod is about to search for the child, to destroy him." Then Joseph got up, took the child and his mother by

---

[1] Hosea 11:1, New Revised Standard Version (NRSV). All Bible verses cited in this book will come from the NRSV unless stated otherwise.

[2] Andrew Alexander Macintosh, *A Critical and Exegetical Commentary on Hosea* (Edinburgh: T&T Clark, 1997), 437.

[3] Ibid., 438.

night, and went to Egypt and remained there until the death of Herod. This was to fulfill what was spoken by the Lord through the prophet, "*Out of Egypt I have called my son.*"[4]

It is the premise of this book that this prophecy is being fulfilled yet again before our eyes. In the fourth chapter of Luke's Gospel, after Jesus stands up in the synagogue and reads the first few verses of Isaiah 61, he declares, "Today, this scripture has been fulfilled in your hearing." I believe that we can say the same of Hosea 11:1 today, at the beginning of the third millennium of the church. Out of Africa, God is calling forth God's church unto Godself for God's mission in the world.

The growth of Christianity in Africa in the twentieth century is nothing short of a miracle. Over five hundred million people have converted to Christianity in the space of one hundred years, with 80 percent of them converting after 1970.[5] Never in the history of Christianity have so many people been converted in so short a time. This conversion of Africa in the twentieth century occurs at a time when Africans—especially African Christians—are migrating to the rest of the world in large numbers. The majority of these African immigrant Christians are settling down in the West. Their presence in the West is proving to be of great missionary significance.

While the Western church has been slowly losing its stronghold, African Christians have come to strengthen it. Many have not realized this yet; as Walter Hollenweger once said, "British Christians prayed for revival, and when it came, they did not recognize it because it was black."[6] It is as if God has preserved

---

[4] Matt. 2:13–15 (emphasis mine). I return to this story later in this chapter.

[5] Todd M. Johnson, Kenneth R. Ross, and Sandra S. K. Lee, *Atlas of Global Christianity, 1910–2010* (Edinburgh: Edinburgh University Press, 2009), 110–13.

[6] Walter Hollenweger, in the foreword to Roswith I. H. Gerloff, *A Plea for British Black Theologies: The Black Church Movement in Britain in Its Transatlantic Cultural and Theological Interaction with Special References to the Pentecostal Oneness (Apostolic) and Sabbatarian Movements*, Studien zur Interkulturellen Geschichte des Christentums (Frankfurt am Main: P. Lang, 1992), ix.

God's church in Africa while it was dying out in Europe and North America, and now, God is calling the church out of Africa to reinvigorate world Christianity. Just like God hid and grew the nation of Israel from seventy people to millions in Africa, and in the same way, hid and grew God's Son in Africa, God has hidden and made to grow the seed of Christianity in Africa, only to call it out for such a time as this. The blessed reflex—whereby the missionaries of old hoped that Christians from the then-unevangelized lands would come to reinvigorate Western Christianity—is here.[7] Missionaries from around the world are proclaiming the gospel in cities that once sent missionaries to Latin America, Africa, and Asia.

Indeed, in the colonial era, Africa was called the Dark Continent. The colonizers called it dark because they believed the Africans to be backward in terms of civilization. Although I do not agree with this notion—knowing for sure that Africans are not backward at all—I have been wondering if God could actually have hidden the seeds of Christianity in the dark to bring them out when needed in what are now being called the spiritually dark continents of Europe and North America.[8] Where else would one hide valuables, if not in the dark? Africa was called dark because most of the continent was practically inaccessible to Westerners until the mid-nineteenth century when explorers were able to penetrate the continent, discovering the correct source of the Nile, the other great rivers of Africa, its beautiful landscape, and massive forests. The explorers opened the way for the missionaries, and sometimes the missionaries made way for the explorers. They spread the gospel and introduced a Western kind of commerce. Today, the continent that was called dark is basking in the light of the gospel and sending its sons and daughters as missionaries to Europe and North America.[9]

---

[7] Kenneth R. Ross, "'Blessed Reflex': Mission as God's Spiral of Renewal," *International Bulletin of Missionary Research* 27, no. 4 (2003).

[8] For instance, see Israel O. Olofinjana, *Reverse in Ministry and Missions: Africans in the Dark Continent of Europe* (Milton Keynes, UK: Author House, 2010). He is a Nigerian minister working in Britain, and he actually calls Europe "the Dark Continent" in the title of his book.

[9] See Andrew F. Walls, "Towards a Theology of Mission," in *African Christian Presence in the West: New Immigrant Congregations and Transnational*

Converting a Continent
to Convert the World

The explosive growth of Christianity in Africa since the 1970s has begun to have a great impact on world Christianity in many ways, even though only a few have noticed. African Christians, with their African expression of Christianity, are now active on every continent. African immigrant congregations that started appearing in the West in the 1970s have in the past twenty years multiplied greatly in number all across the Americas, Europe, and Asia. The two largest churches in Europe at the moment of this writing are African-led. The largest is the Blessed Embassy of the Kingdom of God, located in Kiev, Ukraine. It is led by a Nigerian pastor, Sunday Adelaja. It has 30,000 members, most of whom are actually European. The second largest is the Kingsway International Christian Centre, located in London. It is led by another Nigerian, Matthew Ashimolowo. It is almost entirely African in its 12,000-member base. And of course, the Church of England has Bishop John Sentamu from Uganda as the archbishop of York.

Hundreds of other African immigrant congregations can be found in Germany, Canada, the United States, and elsewhere. Even some strictly African expressions of Christianity, like the so-called African Initiated Churches, are flourishing in Western cities. The *amaZioni* of Southern Africa and *Kimbanguists* of Congo have churches in cities such as New York, Toronto, and Brussels.[10]

Christianity is growing in other parts of the world too—for instance, South America and Asia—and Christians from these continents have also found their way around the world. Some have started vibrant Hispanic or Asian congregations in the West. However, the growth of Christianity in Africa in the past forty years and the massive ripple effects that have resulted warrant some special attention. The pace at which the continent has been converted (especially after 1970) has caused some deep-seated

Networks in North America and Europe, ed. Frieder Ludwig and J. Kwabena Asamoah-Gyadu (Trenton, NJ: Africa World Press, 2011), 407–17.

[10] See Jacob Olupona and Regina Gemignani, *African Immigrant Religions in America* (New York: New York University Press, 2007), 102–29.

societal changes never before seen in the history of Christianity. The effect of these changes will eventually be reflected on a global scale, as African Christians spread around the world in search of better education and living conditions. The Christianization of an underdeveloped continent in this postcolonial age of migration and globalization has created a very mobile yet radically Christianized population that will have a reverse effect on world mission. As such, Africa may easily become a significant force in both the spread and the representation of Christianity in the world in this twenty-first century.

There is a consensus among scholars in the area of missions (and other related fields) that the rise of world Christianity will have an invigorating effect on Western Christianity that has been shrinking for almost a century now. Africans have a large role to play in this phenomenon. The works of Andrew Walls,[11] Roswith Gerloff,[12] Gerrie ter Haar,[13] and others have for several decades commented on the rise of African Christianity in Europe. Following such scholars as David Barrett[14] and Phil Jenkins,[15] we know that this growth of Christianity in Africa has not yet peaked. With half a billion Christians, Africa is only 50 percent

[11]   See Andrew F. Walls, *The Missionary Movement in Christian History: Studies in the Transmission of Faith* (Maryknoll, NY: Orbis Books, 1996). See also Andrew F. Walls, *The Cross-Cultural Process in Christian History: Studies in the Transmission and Appropriation of Faith* (Maryknoll, NY: Orbis Books, 2002).

[12]   Roswith Gerloff, *A Plea for British Black Theologies: The Black Church Movement in Britain in Its Transatlantic Cultural and Theological Interaction with Special References to the Pentecostal Oneness (Apostolic) and Sabbatarian Movements,* Studien zur Interkulturellen Geschichte des Christentums (Frankfurt am Main: P. Lang, 1992).

[13]   Gerrie ter Haar, *Halfway to Paradise: African Christians in Europe* (Cardiff: Cardiff Academic Press, 1998). Also Gerrie ter Haar, *Strangers and Sojourners: Religious Communities in Diaspora* (Leuven: Peeters, 1998). And Gerrie ter Haar, *How God Became African: African Spirituality and Western Secular Thought* (Philadelphia: University of Pennsylvania Press, 2009).

[14]   David B. Barrett, George Thomas Kurian, and Todd M. Johnson, *World Christian Encyclopedia: A Comparative Survey of Churches and Religions in the Modern World,* 2nd ed. (New York: Oxford University Press, 2001).

[15]   Philip Jenkins, *The Next Christendom: The Coming of Global Christianity,* 3rd ed. (New York: Oxford University Press, 2011).

converted. As we go deeper into the twenty-first century, there will be even more growth both from conversions and biological multiplication among the Christians. As it grows in Africa, African Christianity will overflow into the rest of the world.

African Christianity's Impact on Africa

The ever-growing presence of Christianity in a religiously charged continent shapes life in ways that make the secularization theories of the mid-twentieth century appear ill-informed. Indeed, with thousands of conversions taking place on any particular day across the continent, Africa is changing rapidly. Some context: forty years ago, there were one hundred million Christians in Africa. Today, Africa has over five hundred million Christians. Indeed, Africa has added an average of ten million new Christians every year since 1970.[16]

As Christians multiply in number across the continent, Africa's economic, political, and cultural outlooks are also being radically transformed. Even though Paul Gifford focuses only on Ghana in his *Ghana's New Christianity*, the new kind of Christianity that he describes is rising up in all sub-Saharan Africa—and it is a Christianity that is very engaged with African life, both politically and economically.[17] This makes perfect sense for Africans who make no distinctions between their faith and other aspects of life. John Mbiti's assessment that Africans are notoriously religious is true.[18] Their worldview is entirely religious, and so is their culture. The explosion of Christianity at the end of the twentieth century has taken this religiosity to a new high.

In allowing their Christianity to influence everything else around their existence, African Christians are being true to themselves. For instance, the growing involvement of Christians in the arena of politics has effectively eradicated the supposed divide

---

[16] Johnson, Ross, and Lee, *Atlas*, 110–11.

[17] Paul Gifford, *Ghana's New Christianity: Pentecostalism in a Globalizing African Economy* (Bloomington: Indiana University Press, 2004), 23.

[18] John S. Mbiti, *African Religions and Philosophy* (Garden City, NY: Anchor Books, 1970), 1.

between church and state.[19] Alliances between politicians and prophets have become the order of the day. In recent years, many African political figures have been known to frequent Prophet T. B. Joshua's The Synagogue Church of All Nations in Lagos, Nigeria, as a way of consulting the prophetic ministry (which, by the way, is widely popular in Africa), and to be legitimized in the eyes of their Christian citizens.[20] In addition, numerous Pentecostal preachers juggle between the church pulpit and the political podium with ease.

One such Pentecostal preacher-turned-politician is Nevers Mumba of Zambia. He was vice president of Zambia from 2003 to 2004 and continues to be active in politics.[21] At the peak of his political campaigns in the 1990s, he declared, "Zambia shall be saved by the blood (of the Lamb) and by the ballot."[22] His transition between the church and the political scene has been repeated tens of times across Africa. Christian political parties have become increasingly popular in the past two decades as many African Christians have realized that the political sphere is not to be eschewed. They use such scriptures as Proverbs 11:10,

---

[19] African leadership structures have always allowed the political sphere to be shaped by the religious sphere. The local priest or spiritual medium would always be consulted for almost everything taking place in the political realm. As such, the gap between church or the religious structures and state has never really existed in Africa, even in the postcolonial Africa that was supposed to model its governments after Western democracies.

[20] T. B. Joshua is famous for his political prophecies about governments in Africa. His prophetic influence spreads across the entire continent.

[21] Nevers Mumba is currently the president of the opposition party, Movement for Multiparty Democracy (MMD), but he is also an apostle in the Victory Bible Church, which he founded in 1984. The church movement has also grown to become one of the most popular Pentecostal movements in Zambia and Southern Africa. In the late 1990s, he started preaching about political involvement among Christians in Africa. He formed his own party in 1999. He dissolved the party in 2003 just a few days before he joined the MMD and became the vice president of Zambia.

[22] A fuller exploration of the political message of Nevers Mumba, see Kirbey Blair Lockhart, *Zambia Shall Be Saved: The Nevers Mumba Story* (Lusaka, Zambia: Lockhart, 2001). On December 29, 1991, Zambia was declared a Christian nation by its second president, Frederick Chiluba, who was also a Pentecostal preacher.

which states that "when the righteous [people] prosper, the city rejoices," to encourage Christians to seek political positions. During elections, the Christian vote is usually critical, and as such, it is highly sought after by politicians. Most candidates try as much as possible to align themselves with church leaders in order to get their congregations' votes.

Economic and business sectors have also been radically transformed by the conversion of Africa. There is a rising wave of Christian businessmen and women in Africa who are motivated by the desire to be Christ's ambassadors in the marketplace. They want to do business in a *kingdom way*—bringing God's kingship into the business world. Morning devotions and prayer vigils are usually held in corporate offices just as much as they would be in churches and other sanctuaries. Employees are requested to fast and pray for their companies to avoid losses and bankruptcies. Often, spiritual reasons are given for the success or failure of businesses. Kwabena Asamoah-Gyadu gives several examples of such occurrences in his *African Charismatics*.[23]

Indeed, influential apostles and pastors are appointed to chair boards of large conglomerates and statutory bodies in the hope of divine assistance in the running of the company and better accountability, following the belief that followers of God will not be involved in or tolerate any shady management of company finances. Christopher Daza, a Malawian preacher I have known for many years, has recently opened a Prophetic Business College in South Africa that attracts promising young entrepreneurial Christian men and women from the entire continent for one-week intensive courses twice a year on how to be effective business leaders in the face of the corruption that harms the continent. The "Prophetic MBA" that is awarded at the end of the study is fast becoming a trendsetter in business education in Africa.[24] Some have gone so far as attributing the rise of a new middle class in Africa to the rise of Christianity.[25]

---

[23] See J. Kwabena Asamoah-Gyadu, *African Charismatics: Current Developments within Independent Indigenous Pentecostalism in Ghana* (Boston: Brill, 2005), 201–32.

[24] See El-Dabar University, www.eldabar.org.

[25] For instance, Gifford, *Ghana's New Christianity*, 44–82, also 140–60.

On the cultural front, the rise of Christianity has also changed Africa significantly. It has made a culture that was already religious even more openly so. It has, however, moderated this religious enthusiasm in ways that channel the peoples' spiritual energies toward the God of Christianity. Instead of consulting the rainmaker in times of drought, Christians, led by their politicians, now fill stadiums to pray to the God of the Christians for rain. Most believe that this Christian God was present in Africa before the advent of the missionaries and that of Christianity. The names used to describe the traditional gods in many languages were imported into Christianity, and the unknown gods of traditional religions became the known God of Christianity.[26]

As the culture itself becomes more Christian, many of the traditions that were seen as secular have been sanctioned by being re-dressed in Christian clothing or have disappeared altogether. For instance, in the southern part of Malawi, the traditional initiation rites—*chinamwali*—used to prepare young boys and girls for adulthood have almost totally disappeared.[27] They used to be central to the process of attaining adulthood, but Christians started to undermine these practices in the 1970s and '80s, calling them secular traditions that did not sit well with the Bible. To sustain them, there appeared several versions of *chinamwali* that were dubbed Christian.[28] However, these Christian initiation rites were not Christian enough for the Pentecostals and charismatics

---

Also see Terence Ranger and Timothy Samuel Shah, *Evangelical Christianity and Democracy in Africa*, Evangelical Christianity and Democracy in the Global South (New York: Oxford University Press, 2008).

[26] Lamin O. Sanneh, *Translating the Message: The Missionary Impact on Culture*, American Society of Missiology Series (Maryknoll, NY: Orbis Books, 1989).

[27] This is a cultural practice whereby young boys and girls approaching puberty were taken out of the village to a secluded place to be oriented about the responsibilities of adult life. The process would take between three and seven days. Upon their release into the community, the boys and girls were considered adults, and that entailed a great celebration.

[28] In the 1990s, it was common in southern Malawi to hear about Christian initiations, *chinamwali cha chiKhristu*, both among Roman Catholics and mainline Protestants. However, the rise of Pentecostal Christianity, which vehemently demonizes such traditions, has forced even those Christian initiations into obscurity.

in Malawi, and they continued preaching against them until they disappeared.

In many countries, the advent of charismatic Christianity has also changed entire education systems. Christian schools now are educational leaders from kindergarten through tertiary education. They are known to deliver higher standards of academics, matching similar institutions in developed countries. Their teachers and administrators are believed to be honest and accountable. In the case of urban Malawi, especially at the high school level, Christian students are known to perform better. They speak better English. They are more confident and sociable. They are believed to have the discipline to work hard in their classes because of the inspiration they draw from their pastors.

The impact of Christianity on the continent of Africa goes much deeper than we have discussed here. Paul Gifford and other scholars have paid attention to some of these themes.[29] However, it should be noted that the depth of this impact varies from place to place. Not all cultures were open to the spread of the Christian gospel. Missionary work connected with the local Africans at different levels in different places. Nevertheless, generally speaking, the story of the spread of Christianity in Africa has been a success story. Christians constitute more than three-quarters of the populations of most southern African countries. Over 75 percent of Malawi's 14 million people are Christians.[30] The same can be said of other countries like Zambia, Zimbabwe, Kenya, and South Africa. West African countries like Ghana and Nigeria have a slightly lower percentage, between 50 and 60 percent.[31]

African Christianity's Impact in the Diaspora

This Christian impact on African culture has begun to find its way to the African Diaspora.[32] Many scholars such as Andrew

---

[29] See Paul Gifford, *African Christianity: Its Public Role* (Bloomington: Indiana University Press, 1998). See also Paul Gifford, *The Christian Churches and the Democratisation of Africa* (New York: Brill, 1995).

[30] Barrett, Kurian, and Johnson, *World Christian Encyclopedia*, 470.

[31] Ibid., 853.

[32] Gerrie ter Haar has explored the implications of the word "Diaspora"

Walls have already observed that the African type of Christianity has, for the past three decades, begun to make inroads into the Western world. When we look at the numbers of African Christians outside Africa, it is fair to say that African Christianity is no longer just an African phenomenon. It has overflowed to all continents and become global. There are many reasons for this spread of African Christianity outside Africa, but the primary one is the search for better living standards. Political corruption, diseases, droughts, famines, and wars, among many other factors, have displaced Africans both within and without the continent. For these reasons, Africans have become the most mobile people in the world.[33] Out of the 191 million displaced peoples in the world today, a third are African.[34] Of these, millions have migrated out of Africa to the Americas, Europe, and Asia. For example, at the moment of this writing, between 10 and 20 percent of Ghanaians live abroad.[35]

How did this come to pass? In the second half of the twentieth century, the world began to witness a reversal of global migration trends. The expansive migration system that took millions of Europeans to the rest of the world between 1500 and 2000 began to slow down around the turn of the twentieth century.[36] By mid-twentieth century, when the colonial empires began to collapse, Africans, Asians, and Latin Americans began

---

when used to describe the dispersion of Africans around the world. See Haar, *Strangers and Sojourners.* I will not deal with those implications here but simply refer you to her excellent discourse. I will continue to use it, however, to talk about Africans who are resident outside Africa. I am also aware that among Africans, it is also used to describe Africans who are resident outside their home countries, even if they are resident on the same continent.

[33] Jehu Hanciles, *Beyond Christendom: Globalization, African Migration, and the Transformation of the West* (Maryknoll, NY: Orbis Books, 2008), 207.

[34] Ibid., 220–23. See also Aderanti Adepoju and Network of Migration Research on Africa, *International Migration within, to, and from Africa in a Globalised World* (Accra, Ghana: Sub-Saharan Publishers, 2010).

[35] Hanciles, *Beyond Christendom,* 226–28.

[36] In the nineteenth century alone, over 20 million Europeans—and that is one fifth of the entire European population—migrated to the rest of the world. See Dudley Baines, *Emigration from Europe, 1815–1930,* New Studies in Economic and Social History (New York: Cambridge University Press, 1995).

to migrate to the West. Earlier in the 1950s and '60s, most Africans migrated to the countries that colonized them; many Francophone Africans migrated to France and Belgium, and those from Anglophone Africa migrated to Britain, to take advantage of the labor needs in Europe. Some European governments had to import labor to rebuild their economies, especially after losing a great deal of manpower in the two World Wars. By the time of the final collapse of colonialism, many Africans had found new homes in the Europe.[37]

Starting in the 1960s, the United States emerged as a viable option for many Africans, especially for Anglophone Africans. Following the reform of American immigration laws, especially the Hart-Celler Immigration and Nationality Act of 1965, which brought the "National Origins Formula" to an end, Africans were allowed to migrate to the United States in larger numbers.[38] The National Origins Formula had been in place since 1924. Under this law, migration to the United States was more often allowed—if not encouraged—if the immigrants came from Europe, especially noncommunist Europe (after 1945). Africans were greatly disadvantaged under this act. The national origins quota system allowed the citizens of Western and Northern Europe almost unfettered migration rights to the United States while placing limitations on the immigration of citizens of other countries and ethnicities. The provisions of the 1965 act opened the possibility of migration that had been out of reach for most of the non-Western world by giving all countries an apparently equal right to migration to the United States—though some quotas, as seen in the Diversity Visa Program, still silently exist.

It was not until the 1990s that North America began to see a significant increase in African immigration. This wave of African migration to the United States continues to this day and is responsible for the explosion of African immigrant Christianity in the United States. The table below shows the total number

---

[37] See Tiyambe Paul Zeleza, "Contemporary African Migrations in a Global Context," *African Issues* 30, no. 1 (2002).

[38] In general, over against the millions of Europeans who migrated to Europe at the turn of the century, an average of 625 Africans per year were allowed settlement in America between 1870 and 1900.

Table 1. Total foreign-born and African-born
population from 1960 to 2010

Year	Total foreign-born	African-born Share of all foreign-born	Number
1960	9,738,091	0.4%	35,355
1970	9,619,302	0.8%	80,143
1980	14,079,906	1.4%	199,723
1990	19,797,316	1.8%	363,819
2000	31,107,889	2.8%	881,300
2007	38,059,555	3.7%	1,419,317
2010	39,955,673	4.02%	1,606,914

Note: This table has been adopted from Kristine McCabe, "African Immigrants in the United States," in *US in Focus* (Washington, DC: Migration Policy Institute, 2011). It was modified by this writer to include the current data from 2010 Census, which was obtained from the Census Bureau. See US Census Bureau, American Factfinder website, Table B05006: Place of Birth for the Foreign-Born Population in the United States, 2010 American Community Survey 1-Year Estimates, available at http://www.factfinder.census.gov.

of African-born citizens and legal residents in the United States from 1960 to 2010. It reflects a steady rise in percentage from 0.4 percent in 1960 to 4 percent in 2010.

The 2010 US Census reported 1.6 million Africans in the country, a significant rise from 363,819 in 1990 and 881,300 in 2000. The largest migration of Africans to the United States after 1965 occurred between 1990 and 2005. During the 1990s, more Africans immigrated to the United States than in the previous 180 years.[39] Nevertheless, even after this change of law, Africans continue to face a great deal of challenges in migrating to America. The demands placed upon their efforts to secure a visa to travel to the United States are still prohibitive. The costs of applying for visas and travel mean that Africa will still be the

[39] See Susan Hume, "Contemporary African Migration to the United States: Are We Paying Attention?," in *Association of American Geographers* (Los Angeles, 2002), 1.

least represented continent in the United States for the foreseeable future. Africans still represent a mere 4 percent of the total foreign-born population in the United States, and only 0.5 percent of the total US population.

This migration of Africans to other continents continues today, as the same evils of war, disease, bad governance, and poverty still force many Africans away from their continent. The promise of a better life in Europe and America has lured many into illegal migration across unsafe seas on makeshift boats. Thousands have died in the Mediterranean Sea trying to cross into Italy or Spain.[40] Even more Africans have successfully found ways to pursue their migration in a legitimate way. Some have migrated as refugees, while others have moved as students. Still a few have migrated as skilled workers. Among them are millions of Ghanaians and Nigerians. Most of these live in Germany, Britain, Canada, and the United States.[41]

In the United States, just as in Europe, hundreds of African immigrant churches have sprung up in the past twenty years. Most of them are conservative and charismatic in their theology. They also do not employ the spiritual/material dichotomy seen in most of Western Christianity. As they become more visible on the Western Christian landscape, they will slowly become more identified with Christianity itself. Over time, when people hear the word "Christian," they will think not only of white Americans and African Americans. They will also think of immigrant African Christians. Furthermore, when they consider Africans, they will not just think about the unevangelized continent that was once known as the "Dark Continent" saturated with traditional religions. They will also think about Africans as tongue-talking, demon-busting, Bible-thumping Christians who hold revivals and prayer vigils in Western cities. Like the proverbial hare who joined the dance in its dying minutes and yet changed the entire atmosphere with her new dancing style and vigor, the unleashing of African Christianity in the world will invigorate world Christianity, while challenging it in many areas at the same time.

---

[40] See Jenny Cuffe, "African Dream of a Better Life" (BBC News Online, June 16, 2007).

[41] Hanciles, *Beyond Christendom*, 223.

Mission History:
Global Perspectives Needed

The history of Christian missions has so far been told mostly by Western scholars from a decidedly Western perspective. Whether one reads Kenneth Latourette's masterly seven-volume series, *A History of the Expansion of the Church*,[42] or Stephen Neill's *A History of Christian Missions*,[43] or even Herbert Kane's *A Concise History of the Christian World Mission*,[44] one finds a history of mission that is Western. Most of their history is dedicated to the growth of the Western church from its start in the Mediterranean basin to its spread around the world.

This telling of history is not a problem in itself. This perspective is certainly needed. However, we will have a skewed history if this Western perspective becomes the only perspective that informs us.[45] Andrew Walls once complained about "the untroubled rule of palefaces over the academic [or theological] world."[46] This untroubled rule is markedly evident in the field of missiology, and therefore shapes the way the history of the church and mission is told. Walls is of the opinion that the future of the Christian faith—its shape in the twenty-first and twenty-second centuries—is being decided by events that are now, or will be in the near future, taking place in Africa, Asia, and Latin America. His conclusion was that "new agendas for theology will appear in Africa."[47]

While these events continue to unfold, and non-Western Christianity continues to expand, there is still an unjustifiable

---

[42] Kenneth Scott Latourette, *A History of the Expansion of Christianity* (New York: Harper, 1937).

[43] Stephen Neill and Owen Chadwick, *A History of Christian Missions*, The Pelican History of the Church (New York: Penguin Books, 1986).

[44] J. Herbert Kane, *A Concise History of the Christian World Mission: A Panoramic View of Missions from Pentecost to the Present* (Grand Rapids, MI.: Baker, 1982).

[45] See Philip Jenkins, *The Lost History of Christianity: The Thousand-Year Golden Age of the Church in the Middle East, Africa, and Asia, and How It Died* (New York: HarperOne, 2008).

[46] Andrew F. Walls, "Structural Problems in Mission Studies," *International Bulletin of Missionary Research* 15, no. 4 (1991): 152.

[47] Walls, *Cross-Cultural Process*, 85–86.

theological/missiological hegemony by the West over the world. Indeed, fifteen years after Walls talked about the rule of palefaces, and thirty-something years after Mbiti wrote about the provincial nature of theology, non-Western theology still faces an uphill struggle to be heard in the West. Non-Western missiologies are yet to find their ways into the global audience, even when scholars agree that Africa has been evangelized by Africans. Walls later said, "Western theological leadership of a predominantly non-Western church is an incongruity."[48] He is absolutely right. This will have to change. Non-Western theologies and missiologies have to be told even in the West. Timothy Tennent has noted, "We cannot afford to ignore the theological implications inherent in the demographic reality that Christianity is currently in a precipitous decline in the West and that the vast majority of Christians now live outside the West."[49] Indeed, the theological implications of the worldwide spread of Christianity in the twentieth century deserve much greater attention.[50]

The problem with history is that it is usually written by the winners. Or, as my grandfather taught me, *until the lions can tell their stories, the story of the hunt will always glorify the hunter.* Mission history, as it has been told so far, is incomplete. We need to engage non-Western sources in order to have a better picture of how Christianity developed to become a global religion. Some key perspectives from the history of the church are missing. Huge blocks of this missing history include the role of African Christians in the early missionary movements of the first century.

Thomas Oden took upon himself the labor of highlighting this bias in regards to the story of the development of African Christianity and its impact on world Christianity.[51] Any authen-

---

[48] Andrew F. Walls, "Christian Scholarship in Africa in the Twenty-First Century," *Transformation* 19, no. 4 (2002): 221.

[49] Timothy C. Tennent, *Theology in the Context of World Christianity: How the Global Church Is Influencing the Way We Think About and Discuss Theology* (Grand Rapids, MI: Zondervan, 2007), 17.

[50] For a fuller argument on how globalization and theology relate, see Joerg Rieger, *Globalization and Theology*, Horizons in Theology (Nashville, TN: Abingdon, 2010).

[51] See Thomas C. Oden, *The African Memory of Mark: Reassessing Early*

tic telling of the history of the expansion of Christianity must engage the voices of non-Western Christianities like that of Africa, India, and Asia. In such a telling of church history, African Christianity is no longer a side story. It is central to the development of world Christianity.

Of African Missionaries in the Early Church

Because of the bias of popular mission history, when one reads church history from the first five centuries, the presence of Africans is not clearly visible. Even those Christian leaders who are definitely African, such as Tertullian, Cyprian, Athanasius, and Augustine, have been made to appear more Western than African. For instance, it was because of his African origin and black skin that Athanasius was called the "black dwarf" by his enemies.[52] Another example is the catechetical school of Alexandria—a theological school that significantly influenced the entire development of Christian theology—which is usually presented in the shadows of the theological developments taking place in Rome and elsewhere in Europe, with little recognition of its location in Egypt. When the stories of the influence of Alexandria on early Christianity are told, they are said to be based on tradition—and therefore, not as credible as those of Antioch, Constantinople, and Rome, which are believed to be based on verified historical facts.

Luckily, some Western scholars such as Thomas Oden are pointing out the significant role of Africa in the development of Christianity. Oden's *How Africa Shaped the Christian Mind* recognizes the African contributors for who they were—Africans.[53]

Church Tradition (Downers Grove, IL: IVP Academic, 2011). Also see Thomas C. Oden, *How Africa Shaped the Christian Mind: Rediscovering the African Seedbed of Western Christianity* (Downers Grove, IL.: IVP Books, 2007).

[52] Justo L. González, *The Story of Christianity, Volume 1: The Early Church to the Reformation* (New York: HarperCollins, 2010), 199.

[53] See Oden, *How Africa Shaped the Christian Mind*. I agree with Oden that tradition is not necessarily the best way to describe the history that has not come to us through Western sources. The word "tradition" is used to enforce Western suspicions of other ways of passing knowledge.

By this line of reasoning, African missionaries have worked in the West before, only in a different Western context.[54] In his now famous book, *Drums of Redemption,* Harvey Sindima also explores the two-thousand-year existence of Christianity in Africa, and how Africa has not only been a recipient of missionaries but has also been involved in sending missionaries to the rest of the world.[55] History is coming full circle with the current movement of missionaries from Africa to Europe and North America.

In order to be able to tell an accurate history of world Christianity, we must acknowledge the role played by African Christians in its establishment and growth right from the first century, and this includes their missionary work in the first few centuries of Christianity's existence.[56] African missionary work in the West should be understood to have taken place in two phases. The first phase is recorded in the New Testament and other historical works of church history covering the first five hundred years of the church. The second phase—which is the immediate interest of this book—started in the 1960s and is still rising.

The New Testament mentions several Africans who were involved in early missionary work with Paul and the other apostles. African Christians were not only recipients of "Western missionaries" but were missionaries themselves who participated in missionary work in Europe and Asia Minor—Antioch, Cyprus, Corinth, Rome, and many other places. They actively participated in the spread of the church in the Middle East as well as Europe itself. From being the place of refuge for the young Jesus fleeing Herod's jealous wrath, to Simon of Cyrene helping carry Jesus' cross on the way to Calvary, Africa and its people contributed to the founding of the church in some remarkable ways. A faithful telling of the spread of Christianity in antiquity must acknowledge that the contributions of Africans to its growth were significant right at the birth of Christianity, in the gospels, in the Book of Acts (the Ethiopian eunuch

---

[54] See Harvey J. Sindima, *Drums of Redemption: An Introduction to African Christianity,* Contributions to the Study of Religion (Westport, CT: Greenwood Press, 1994).

[55] Ibid.

[56] Ibid.

in Acts 8:26–40, Luke the Niger in Acts 13:1–2, and Apollos in Acts 18:24–28).

The *History of the Patriarchs of Alexandria* suggests that Mary and her husband, Aristopaulus—the parents of John Mark, the writer of the second gospel—had lived for an extended period in Cyrene, Libya—modern day Shahhat—before returning to Jerusalem a few years before the founding of the church.[57] Their worldview was shaped to a considerable extent by their experience of the African way of life in Libya. An internalized sense of African hospitality provided a safe place for the birth of the movement. Mark, himself, was born in Cyrene.[58] He moved with the family to Jerusalem when he was a young man. Some commentators have identified Mark as an African native of Jewish heritage. In addition, there were many Africans—if only African Jews—in Jerusalem on the Day of Pentecost. Luke mentions the presence of people from Egypt and Libya (Cyrene had a huge Jewish presence).

The significance of this Cyrenian Mary's house in early Christianity should not be underestimated. The scriptures suggest that Mary was influential among the early disciples in Jerusalem.[59]

---

[57] Severus of Al'Ashmunein, *History of the Patriarchs of the Coptic Church of Alexandria: Saint Mark to Theonas (300 AD)* (Paris: P. FAGES, v. g.), http://www.tertullian.org.

[58] E. L. Butcher, *The Story of the Church of Egypt: Being an Outline of the History of the Egyptians under Their Successive Masters from the Roman Conquest until Now* (New York: AMS, 1975), 20. Since Aristopaulus, sometimes called Christopaulus, is not mentioned anywhere in the scriptures, it is possible that he died before the events recorded in the gospels and Acts. Most of the recent Western scholarship going back two centuries is skeptical about Mark's African history, calling it mere hagiography. However, the old sources like Eusebius are clear that Mark spent almost his entire life in Africa. See Eusebius, *Eusebius: The Church History,* ed. Paul L. Maier (Grand Rapids, MI: Kregel Publications, 2007).

[59] See Acts 12. Mary must have been affluent, for her home was relatively large—large enough to hold the "many" who gathered there when Peter was imprisoned, in addition to the upper room. The typical house in Jerusalem was quite small and would not have provided room for a number of people to gather. She also had a household maid, Rhoda, which further suggests that she was a member of the upper class. The fact that Peter went immediately to her home when an angel released him from prison indi-

Coptic Christian history has it that Jesus and the disciples had the Last Supper in the upper room of her house.[60] Thus, both she and Mark were evidently known to Jesus. After the ascension, the disciples continued to stay in that upper room while they hid from the Jewish authorities.

Peter preached the famous first sermon from the patio of Mary's house—and in his audience are mentioned Libyans and Egyptians (Acts 2:10). Later on, when Herod tried to have Peter killed, the Christians were gathered together in prayer at Mary's house. As a gathering place for the early church, it brought together various leaders and developed relationships that would later on take the gospel to the entire Mediterranean region. Barnabas, Paul, and Peter are all mentioned in connection with Mary's house. Mark's connection to the early missionary movement began in the same dwelling and spread to Antioch, Cyprus, and Rome. Even Eusebius acknowledges Mark as the first bishop of the see of Alexandria in Egypt, adding that he was martyred in Alexandria somewhere around 68 CE.[61]

It is likely that Mark's close relationship with his uncle, Barnabas (who may also have been related to Peter), opened doors for his missionary work around Europe. He traveled first with Barnabas and Paul, and then with Barnabas alone after Paul refused to take him along (Acts 15:36–41). In his letters to the Colossians and Philemon, Paul sent greetings from Mark (Col. 4:10; Philem. 1:24). In his second letter to Timothy, Paul called for Timothy to bring Mark along with him, saying, "for he is useful to me in the ministry" (2 Tim. 4:11).

The African history of Mark has it that he was Peter's interpreter and wrote his gospel based on what he heard from Peter.[62] In 1 Peter 5:13, Peter identified Mark as "my son." Out of Peter and Mark's relationship during their missionary work in Europe, then, came the Gospel of Mark, the first gospel to be written.[63] If

---

cates that she was close to the leadership of the church and an important member of the local body.

[60] Severus of Al'Ashmunein, *History of the Patriarchs.*

[61] Eusebius, *Eusebius*, ed. Maier, 64.

[62] Oden, *African Memory*, 185–216.

[63] There are some doubts in some scholarship about Mark's authorship

indeed John Mark is the author of this gospel, then he provided much of the material that both Matthew and Luke used to write their gospels.

Along with Mark, several other Africans are mentioned in the missionary endeavors in Acts and the Epistles. First among them is the Ethiopian eunuch who was a man of great authority under Candace, the queen of Ethiopia (Acts 8:26–40). He had come to Jerusalem to worship, and by divinely orchestrated miraculous circumstance, met Philip, who preached the gospel to him and eventually baptized him. He became the first missionary to take the gospel to Ethiopia. A strong church was birthed in Ethiopia because of this one man's conversion.

Second, in Acts 11:20, Luke mentions the presence and influence of men from Cyrene among those who began to intentionally preach the gospel to Gentiles. Simeon, who is also called "the black," is mentioned in Acts 13:1, when the church in Antioch dedicated Paul and Barnabas for their first missionary trip. His identity as an African is based on the nickname, *Niger*, which suggests that he was a black man. Following Simeon is Lucius, who, Luke expressly says, was from Cyrene and thus was of African descent (Acts 13:1). These two were mentioned among the prophets and the teachers of the Antioch church, second and third in the list, which suggests that they may have been senior in the ranks. In Romans 16:21, Lucius is mentioned in Paul's final greetings to the church in Rome. Just like several other apostles, Lucius may have moved to Rome some time after Antioch. It is possible that both Simeon and Lucius were part of this first group of Christians from Cyprus and Cyrene who preached to the Gentiles (Acts 11:20), and while many of these may have been Jews like Barnabas, some may have been Africans.

Mark also mentions Alexander and Rufus, the two sons of Simon of Cyrene, the African who helped Jesus with his cross to Golgotha (Matt. 27:34), suggesting that they were well known to Mark's audience. Paul mentions Rufus in the sixteenth chapter of

---

of this gospel. However, both Eusebius's *Church History* and Severus's *History of the Patriarchs* suggest that it was this Mark who was an apprentice to Peter who established the Alexandrian church and authored the gospel.

his letter to the Romans. Paul salutes Rufus's mother as his own mother, indicating a close relationship with the family (Rom. 16:13).

Another prominent African in early missionary circles was Apollos. He was a Jew, born and raised in the Egyptian city of Alexandria. His name is first mentioned in Acts 18:24–25, where he was a visiting preacher who was "fervent in spirit and taught with great accuracy the things concerning Jesus though he knew only of the baptism of John." Priscilla and Aquila, a ministering couple that had come to Ephesus with Paul, called Apollos aside and explained to him more accurately the way of God (Acts 18:27). As we follow his life in the records of the scriptures, Apollos later moved to Achaia and Corinth (which was the capital of the Achaian province). Luke says that Apollos went to Achaia with letters of recommendation from the Ephesian Christians. He is said to have "greatly helped those who through grace had believed, for he powerfully refuted the Jews in public, showing by the Scriptures that the Christ was Jesus" (Acts 18:27–28). His work at Corinth was commended by Paul who said, "I planted, Apollos watered, but God gave the increase." He is finally mentioned in the Epistle to Titus where the recipient is asked to send Zenas and Apollos on their journey with haste (Titus 3:13).

After the Apostles

By the time of the spread of early Christianity, North Africa had become the breadbasket of the Roman Empire, producing and exporting vast quantities of wine, olive oil, and wheat to the entire empire. North Africa was at the time identified as "Roman Africa." Much of its territory covered the four billion square miles that stretch from Eritrea to Morocco.[64] There is often pushback against the claim that this territory of Roman Africa was "actually" Africa, as in black Africa. However, this prejudice is unnecessarily cynical and obviously misguided. Ogbu Kalu has observed, "Since North Africa used to be a strong Christian territory until the seventh and eighth centuries, many Europeans did

---

[64] See Elizabeth Isichei, *A History of Christianity in Africa: From Antiquity to the Present* (Grand Rapids, MI: Eerdmans, 1995), 35.

not consider it to belong to Africa. It suited their prejudices to consider Africa as beginning at the Sahara desert."[65] There were black people in North Africa just as there were black people in the Roman Empire. We know with certainty that Augustine's mother, Monnica, was a Berber, and her Africanness had a great influence on Augustine's theology.[66]

The presence of a large Jewish population in North African cities like Alexandria and Cyrene provided Christianity with an immediate connecting point for the new religion. As a result, Christianity spread in the Maghreb rather quickly.[67] The trade routes (used for the export of flour from North Africa, among other things) also made it easier for Christian missionaries to travel throughout North Africa and around the empire. Consequently, for the first six centuries of church history, North Africa was a strong Christian heartland that was deeply involved in the growth and development of Christianity within the Roman Empire. It was the invasion of Islamic jihadists in the seventh century that gradually destroyed certain aspects of North African Christianity and forced it to retreat into Coptic villages and in the deserts south of Egypt.[68]

In the first six centuries of Christianity, African leaders were deeply involved in Christian work in Europe. For instance, Pope Victor who was bishop of Rome from around 189 to 199 CE was an African (probably from Tripoli).[69] He was the first pope to use Latin, which was his native language, instead of Greek, which had been used until then. There were two other African popes in the history of the Roman Catholic Church: Melchiades (311–314) and Gelasius (492–496).[70]

---

[65] Ogbu Kalu, *African Christianity: An African Story* (Trenton, NJ: Africa World Press, 2007), 124.

[66] John Baur, *2000 Years of Christianity in Africa: An African Church History*, 2nd rev. ed. (Nairobi, Kenya: Paulines, 1998), 28.

[67] Maghreb was the common name for entire northwestern region of Africa, west of Egypt.

[68] Sindima, *Drums*, 23–24.

[69] See González, *Story of Christianity, vol. 1: The Early Church to the Reformation*, 91–93.

[70] See Sindima, *Drums*, 23.

Tertullian (160–225 CE) was an African from Carthage.[71] Like Pope Victor, he wrote his theology in Latin. He is known as the father of Latin Christianity and the founder of Western theology.[72] His famous contribution to theology is the formation of the Trinity.[73] He was followed by another Carthaginian, Cyprian, who was bishop of Carthage from 248 to 258 CE. Cyprian, who is one of the hundreds of African bishops mentioned in various documents, is said to have spoken confidently to Rome and to the wider ecclesial world on matters ranging from the sacraments to pastoral responses to persecution.[74] He is especially remembered for *extra ecclesiam nulla salus*—a Roman Catholic doctrine that suggests that there is no salvation outside (the Catholic) church.[75]

To underestimate the influence of the catechetical school of Alexandria, also known as the Didascalia, is to miss a very important portion of church history. This catechetical school is undoubtedly the earliest important institution of theological learning in Christian history. It is for a good reason that Eusebius gives it detailed attention in his *Church History*.[76] During the years when the Didascalia had the greatest theological influence in the world, Alexandria was the intellectual and philosophical capital of the world and naturally would be the center where the theological thought of the time was formulated. Amir Nasr states that it was Mark's ministry in Egypt that created a center for the discipleship and education of the early Christians—the beginnings of what was to become the famed catechetical school that would shape Christian theology for five centuries.[77] From

---

[71] For Tertullian's biography, see Geoffrey D. Dunn, *Tertullian* (New York: Routledge, 2004).

[72] See Eric Francis Osborn, *Tertullian, First Theologian of the West* (New York: Cambridge University Press, 1997).

[73] Dunn, *Tertullian.*

[74] Isichei, *History of Christianity*, 60.

[75] Cyprian and M. Bâevenot, *The Lapsed: The Unity of the Catholic Church*, Ancient Christian Writers, no. 25 (London: Newman Press, 1957), 48–49. See also Peter Bingham Hinchliff, *Cyprian of Carthage and the Unity of the Christian Church* (London: G. Chapman, 1974), chap. 8.

[76] Eusebius, *Eusebius*, ed. Maier.

[77] Amir Nasr, *St. Mark the Apostle and the School of Alexandria* (Cairo: Bishopric of Youth, 1993), 22. Also see Otto Friedrich August Meinardus,

this school came some of the greatest thinkers and leaders of the early church, whose influence has been felt throughout church history. We have some important names like Pantaneus, Dionysius, Clement, Origen, and Athanasius, all of whom were great theologians of the early church who attended the Alexandrian catechetical school.[78] Augustine of Hippo is another monumental African theologian whose influence in Western theology continues. Augustine's *Confessions* and *The City of God* are among the most influential books from late antiquity.[79]

All these theologians had a great impact, not just in Africa, but also in Asia and Europe. Later in the fourth century, the main voices in the debates at the Council of Nicaea were African, and were actually discussing other Africans: Tertullian, Sabellius, Arius, Athanasius, and Origen.[80] Most of the issues that shaped the theological and ecclesiological conversations of those centuries had been first raised by Demetrius of Alexandria, Cyprian of Carthage, Optatus of Milevis, and Augustine of Hippo.[81] When we read early church history and theology, it becomes apparent that real Western theologians (from Rome) appear much later, probably starting with Pope Leo the Great, who reigned from 440 to 461 CE.[82] What has been claimed as Western theology originally started as African theology.[83]

Even in the secular realm, Africans were involved in the wider world of the Roman Empire. For example, Terence, the great Roman playwright, was from North Africa, and first came to Rome as a Berber slave.[84] The Emperor Septimius Severus was

---

Two Thousand Years of Coptic Christianity (Cairo: American University in Cairo Press, 1999), 38.

[78] Kalu, *African Christianity*, 50–52.

[79] See Augustine, *The Confessions, The City of God, On Christian Doctrine*, ed. Marcus Dods, J. F. Shaw, and E. B. Pusey, Great Books of the Western World 18 (London: Encyclopaedia Britannica, 1952).

[80] Sindima, *Drums*, 9–23.

[81] Ibid., 14–21.

[82] See Roger E. Olson, *The Story of Christian Theology: Twenty Centuries of Tradition and Reform* (Downers Grove, IL: InterVarsity Press, 1999), 228–29.

[83] Ibid., 81–83.

[84] William Smith, *A Dictionary of Greek and Roman Biography and*

from North Africa,[85] as well as the novelist Apuleius, whose novel, *The Golden Ass*, is one of the masterpieces of the ancient world.[86]

The ability to travel around the Roman Empire was one of the key factors that allowed Africans to engage in missionary work in the West. Of course, the Roman Empire had an excellent transportation system—remember "All roads lead to Rome." In addition, the quietness of the period of the Pax Romana allowed people to travel and engage each other easily.[87] In *Contra Celsum*, Origen of Alexandria saw in the stability of the Pax Romana a divinely ordered space within which the church could spread:

> God was preparing the nations for his teaching, that they might be under one Roman emperor, so that the unfriendly attitude of the nations to one another, caused by the existence of a large number of kingdoms, might not make it more difficult for Jesus' apostles to . . . "Go and teach all nations."[88]

These two conditions contributed greatly to the spread of Christianity. As seen in the Book of Acts, many of the Christian leaders were constantly traveling from one city to another. We meet some in Thessalonika, only to meet them later in Corinth, Ephesus, and then Rome. Once connected with these itinerant missionary networks, an African could go around the empire with relative ease. Apollos's missionary travels might have benefited from such networks. Almost four hundred years after Apollos, Augustine's life followed the same trajectory, starting even before Augustine was converted to Christianity. In a fashion common in his time, and despite his dislike of sea travel, he moved from Tha-

---

Mythology, "Lucanus, Terentius" (London: J. Murray, 1876).

[85] "Septimius Severus," Encyclopedia Britannica Online, http://www.britannica.com.

[86] "Lucius Apuleius," Encylopedia Britannica Online, http://www.britannica.com.

[87] See Calvin J. Roetzel, *The World That Shaped the New Testament*, rev. ed. (Louisville, KY: Westminster John Knox Press, 2002).

[88] Origen and Henry Chadwick, *Contra Celsum* (Cambridge: Cambridge University Press, 1953), 92.

gaste to Carthage, Rome, Milan, and finally back to North Africa, to a city called Hippo—modern Annaba in Algeria—where he became bishop.[89] The Roman roads once traveled by our early church fathers were foreshadowing the worldwide travel network that exists today, in this age of migration. For contemporary Africans, the need to migrate (to escape poverty, wars, diseases, to seek better education, among many other things) and the ease with which migration is possible now through asylum, study, and skilled workers' permits, makes African missionary work in the West possible again.

A Theology of Migration

Central to the argument of this book is the issue of migration. It is the migration of Africans to the West that makes possible the presence of African Christians and missionaries in the West. I see the theme of migration throughout the Bible, and yet migration has not always been a subject of serious interest among theologians and missiologists. Although the study of migration and religion attracts voices from many academic disciplines including history, sociology, psychology, economics, law, human rights, and anthropology, the subject of migration and mission is an isolated conversation. Even in Christian disciplines such as theology, religious studies, and missiology, migration does not feature as a prominent conversational subject. In the context of North America, where both the United States and Canada are known to be nations of immigrants, theologies of migration have recently out of necessity become more relevant in theological discourse. This is a vital and positive development in the face of the current migration trends and the political, economic, and social controversies that the presence of immigrants can create.

There is a direct link between migration and the mission of God—*missio Dei*.[90] It is *missio Dei* that makes Christians pilgrims

[89] A journey that Augustine explores in his *Confessions*. See Augustine, *Confessions,* ed. Henry Chadwick (New York: Oxford University Press, 1992).

[90] See Andrew F. Walls, "Mission and Migration: The Diaspora Factor in Christian History," *Journal of African Christian Thought* 5, no. 2 (2002). Also

on earth.[91] Just like many immigrants who live in countries they did not originally belong to, Christians are in the world, but not of it. The kingdom calls people into movement, making church members exiles on earth, strangers in this world, and sojourners en route to another place. In the words of the second-century letter to Diognetus, "They [Christians] dwell in their own countries, but simply as sojourners. As citizens, they share in all things with others, and yet endure all things as if foreigners. Every foreign land is to them as their native country, and every land of their birth as a land of strangers."[92]

Hanciles contends that "in order to claim that the God of the Bible is a God of mission is to accept that he makes himself known to human beings through ordinary, culturally conditioned experiences like migration."[93] Talking about migration, Silvano Tornasi observes that "it is a symbol that reveals the underlying reality of the church as a pilgrim people . . . almost a sacrament, for it is like a mirror in which the People of God views its own reality not only as a problem but also a grace."[94] Later, he adds, "They [migrants] are thus part of God's plan for the growth of the human family in greater cultural unity and universal fraternity [sic]."[95]

---

see Christine D. Pohl, "Biblical Issues in Mission and Migration," *Missiology* 31, no. 1 (2003).

[91] *Missio Dei* is the Latin for "the mission of God." The term *missio Dei* was coined in 1934 by a German theologian, Karl Hartenstein, in response to Karl Barth's 1932 presentation at the Brandenburg Missionary Conference in which Barth envisioned mission as an activity of God—*actio Dei*. Hartenstein, however, in 1934 moved beyond identifying mission as the action of God to understanding it as the mission of God.

[92] Letter to Diognetus cited in David Bosch, *Transforming Mission: Paradigm Shifts in Theology of Miossion,* American Society of Missiology Series (Maryknoll, NY: Orbis Books, 1991), 211.

[93] Hanciles, *Beyond Christendom,* 140.

[94] Silvano Tornasi, "The Prophetic Mission of the Churches: Theological Perspectives," in *The Prophetic Mission of the Church in Response to Forced Displacement of Peoples: Report of the Ecumenical Consultation, Addis Ababa, November 6–11, 1995,* ed. World Council of Churches (Geneva: World Council of Churches, 1996), 36–43.

[95] Ibid., 46.

Migration and the Biblical Story

Although we find examples and expressions of every form of migration in the scriptures,[96] migration and God's mission are specifically and conspicuously linked together in both the Old and the New Testament. For instance, Andrew Walls correctly states that the book of Genesis might as well be called "Migrations."[97] In it is found the story of Adam and Eve being expelled from Eden—the first story of human migration in the Bible (Gen. 3), immediately followed by the curse pronounced upon Cain, that he would be a wanderer—a perpetual migrant—on the earth (Gen. 4). Following this is the migration of the nations from the Tower of Babel, when the separation of their languages pushed the people to scatter in all directions on earth (Gen. 11). However, as Walls also observes, migrations are part of every major story in Genesis. Abraham, Isaac, Jacob, Joseph, the nation of Israel—all are constantly mentioned as being on the move. Indeed, these migrations set the tone for the rest of the Bible: Exodus, the Babylonian Captivity, the Incarnation, the Diaspora, the second coming of the Christ, even the rapture of the believers and the inhabiting of the Golden City to come.

Abraham, the Wandering Aramaean

The migration of the patriarchs, starting with that of Abraham, solidifies the theme of migration in the biblical story. God brought Abraham out of his father's land to start the pilgrim life that would characterize him and his descendants for many generations. Abraham left his father's land, following God's command to "go to a land that I will show you" (Gen. 12:1). He wandered in Palestine as a nomadic pastoralist for many years, possessing no land apart from a small plot to bury his dead (Gen. 23). Walls observes that "it is as a nomadic pastoralist that he experiences those divine encounters that became the basis for Israel's religion. . . . Maybe he could never have heard the voice of God of Heaven so clearly in Ur or in Haran [where] the gods of the land

---

[96] Hanciles, *Beyond Christendom*, 140.
[97] Walls, "Mission and Migration."

would have obtruded too much."[98] Abraham's role as a faithful perennial migrant with a promise of a land that he never settles in establishes him as a model for New Testament teachings about faith and obedience. The writer of Hebrews has this to say about Abraham:

> By faith Abraham obeyed when he was called to set out for a place that he was to receive as an inheritance; and he set out, not knowing where he was going. By faith he stayed for a time in the land he had been promised, as in a foreign land, living in tents, as did Isaac and Jacob, who were heirs with him of the same promise. For he looked forward to the city that has foundations, whose architect and builder is God. (Heb. 11:8–10)

When famine struck in Canaan, Abraham and his family went down to Egypt, a move that started to unfold the fulfillment of God's word to Abraham: "Know this for certain, that your offspring shall be aliens in a land that is not theirs, and shall be slaves there, and they shall be oppressed for four hundred years" (Gen. 15: 13). Following the footsteps of Abraham, Isaac was also a wanderer in search of water for his animals. Jacob's wanderings also took him away from his family to his uncle's home. In *A History of Israel,* John Bright points out that the patriarchs "lived a semi-nomadic life, living in tents, wandering up and down Palestine and its borderlands in search of seasonal pasture, and on occasion, making longer journeys to Mesopotamia or Egypt."[99]

Later, when Jacob was brought to Egypt during a famine in Canaan, the prophecy given to Abraham would clearly begin to unfold. Jacob's migration to Egypt would lead to four hundred years of the Israelites being immigrants and strangers in Egypt. One can confidently argue that to identify God as the God of Abraham, Isaac, and Jacob is to identify God as the God of the wandering migrant. Indeed, the God of Israel was not ashamed

---

[98] Ibid.

[99] John Bright, *A History of Israel* (Louisville, KY: Westminster John Knox, 2000), 80.

to be called their God because they lived on earth as if they were strangers. Of these three patriarch wanderers and many other migrants in the Bible, the writer of Hebrews suggests that:

> All of these died in faith without having received the promises, but from a distance they saw and greeted them. They confessed that they were strangers and foreigners on the earth, for people who speak in this way make it clear that they are seeking a homeland. If they had been thinking of the land that they had left behind, they would have had opportunity to return. But as it is, they desire a better country, that is, a heavenly one. Therefore God is not ashamed to be called their God; indeed, he has prepared a city for them. (Heb. 11:13–16)

The Exodus

Four centuries after Jacob's migration to Egypt, another major migration took place: the Exodus. In this migration, following a massive intervention of the God of their fathers and mothers (the patriarchs and matriarchs), a nation of twelve tribes left Egypt to migrate back to Palestine (Exod. 12:31–42). These too wandered in the deserts for a long time, having to depend on divine providence for sustenance and protection from enemies and the desert weather. This experience as strangers in Egypt and as wanderers in the wilderness would forever be in their minds and was to shape their understanding of any strangers who would come among them. On establishing their covenant with Yahweh in Exodus, they were told, "You shall neither mistreat a stranger nor oppress him, for you were strangers in the land of Egypt" (Exod. 22:21). On approaching the entrance of the Promised Land, the instructions are repeated. Israel was to always remember its historically vulnerable past as an immigrant stranger in Egypt.[100] At the beginning of every harvest season, they should recite together:

---

[100] Ibid., 91.

A wandering Aramaean was my ancestor; he went down into Egypt and lived there as an alien, few in number, and there he became a great nation, mighty and populous. When the Egyptians treated us harshly and afflicted us, by imposing hard labor on us, we cried to the Lord, the God of our ancestors; the Lord heard our voice and saw our affliction, our toil, and our oppression. The Lord brought us out of Egypt with a mighty hand and an outstretched arm, with a terrifying display of power, and with signs and wonders. (Deut. 26:5–8)

Even after Israel finally settled down in the Promised Land, Yahweh wanted them to remember that they were still strangers in the land that belonged to Yahweh. Indeed, Yahweh said to them, "The land is mine, for you are strangers and sojourners with me" (Lev. 25:23). The Israelites were to always view themselves as resident aliens in their own land, for it belonged to God. They would be only stewards, taking care of God's land. Even though they were chosen people living in their Promised Land, they were still aliens.

The Babylonian Captivity

Another major story of migration in the Bible is that of the Babylonian Captivity. In 597 BCE, King Nebuchadnezzar of Babylon conquered Judah and Jerusalem and took the best of the country's political, ecclesiastical, and intellectual leadership to Babylon.[101] The extent of the devastation and the number of the Jews taken captive are not confidently known (2 Kings 24:14, 16 and Jer. 52:28). However, the event itself involved all the shame and pain of being forcefully dispossessed from their homeland and taken as refugees by a Gentile power. Many of the Jews were killed in battle; many more were taken to Babylon, while others went down to Egypt and other lands.[102] In effect, the Jews were scattered so far and wide that it would be impossible for them all to return to their Promised Land. While in Babylon, the wor-

---

[101] Ibid., 345.
[102] Ibid., 346.

ship of Yahweh was impossible, and they were often required to worship the captor-kings (Dan. 3 and 6). The Psalmist suggests that they were mocked by being forced to sing their religious songs to entertain their captors (Ps. 137). They were surrounded on all sides by symbols of a powerful secular empire and were constantly taunted about the defeat of their God.

Some found ways to live comfortably, as Jeremiah had exhorted them to live peaceably and to pray for the peace of their cities (Jer. 29). The stories of Daniel, Esther, and Ezekiel display the exiles' uncomfortable state of uprootedness and longing to remain faithful to their religion, as they anticipated returning to the land where they could worship Yahweh freely. While in exile, Bright says, "They eagerly awaited Yahweh's judgment on proud Babylon and their eventual release. The ruins of the Holy City pressed upon their hearts; confessing their sins, they prayed for its restoration and for Yahweh's intervention as in the Exodus days."[103] With the help of the prophet generally known as Second Isaiah, the exiles were encouraged to hear God's plan to restore Israel to its original land of the promise (Isa. 40–43). Eventually, upon returning, the exiles were the ones who would restore the temple and the city. It is they, and not the people who had remained in Palestine, who "would shape Israel's future, both giving her faith a new direction and providing the impulse for the ultimate restoration of the Jewish community in Palestine."[104]

The Incarnation

A prime New Testament example of the connection between migration and *missio Dei* is the story of the Incarnation, whereby God actually "moved [also translated "migrated"] into the neighborhood" (John 1:14 [The Message]). Indeed, in the Incarnation, God came and pitched God's tent among us. John 1:14 uses the Greek word *skēnoō,* translated as "to dwell in a tent." Young's Literal Translation of the Bible says, "and [the Word] did *tabernacle* among us," to highlight the connection between the Incarnation and the enduring physical presence of the tabernacle of the Old

---

103 Ibid., 351.
104 Ibid., 345.

Testament. This is both mission at its best and migration at its core, with the missionary God coming down to identify with our neighborhood and to serve and save humankind. It is a border-crossing event in which God becomes the migrant who takes the form of a slave in order to fully identify with human beings (Phil. 2:7). In essence, in the Incarnation, Jesus Christ becomes God's migrant Son. Karl Barth recognizes the Incarnation as "the way of a Son of God into the far country."[105] Jesus was an immigrant, not only as a Galilean carpenter-turned-rabbi ministering in Judea, but also as "the Word made flesh" living in this world among humankind (John 1:14).[106] *Missio Dei*, when understood as the sending of God, is rooted in God's migration.

David Bosch observes a recent rooting of Christian mission in terms of the incarnate Christ, the human Jesus of Nazareth who wearily trod the dusty roads of Palestine to have compassion on the marginalized.[107] Daniel Groody states that no aspect of a theology of migration is more fundamental, and more challenging in its implication, than the Incarnation.[108] The Triune God of heaven, who is a missionary God, became an immigrant God who came to dwell on earth, and the Spirit of God itself continues to be a migrant God who dwells with God's people in the world. Indeed, Groody adds, "God migrates into a world that is poor and divided, not because God finds something good about poverty and estrangement, but because it is precisely in history's darkest place that God can reveal hope to all who experience pain, rejection, and alienation."[109] As such, human migrations are avenues where possibilities for the embodiment of *missio Dei* exist. Jesus' exhortation for the disciples to be his witnesses in Jerusalem, Judea, Samaria, and to the ends of the earth suggests that *missio Dei* would involve migration, as the Great Commis-

---

[105] Karl Barth, *Church Dogmatics*, vol. 4.1: *The Doctrine of Reconciliation* (Edinburgh: T&T Clark International, 1956), 157.

[106] Galilee is also know as Galilee of the Gentiles (Isa. 9:1) and was inhabited by migrants and more gentiles than Jews in the time of Jesus.

[107] Bosch, *Transforming Mission*, 513.

[108] Daniel G. Groody, "Crossing the Divide: Foundations of a Theology of Migration and Refugees," *Theological Studies* 70, no. 3 (2009): 649.

[109] Ibid., 650.

sion says, "Go therefore and make disciples of all nations" (Matt. 28:19).[110]

Human migrations have been a huge part of the spread of religions around the world. Since its birth, Christianity's growth has been connected to the migrations of its adherents. As the disciples scattered into Europe, North Africa, Arabia, and Asia, they took the gospel with them. Recent missionary advance has been achieved through the migration of Europeans to the New World, and then of the Europeans and North Americans to the rest of the world. Now, at the beginning of the twenty-first century, it is the Africans, the Asians, and the Latin Americans who are on the move—moving to Europe and North America. Incidentally, Latin America, Africa, and Asia are also promising to be the Christian heartlands of this century.

We have explored in this chapter how Africans were part of this enterprise right from the beginning of Christianity, and are now joining the missionary movement once again. In the next chapter, I focus on African agency in the missionary movement of the twenty-first century. I suggest that we are witnessing the rebirth of a multiracial multicontinent missionary movement. The blessed reflex is here.

---

[110] Several scholars such as Schroeder have suggested that the emphasis in the Great Commission is on baptizing and not on going. See Roger Schroeder, *What Is the Mission of the Church?: A Guide for Catholics* (Maryknoll, NY: Orbis Books, 2008). This move discourages the urge to go into foreign lands to spread the gospel, and supports the argument that Christians ought to be missionaries in their contexts. However, a majority of non-Western mission scholars insist that "go means go." Lazarus Chakwera of the Assemblies of God in Malawi is famed for telling the 2007 General Council of the Assemblies of God in the USA, in relation to the Great Commission, "Which part of 'Go' do you not understand? Stop analyzing it and start obeying it."

Chapter Two

African Missions in History

We saw in the preceding chapter that the involvement of African Christians in mission goes back to the very early days of Christianity, through figures mentioned in the Book of Acts and the Epistles as part of the great missionary movement that spread Christianity from Jerusalem to Asia Minor and Europe. Down through the decades and centuries, the influence of other African Christians, theologians, and missionaries—such as Tertullian, Pope Victor, Athanasius, and Augustine—is seen all over Western Christianity. This first African missionary movement died with the demise of North African Christianity at the hands of the militant Islam that rose up in Arabia in 632 CE. The period between the seventh and the fifteenth centuries saw very little missionary activity in Africa. Both the Coptic Church in Egypt and the Ethiopian Church continued to exist, but there is little evidence of any missionary activity outside their own communities. It was not until the Portuguese "discovered" sub-Saharan Africa again in the fifteenth century that missionary work began to emerge again in Africa. Almost immediately, African converts started to engage in mission again, and the seeds for a second African missionary movement were planted. This movement would be only marginally successful due to the rise of slavery and racism.

African Agency in Mission in Africa

Writing this story at the beginning of the twenty-first century, it is important to note that the continent of Africa has been evangelized by Africans. Any faithful writing of the history of Christianity in Africa will have to account for the agency of

Africans in its growth—the agency that, as I have suggested above, can be seen in African Christianity since the fifteenth century. Whether one reads Ogbu Kalu's *African Christianity*,[1] Elizabeth Isichei's *A History of Christianity in Africa*,[2] or Adrian Hastings's two books, *The Church in Africa, 1450–1950*,[3] and *A History of African Christianity, 1950–1975*,[4] the role played by Africans in spreading the gospel in Africa is evident. Although only a few names of African leaders, such as David Asante of Ghana (1834–1892), Samuel Ajayi Crowther of Nigeria (1809–1891), and William Wade Harris of Liberia (1860–1929), are recognized, mentioning them highlights the early evangelistic efforts of Africans among other Africans, even when the Western missionary movement of the nineteenth century was just beginning in Africa. In addition to these few names, there were hundreds—probably thousands—of other African evangelists and leaders who contributed just as much as these, even though their names did not make it into the books of history. Naturally, this fact will be of great importance to any understanding of African missionary work, since it shapes the African understanding of missions.

A careful study of the development of Christianity in Africa reveals the agency of African Christians in evangelizing the continent going back to the reintroduction of the religion in Africa during the Portuguese Voyages of Discovery in the fifteenth century. With the blessings of the pope and Prince Henry, Portuguese sailors and traders sought to convert the Africans they met on the West African coast. Prince Henry, who was a devout Catholic, believed that it was his duty to spread the Catholic faith in Africa, as this would, in a way, prevent the Muslims from taking over sub-Saharan Africa. In the process, many Africans were taken to Portugal; most were slaves, but a few were sent by the mission-

---

[1] Ogbu Kalu, *African Christianity: An African Story* (Trenton, NJ: Africa World Press, 2007).

[2] Elizabeth Isichei, *A History of Christianity: From Antiquity to the Present* (Grand Rapids, MI: Eerdmans, 1995).

[3] Adrian Hastings, *The Church in Africa: 1450–1950*, Oxford History of the Christian Church (Oxford: Oxford University Press, 1994).

[4] Adrian Hastings, *A History of African Christianity, 1950–1975*, African Studies Series 26 (Cambridge: Cambridge University Press, 1979).

aries to receive a theological education in Lisbon. Isichei mentions "one little Moor who became a friar of Saint Francis and a lay missionary at St. Vincent de Cabo as early as 1444."[5] Charles Boxer points out that by 1494, there were already hundreds of young black men from West Africa studying Latin and theology in Portugal with the aim of returning to São Tomé, Congo, and elsewhere as missionaries.[6] This would cause one German visitor at the time to say, "It seems likely that in the course of time, the greater part of Ethiopia [referring to all of sub-Saharan Africa] will be converted to Christianity."[7] For a brief time in the mid-sixteenth century, another seminary was established in Cape Verde. Later, in 1571, a seminary for the training of local youths was opened in São Tomé by the bishop of the island. By 1600, it was reported that all the priests who were then active on the island had graduated from this seminary.[8]

In 1518, Pope Leo X had consecrated an African bishop, Dom Henrique, the son of King Afonso of Kongo, who had been studying in Lisbon for thirteen years, as Bishop of Utica (and not in his native Kongo).[9] Several other young men from the king's family were also sent to Lisbon for theological training. Dom Henrique died in 1530, having achieved very little as a bishop because "he was marginalized by the Portuguese clergy."[10] Another prominent figure was Philip Quaque (1741–1816). Quaque (also known as Kweku) was an African from Cape Coast (Ghana) who was trained in theology in London and ordained as an Anglican priest—the first African Anglican minister—in 1765 before returning to Africa for missionary service.[11] He worked as a chaplain at the Cape Coast Castle but had forgotten his mother tongue, Fante, and so could not be effective as a missionary.

---

[5] Isichei, *History of Christianity*, 55.

[6] Charles R. Boxer, *The Church Militant and Iberian Expansion, 1440–1770* (Baltimore: Johns Hopkins University Press, 1978), 3.

[7] Ibid.

[8] Ibid., 6.

[9] John Baur, *2000 Years of Christianity in Africa: An African Church History,* 2nd rev. ed. (Nairobi, Kenya: Paulines, 1998), 59–60.

[10] After his death, it took the Roman Catholic Church centuries to appoint another West African bishop, who was actually consecrated in 1970.

[11] Baur, *2000 Years of Christianity in Africa,* 117.

I find it amazing that, as Charles Boxer puts it, there was once a time when there were no color barriers involved in the development of an indigenous clergy. Unfortunately, it was not long before racial prejudice made itself known.[12] In those days, the potential for an African agency was evident, but it was not until after the influx of missionaries in the second half of the nineteenth century that one finds some intentionality in developing an indigenous church that would depend on indigenous evangelists for its propagation.

The idea of indigenous agency in missions had already been mentioned in the works of some early missionaries, such as Henry Venn and William Hughes. Venn was secretary of the Church Missionary Society from 1841 to 1873. With the help of an American contemporary by the name of Rufus Anderson, Venn developed a "three-self formula" for indigenizing the church, which they would test in Africa. He was of the vision that missionary work in the unevangelized world should produce a self-governing, self-supporting, and self-propagating indigenous church.[13] In this way, Venn put his trust in the agency of the indigenous converts in propagating their newly found religion.

William Hughes, a Welsh missionary in Congo in the 1880s, established the Colwyn Bay African Institute (originally called the Congo Institute) in 1891 in Wales with the aim of "training Africans in Britain, where they would be raised in a Christian environment and receive practical training from local tradesmen and professionals,"[14] in such fields as carpentry, printing, tailoring, and blacksmithing. This, argued Hughes, would enable them to become self-supporting missionaries in Africa. In so doing, they would help realize Henry Venn's vision of a self-governing, self-supporting, and self-propagating African church.[15] However, one might reasonably assume that Hughes was actually hoping

---

[12] Boxer, *Church Militant and Iberian Expansion, 1440–1770*, 4–5.

[13] See Gailyn Van Rheenen, *Missions: Biblical Foundations and Contemporary Strategies* (Grand Rapids, MI: Zondervan, 1996), 179–205.

[14] Jeffrey Green, "009: Colwyn Bay's African Institute: 1889–1912" (London), http://www.jeffreygreen.co.uk.

[15] C. Peter William, *The Ideal of the Self-Governing Church: A Study in Victorian Missionary Strategy* (Leiden: Brill, 1990), 1.

to Westernize—or "civilize"—the Africans to make them better missionaries.[16]

Zana Etambala suggests many missionaries brought Congolese children to Europe in the late 1800s for education, hoping to send them back to Africa as missionaries.[17] In addition to Hughes's school in Wales, Etambala mentions other schools in Italy, Sweden, and the United States. Fathers Don Mazza and Daniel Comboni established the Istituto per le Missioni della Nigrizia in Verona, Italy; later, Cardinal Lavigerie established the Institut des Jeunes Noirs in Malta.[18] The impact of these schools and institutes on the development of African Christianity is not well documented. We do not even know how many of these African students returned to Africa or what they did when they returned.

From my home in Malawi, we have a legendary story of a man called John Chilembwe, a Baptist minister who was taken from Malawi by a missionary named Joseph Booth for training in the United States between 1897 and 1900.[19] Upon his return to Malawi (then called Nyasaland), he started the Providence Industrial Mission at Nguludi in Chiradzulu. He was very critical of the treatment that the locals received from the colonial government. In January 1915, he led a local uprising against the government, during which several white farmers and colonialists were killed. Chilembwe himself was killed a few weeks later by the colonial government.[20] It is likely, however, that some of

---

[16] See William Hughes, *Dark Africa and the Way Out: Or a Scheme for Civilizing and Evangelizing the Dark Continent* (New York: Negro Universities Press, 1969).

[17] Zana Aziza Etambala, "Congolese Children at the Congo House in Colwyn Bay (North Wales, Great Britain) at the End of the 19th Century," *Afrika Focus* 3, no. 3–4 (1987): 240.

[18] Ibid., 241.

[19] D. D. Phiri, *John Chilembwe*, Malawians to Remember (Lilongwe: Longman Malawi, 1976). Also D. D. Phiri, *Let Us Die for Africa: An African Perspective on the Life and Death of John Chilembwe of Nyasaland*, exp. ed. (Blantyre, Malawi: Central Africana, 1999).

[20] George Shepperson and Thomas Price, *Independent African: John Chilembwe and the Origins, Setting, and Significance of the Nyasaland Native Rising of 1915*, Edinburgh University Publications: History, Philosophy, and Economics (Edinburgh: University Press, 1958).

the Western-educated Africans returned home and contributed in various ways to their country's development and evangelism. In addition, Etambala has also suggested that these African students were involved in the struggle for the decolonization of Africa while they were in Europe and North America.[21] For instance, Etambala suggests that the first Pan-African conference, which took place in London in 1900, involved many such African students.[22]

The Three Tracks of African Christianity

The development of African Christianity in the past two centuries has taken place on three parallel tracks. First, we have the mainline or missionary churches that have followed the Western denominations brought to Africa by the missionaries. In this group, we find the Presbyterian, Methodist, Lutheran, Anglican, and Roman Catholic churches, among others. The independence of most of these mission churches came about in the 1970s, after the political decolonization of Africa. The second group comprises what has been called the African Independent Churches. These were formed by African prophets and evangelists who for various reasons broke away from the mission churches. These churches started to emerge as early as 1880, but their growth exploded in the 1920s. Many such African Initiated Churches led by African evangelists have spread across sub-Saharan Africa for the past one hundred years and have converted millions of Africans from traditional religions to Christianity. Two such churches are the Aladura of Nigeria and the Kimbanguists of Congo. The third type of African Christianity, which has fully emerged in the second half of the twentieth century, mainly consists of Pentecostals and charismatic Christians. These have maintained a strong sense of Africanness and are independent in their work, but they also maximize their network connections with the global evangelical community.[23]

---

[21] Etambala, "Congolese Children at the Congo House," 242.

[22] Ibid.

[23] For a thorough explanation of this development, see J. Kwabena Asa-

Each of these three types of African Christianity has grown largely owing to the work of African evangelists, prophets, and apostles. Knowing this, the growth of African Christianity after 1970 begins to make sense: African Christianity has thrived independently of the missionaries' lead. For example, in the case of the African Independent Churches, early evangelists such as Samuel Ajayi Crowther and William Wade Harris had great success converting other Africans where it had proved difficult for Western missionaries. Furthermore, in the Buganda revival of the 1890s, hundreds of African evangelists carried vernacular scriptures to every district. Later, in the 1930s, during the famous East African revivals, which originated in Rwanda through the Anglican Church of Uganda, the local *balokole*—translated "saved ones"—were the evangelists. It was a local Luganda chorus, *tukutendereza Yesu* (meaning "we praise you, Jesus") and not a Western hymn, that became the theme song of these revivalists as they spread throughout the Swahili-speaking region.

Mission in Africa's Postcolonial Christianity

To highlight this aspect of the history of African Christianity is not to overlook the many Western missionaries who planted the seeds of Christianity in African countries between 1850 and 1970, or those who stayed after 1970 to see the fruition of their efforts. That history, however, is not complete without acknowledging that Africa has been most actively converted by the thousands of African evangelists who traversed the continent with the gospel after 1970 with the intensity and fervor of an eleventh-hour evangelism movement, one perhaps unprecedented in the history of the church. The result of their evangelization efforts is the conversion of about ten million people every year in sub-Saharan Africa, on average.[24] The multitudes of African evangelists

---

moah-Gyadu, *African Charismatics: Current Developments within Independent Indigenous Pentecostalism in Ghana* (Boston: Brill, 2005). There is a growing conversation among scholars of African migration about the transnational nature of the immigrants' existence whereby they are involved in both their home countries and in the Diaspora.

[24] See Todd Johnson, Kenneth R. Ross, and Sandra S. K. Lee. *Atlas*

have unleashed millions of energized "missionaries"—and by that
I mean local evangelists, most of them lay Christians—who have
effectively proclaimed the gospel, shared their faith, and planted
millions of churches in their neighborhoods and townships across
Africa. The priesthood—or should I say "evangelisthood"—of all
believers is a missionary strategy that has received new life among
African Christians.

The African evangelists, apostles, and their followers who
have, in a way, converted the continent rarely call themselves missionaries. For them, evangelism and mission are an inherent part
of what it means to be Christians. Without being involved in
both these endeavors, their sense of "being a Christian" is incomplete. Even when they cross national borders to serve on foreign
mission fields, they identify themselves simply as Christians doing
their Christian duty to evangelize.

This concept of the *evangelisthood* of all believers in African
Christianity has, to a great extent, been a result of Africa's contextualization of Christianity. It draws from the African traditional
religions where people were involved in the acts of worship and
ritual sacrifices as communities, not as individuals. Religion for
Africans is a cultural event that involves entire communities. Talking about the traditional religions in Kenyan culture, John Mbiti
portrays a culture that is notoriously religious—in which religion
covers everyone and everything.[25] The communal nature of African religions allowed for a very narrow gap between the clergy
and the laity.[26] Everyone in a culture like this was a *lay* priest and

---

of Global Christianity, 1910–2010 (Edinburgh: Edinburgh University Press,
2009), 110. There has been a sense of urgency for evangelism typically
aligning African Christianity with the charismatic and Pentecostal movement. One can see this urgency in the names of some of the churches
and ministries. The Eleventh-Hour Institute is an evangelistic arm of the
Assemblies of God in Africa, headed by Lazarus Chakwera, the president of
the Assemblies of God in Malawi.

[25] John S. Mbiti, *African Religions and Philosophy* (Garden City, NY:
Anchor Books, 1970), 1.

[26] Recent years of African Christianity have brought some Western
influences, and there has been a surge of complaints among many local
African Christians about the dominance of the type of prosperity gospel
that comes from America. See Paul Gifford, *Ghana's New Christianity: Pente-*

an evangelist. One did not have to be anointed as a priest to be able to spread the good news about religion (and culture). The priestly duties were naturally guided by the officially ordained priests, but they were everybody's responsibility and were performed by entire communities. Lay people were just as involved in the religious rituals as the priests themselves.

In a sense, the entire community was a community of priests, something similar to Peter's notion of "a kingdom of priests" (1 Pet. 2:9).[27] They were communities of evangelists where a majority of the members are able to proclaim the gospel and perform basic religious rituals. Contemporary African Christianity has brought this participatory nature of religion into contact with the church at large and, in doing so, turned new converts into immediate witnesses and evangelists who constantly "proclaim the mighty acts of him who called [them] out of darkness into his marvelous light" (1 Pet. 2:9). In Africa, every Christian is a potential evangelist, and a majority of them take this evangelistic calling seriously enough to talk freely about faith in the public arena.

In embracing this priesthood of all believers, African Christianity has overcome some of the most problematic dichotomies that encumber Western Christianity. For instance, it overcomes the divide between the clergy and the laity. Most of the duties of the clergy are also accessible to their lay members. In most cases, the clergy are there for the sake of structure, while everything that they do can also be done by their members. Most African clergy will spend a great deal of their energy training, equipping, and encouraging their members for the work of the ministry. Under normal circumstances, it is the lay Christians who do the work of evangelism, visitation, and praying for the sick, among other ministry duties. In their small groups—or "home-cells," as they are usually called—lay Christians engage in neighborhood evangelism on a constant basis. These home-cells organize their own prayer vigils, community get-togethers, and ministry schools.

---

costalism in a Globalizing African Economy (Bloomington: Indiana University Press, 2004).

[27] The NRSV interprets this as a royal priesthood. The concept also appears in Revelation 1:6 where John the Revelator suggests that Christ has made "us"—his followers—to be kings and priests to his God and Father.

In this way, African Christianity has taken much of the work of the ministry away from the clergy and given it to the laity where, some would argue, it belongs.[28]

In addition to the narrowing of the clergy-laity gap, and the subsequent rise of millions of lay evangelists on the continent, this priesthood of all believers has also avoided the Western dichotomy of sacred-versus-secular spaces. Lay African Christians share their faith in any circumstance. Every Christian is a potential evangelist, and thus a missionary, and the gospel can be proclaimed anywhere. The preaching of the gospel is seen in places that would make some Western Christians uncomfortable, like the hospital ward, or a moving bus, or even at the farms during lunch breaks.

Like evangelism, ministry to the needy is a corporate effort. Laying hands on the sick, just like exorcising the demon-possessed, is every believer's portion. Pastors and elders are called for help after their lay members have already done their part. Exploring these tendencies among Ghanaian Christians, Asamoah-Gyadu says that lay African Christians have the world as their parish.[29] Sunday morning services are for formal worship, where Christians gather together to recharge their missional zeal. However, midweek fellowships that take place in homes are where most of their missional efforts occur. Away from the ecclesiastical bounds of their denominations, most lay Christians participate in nondenominational midweek fellowships where they embody the Christianity they see in the New Testament without the guidance or the supervision of their clergy. This is where most of the church growth occurs, when the gospel is made accessible to neighbors in a nonthreatening atmosphere.

I say this to highlight an important aspect of African Christianity that might speak to our quest to understand the role of Africans in Christian mission. As mentioned earlier, although African Christianity is truly missional in nature, very few African Christians identify themselves as professional missionaries. This has always been so. Long ago, in 1897, when the Nigerian

---

[28] See Asamoah-Gyadu, *African Charismatics*, 127–31.

[29] Also see Allan Anderson, *African Reformation: African Initiated Christianity in the 20th Century* (Trenton, NJ: Africa World Press, 2001).

Archbishop Ajayi Crowther spoke at a Keswick Convention in England, he said it was a rule in the native churches that all who came to the Lord's table must be missionaries.[30]

The African belief in its own agency in the spread of Christianity, nevertheless, has not been well appreciated in mission history. When Western scholars report on the role of indigenous Africans in evangelizing the continent, their objectivity is usually overcome by skepticism. For example, in the case of the growth of Malawian Christianity, the story of the powerful Malawian *alaliki*[31] of the 1970s and '80s is often overshadowed by mentions of their age, syncretism, and power struggles, and the charismatic tendencies of their Christian practice. Writing about the "young puritan preachers," of Malawi, Richard van Dijk agrees that the City of Blantyre saw an explosion of "born again churches, ministries, and fellowships" led by young Malawian men in their twenties and thirties.[32] However, while he offers an outsider commentary that is generally true in its observations, his interpretations seem too skeptical to warrant any credibility for both the "Born-Again movement" and those interested in its study. While focusing on what seemed abnormal to him about these young preachers, Van Dijk missed the explosive growth that Christianity experienced in Blantyre and the surrounding districts in the 1980s and '90s. In addition, Van Dijk's claim that the movement was confined to the cities and was characterized by a dislike of village life[33] proved to be wrong. The movement spread like a bushfire across Malawi, and the by the mid-1990s had reached Mozambique, where Living Waters (one of the churches mentioned in Van Dijk's article) planted hundreds of churches.

---

[30] *Keswick Week, 1897*, 191.

[31] Literal translation: preachers. However, the word was used to describe local itinerant evangelists who were popular in the country in those decades. It should be noted that this word has been misspelled in most African Christianity literature. *Alaliki,* as we have it here, is the correct spelling.

[32] Richard van Dijk, "Young Puritan Preachers in Post-Independent Malawi," *Africa* 62, no. 2 (1992).

[33] Ibid., 159.

Did You Say "Mission"?

Because very few African Christians identify themselves as professional missionaries, when the word *missionary* is used even today, it evokes for Africans a Western foreigner: a Roman Catholic priest from Belgium, a white Southern Baptist pastor from the United States, or a Canadian Pentecostal teaching at a mission school, working at a village clinic, or even heading a parish in rural Africa. For most Africans, a missionary has to be white, coming from Europe, North America, or Australia. He—the term "missionary" was almost exclusively used for males—must also be serving the church in Africa for an extended period. For Africans, missionary work involves incarnation and longevity. One has to identify with the people he or she is trying to reach in all aspects of life, especially by living among them.

Unfortunately, such missionaries are not as available today as they were half a century ago. Certainly, there are still hundreds of white missionaries across the continent, but most Western missionaries left the continent in the 1960s and 1970s when colonialism came to an end. Neither they nor their children returned to Africa to continue with the missionary work they had started. If they visited again, it was usually on short-term mission trips, which Africans rarely consider missionary trips. African Christianity is certainly very committed to the expansion of the kingdom of God, but luckily, this commitment is manifested in ways that are radically different from those of the Western Christianity associated with colonialism.

The growth of Christianity in Africa since the early 1970s has coincided with the end of most forms of political colonialism, which also triggered the liberation of the African church from Western leadership. By 1960, in chorus with African nationalists, African Christians also started to talk about the need to decolonize the African church. The popular works of great writers such as Mzee Jomo Kenyatta, Mongo Beti, and Chinua Achebe revealed some of the struggles that Africans had with Western missionaries. Mongo Beti's *The Poor Christ of Bomba* summarizes these struggles with masterly narrative eloquence. By depicting missionary superiority and outright brutality, as well as conflicts with colonial agents in the face of forceful or fake conversions intended to gain missionary favors, he makes it evident that colonialism and authentic missionary efforts could not go together.[34]

By the time the process of political decolonization reached its peak, native sentiments toward missionaries in Asia and Africa were often not amicable. The atrocities of colonial governments and their agents were associated with the activities of the missionaries. As a result, Africans and Asians cried out together in chorus against the colonization of the church—the Western leadership of the church—on their continents. When the Philippine missionary theologian Emerito Nacpil wrote about the "death of mission" in 1971, he spoke of mission as symbolizing the "universality of Western imperialism and racism . . . and Western technology and gadgetry."[35] For him, as well as for many Asians, what they saw in the missionary was not "the face of the suffering Christ, but a benevolent monster."[36] He concluded his now-famous speech at a missionary conference in Kuala Lumpur in February 1971 with a declaration, "The present structure of modern mission is dead. . . . The first thing we ought to do is eulogize it and then bury it. . . . The most *missionary* service that a missionary under the present system can do today to Asia is to go home!"[37]

On the African continent, Adrian Hastings said that by 1970 it had become clear that the foreign missionary was essentially irrelevant or had become something vastly more marginal to African Christianity than ever before.[38] Most foreign missionary leaders by this time had stepped down to make way for African successors, and many missionaries had returned to Europe and North America. Just like the decolonization of African politics,

---

[34] For instance, see Father Drummond's manhandling of Sanga Boto. Mongo Beti, *The Poor Christ of Bomba* (Long Grove, IL: Waveland, 1971), 73.

[35] Emerito P. Nacpil, "Mission but Not Missionaries," *International Review of Mission* 60, no. 239 (1971): 359.

[36] Ibid.

[37] Ibid., 360. See also David J. Bosch, *Transforming Mission: Paradigm Shifts in Theology of Mission,* American Society of Missiology Series (Maryknoll, NY: Orbis Books, 1991), 518.

[38] Hastings, *History of African Christianity, 1950–1975,* 224.

the independence of the African church was not freely given. It had to be fought for. Many Westerners did not trust that the "younger churches" would be capable to stand without them. Therefore, the decolonization of the African churches took much longer. It was the General Secretary of the Presbyterian Church of East Africa, John Gatu of Kenya, who shocked the world at a missions festival in Milwaukee, Wisconsin, USA, in October 1971 when he suggested that no missionaries or money should be sent to Africa for at least five years.[39] These thoughts had been in circulation for quite a while.[40] Adrian Hastings adds that the concept of the moratorium had originally been suggested by Professor Walter Freytag in 1958, and had been discussed on several platforms since then. However, Gatu garnered the courage to bring the message home to the United States to call for Western churches to stop helping the African church "so that the short man could learn to hang his knapsack within reach."[41] He went on to suggest a withdrawal of all Western missionaries from Africa.

> The time has come for the withdrawal of the foreign missionaries from many parts of the Third World, that the churches of the Third World must be allowed to find their own identity and that the continuation of the present missionary movement is a hindrance to this selfhood of the church.[42]

Cited elsewhere, he continued:

> We cannot build the church in Africa on alms given by overseas churches. Nor are we serving the cause of the

---

[39] R. Elliott Kendall, *The End of an Era: Africa and the Missionary* (London: SPCK, 1978), 90.

[40] Hastings, *History of African Christianity, 1950–1975*, 225.

[41] Ogbu Kalu, "The Anatomy of Reverse Flow in African Christianity: Pentecostalism and Immigrant African Christianity," in *African Christian Presence in the West: New Immigrant Congregations and Transnational Networks in North America and Europe*, ed. Frieder Ludwig and J. Kwabena Asamoah-Gyadu (Trenton, NJ: Africa World Press, 2011), 35.

[42] Bengt Sundkler and Christopher Steed, *A History of the Church in Africa*, Studia Missionalia Upsaliensa 74 (New York: Cambridge University Press, 2000), 1027.

Kingdom by turning all bishops, general secretaries, moderators, presidents, and general superintendents into good enthusiastic beggars, always singing the tune of poverty in the churches of the third world.[43]

Later on, he adds,

We must ask missionaries to leave. . . . I started by saying that the missionaries should be withdrawn from the Third World for a period of at least five years. I will go further and say that the missionaries should be withdrawn, period.[44]

The moratorium debate lasted five years. As mentioned, its main thrust was that the European and North American churches should stop sending missionaries and money to Third World churches.[45] It was met with fierce resistance from the West. Nevertheless, it opened up conversations, especially among the Majority World Christians who loudly mused whether cross-cultural mission is biblically mandated for white people only. Non-Western Christians began to wonder, "Is the missionary nature of the church imparted to the non-Western churches as well? Were the Christians from the Third World churches also mandated to be missionaries, both in their own world, and in the West?" As a result of the moratorium debate, missionary movements among non-Western nations began to rise. The moratorium generated the reverse flow concept—"the blessed reflex"—grounding its rationale, and determining its characteristics.[46] Later, at the All

---

[43]   Emele Mba Uka, *Missionaries Go Home?: A Sociological Interpretation of an African Response to Christian Missions* (New York: Lang, 1989), 192.

[44]   Cited in Kendall, *End of an Era*, 90–91.

[45]   See R. Elliott Kendall, "On the Sending of Missionaries: A Call for Restraint," *International Review of Mission* 64, no. 253 (1975). In addition to Emilio Nacpil, Gerald Anderson adds two other voices calling for the moratorium, one is that of Father Paul Verghese from India, who is reported to have said that, "the mission of the church is the greatest enemy of the gospel. The other one is José Miguez-Bonino from Argentina. See Gerald H. Anderson, "A Moratorium on Missionaries" (Chicago: Christian Century), http://www.religion-online.org.

[46]   Frieder Ludwig and J. Kwabena Asamoah-Gyadu, *African Christian*

Africa Council of Churches in Lusaka in 1974, under the leadership of Burgess Carr, it was declared:

> To enable the African Church to achieve the power of being a true instrument of liberating and reconciling the African people, as well as finding solutions to economic and social dependency, our option as a matter of policy has to be a moratorium on external assistance in money and personnel. We recommend this option as the only potent means of becoming truly and authentically ourselves while remaining a respected and responsible part of the Universal Church.[47]

Third World churches began to gain confidence that they also had the mandate to do missionary work, both among themselves and in the West. Indeed, most of the non-Western missionaries today are serving in the non-Western world. A member of John Gatu's previous congregation recently informed me that the Presbyterian Church of Kenya actually sent missionaries to London at the end of the 1970s. The Lutheran World Federation sent five pastors from Tanzania to work in Europe in 1982. Kalu reports that these missionaries "were received politely and patronized."[48] Apparently, mainline reverse mission would struggle to gain ground until the Pentecostal and charismatic movement provided an impetus in the 1990s. African missionary work outside the continent of Africa grew to become a worldwide phenomenon during this final decade of the twentieth century.

Gatu met resistance from all directions, both on theological and humanitarian grounds. The West was not ready to recognize that the African churches were capable of standing on their own. The moratorium was never effected. However, by the late 1960s, amid a climate of self-doubt and reevaluation, the number of professional Western missionaries from the older Western main-

---

Presence in the West: New Immigrant Congregations and Transnational Networks in North America and Europe (Trenton, NJ: Africa World Press, 2011), 36.

[47] See Hastings, *History of African Christianity, 1950–1975*, 225.

[48] Ludwig and Asamoah-Gyadu, *African Christian Presence*, 36.

line denominations began to plummet.[49] Phil Jenkins observes: "It was precisely as Western colonialism ended that Christianity began a period of explosive growth that still continues unchecked in Africa."[50]

The Western Missionary Movement Slows Down

Similarly, Western Christianity underwent a crisis in its missionary work throughout the world. The African moratorium on foreign missionary aid represented a view echoed by many voices in the non-Western world. In most of the colonies, the fight for political independence was led by Christians who had been educated in mission schools. Robert Mugabe, for instance, was educated at the Katuma Jesuit Mission near Salisbury in Zimbabwe (then called Southern Rhodesia).[51] Like many African nationalists of his generation, his missionary education helped him fight against colonialism—a struggle that also led to the decolonization of the African church. In the face of this resistance, the Western missionary movement lost a great deal of confidence. Many Westerners took the rejection personally, and could not believe that their own students and disciples were forcing them out. Some non-Western countries like China expelled all Western missionaries. Other countries simply denied them return visas.

The second problem that the missionary movement faced was theological, and it was primarily a Western problem. Arising in Europe in the 1960s, an influential Dutch theologian by the name of Johannes Hoekendijk began to argue against colonial missions. In *Kirche und Volk,* Hoekendijk said that for more than a thousand years, Europe had played the crusader by maneuvering itself ideologically into a position of power and using this position to tyrannize the world.[52] He believed it was now time

---

[49] Dana Lee Robert, *Christian Mission: How Christianity Became a World Religion* (Malden, MA: Wiley-Blackwell, 2009), 69.

[50] Philip Jenkins, *The Next Christendom: The Coming of Global Christianity,* 3rd ed. (New York: Oxford University Press, 2011), 56.

[51] Andrew Norman, *Robert Mugabe and the Betrayal of Zimbabwe* (Jefferson, NC: McFarland, 2004), 35–37.

[52] Johannes Christiaan Hoekendijk and Erich Walter Pollmann, *Kirche*

to change that. In his *Church Inside Out*, he went further to argue for the place of the secular world in mission—claiming that the world should set the church's agenda for mission.[53] He showed a great discontent with the church as it was then. He believed God's activity in the world consisted of bringing God's kingdom and shalom to the world, and this could be done without the church. The church was thus, in his opinion, irrelevant for mission. In arguing like this, Hoekendijk further weakened the prevalent understanding of mission in his day. Many mainline churches would end up calling their missionaries back. They also found it difficult to recruit new missionaries.

Redefining the Missionary

For better or for worse, in the eyes of most Africans, the term *missionary* still struggles to shake off its identification with colonialism. The connections between the missionary movement and colonialism have deep and long-lasting implications for the spread of the gospel in the postcolonial world. In the same way that the missionary enterprise was closely associated with the imperial expansion of the West, the word *missionary* was also attached to this expansion effort and was often taken to imply "the earliest foot-soldiers of colonial empires,"[54] or as "colonial administrators."[55] Even in this day and age, when the typical missionary is no longer a seminary-educated white European or North American male serving in some distant country across the oceans, Africans are wary of the West's use of mission to help colonialism. Indeed, even if anyone from any part of the world, regardless of color, education, class, or country of origin, can now serve on the mission field in any part of the world, this change

---

und Volk in der Deutschen Missionswissenschaft (Munich: Kaiser, 1967), 317.

[53] See Timothy C. Tennent, *Invitation to World Missions: A Trinitarian Missiology for the Twenty-First Century* (Grand Rapids, MI: Kregel Publications, 2010), 59.

[54] John H. Darch, *Missionary Imperialists?: Missionaries, Government and the Growth of the British Empire in the Tropics, 1860–1885* (Colorado Springs: Paternoster, 2009), 1.

[55] Beti, *Poor Christ of Bomba*, 153.

of identity is only beginning to disassociate the work of the missionary from its colonial/Western connotations.

In light of this, the terms *mission* and *missionary* that were relevant to the kind of Christianity that was spread with Christendom may now be outdated in the current post-Christendom world in which we live. It is not the word *mission* in itself that is problematic, but the way in which it has been used in the past centuries. Both the terms *mission* and *missionary* have to be stripped of their colonial robes and reinterpreted through both postcolonial and post-Christendom—or pre-Christendom— lenses. I suspect that this may be simpatico with the type of mission that we see in the New Testament. *Mission* is translated from Latin *missio* which means "to send." The New Testament seems to envision the entire church as a sent community. The contemporary (and popular) usage that connects mission to both a special group of designated people as missionaries and to the Great Commission, whereby people leave their homelands to share their faith across the seas, and thereby to extend the church, is a more recent one and does not reflect the complete reality of *missio Dei*. It came into use in the sixteenth century among the Jesuits who began to use "mission" to refer to the spreading of the Jesuit movement to bring the gospel to the unevangelized, mostly outside Europe. Before that time, "mission" was "used exclusively with reference to the doctrine of the Trinity, that is, of the sending of the Son by the Father, and of the Holy Spirit by the Father and the Son."[56] That is to say, the origin of "mission" was about the Trinity and God's redemptive work in the world, and had nothing to do with the activities of one dominant group among the nations of the world.

Where the term *mission* has been adopted in Africa (especially among Pentecostals who take it from their Western counterparts), it has to do with the intentional sending of pastors to foreign countries, usually to take spiritual care of their countrymen and countrywomen who have migrated to those countries.[57] In these

---

[56] Carlos F. Cardoza-Orlandi, *Mission: An Essential Guide* (Nashville, TN: Abingdon Press, 2002), 24–25.

[57] This could be largely attributed to the globalized nature of Pentecostal Christianity. As will be argued in chapter 5, a majority of African

cases, the identity of the "missionary" is given almost exclusively to the leaders (pastors and evangelists), and not the members. For the rest of African Christians, mission is inherent in their Christianity.

African Agency in Missions in the World

In the process of rejecting the Western missionary work that was tied closely to the colonization of the continent, a type of African Christianity has emerged—one that has little to do with Christendom and imperial powers. Like Latin American Christianity, it is shaped by a liberation mentality—liberation from oppression, exploitation, poverty, and diseases. It is a Christianity that has grown in an intensely religious culture amid many other competing religions. In most cases, it is the religion of the powerless, the poor, and the uneducated. Despite these disadvantages, African Christians are passionate about taking the gospel to other continents. They are passionate about doing God's missionary work in the world even though they rejected the colonial missions of the last century and understand mission in a way that is different from the way the Westerners that brought Christianity to Africa understood it. The remaining section of this chapter is dedicated to discussing how this movement of African Christians and missionaries to the West came about. First, it explores the origins and meaning of the term *blessed reflex*. After that, it explores how it has developed so far.

Blessed Reflex

In the final decade of the eighteenth century, William Carey popularized the idea of voluntary missionary associations. Carey founded the Baptist Missionary Society (BMS) in 1792. In the following year, he left England for India, where he spent the remaining years of his life, never to return to his beloved Britain.[58]

---

missionaries are working in African ethnic congregations among people of their own cultural heritage.

[58] For Carey's biography, see Timothy George, *Faithful Witness: The Life and Mission of William Carey* (Birmingham, AL: New Hope, 1991).

Within a decade of the formation of the BMS, more than ten other missionary associations were formed on both sides of the Atlantic Ocean.[59] A renewed fervor around mission spread among Western Christians, resulting in remarkable growth in both human and financial resources dedicated to the cause of overseas missions. Throughout the nineteenth century, mission was the new orthodoxy. The key to this radical change in the church's engagement with mission was in the new possibilities opening up for lay Christians to form associations among themselves to send missionaries to the unevangelized world. In the first half of the nineteenth century, thousands of European and North American Christians left their homelands to serve as missionaries in South America, Africa, and Asia.

As these developments were taking place, there was expressed some expectation of the "blessed reflex" or "reflexive action," that at some time in the future Christians from the rest of the world would invigorate Western Christianity in one way or another. The term *blessed reflex* itself was used in the early nineteenth century by Western missionary leaders to talk about the hope of a time when the "sending" churches of the West would be challenged and renewed by the churches then springing up in Latin America, Africa, and Asia.[60] The Western missionaries believed that the impulse that energized the missionary movement of the nineteenth century would create a reflex action in the rest of the world that would, in return, benefit the Western sending churches. However, these benefits that the Western missionaries thought about were never fully explained.

In his article on the blessed reflex, Kenneth Ross suggests a sort of "conversion" of the Western missionary as one possible benefit.[61] A

---

[59] For instance, London Missionary Society (1795), Friends' Missionary Society (1795), Scottish Missionary Society (1796), Church Missionary Society (1799), and New York Missionary Society (1800).

[60] Wilbert R. Shenk, "Recasting Theology of Mission: Impulses from the Non-Western World," *International Bulletin of Missionary Research* 25, no. 3 (2001): 106. Also see Kenneth R. Ross, "'Blessed Reflex': Mission as God's Spiral of Renewal," *International Bulletin of Missionary Research* 27, no. 4 (2003): 162–68.

[61] Ross, "'Blessed Reflex,'" 163.

similar interpretation is given by Michael Goheen, who in his article, "Toward a Missiology of Western Culture," talks about a hypothetical scenario of a Western missionary who is "converted" while working overseas.[62] Goheen's hypothetical missionary in India becomes increasingly aware of the impact of the particular culture's worldview on its understanding of the gospel. In this way, the missionary is challenged to see how her own understanding of the gospel is shaped by her culture—and there her conversion begins. A similar line of thought appears in the works of Anthony Gittins, a Catholic missionary, who wrote about the impact the "converted missionaries" would have back home when they return.[63] Although there may have been an expectation that non-Western Christians would come to engage in missionary work in Europe and North America, this is not explicitly mentioned anywhere. The renewal that the missionaries spoke about remained an abstraction. It appears to me that the growing presence of non-Western Christians (and missionaries) in Western cities was not expected at all.

As the Western missionary movement gained momentum, the expectation of a blessed reflex gradually disappeared from missiological conversations. The Western impulse to dominate the world and the success with which this was carried out in the second half of the nineteenth century meant that mission was monopolized by the West well into the twentieth century. In addition, it meant that the hope of the "younger churches"—as they were called then—for affecting Western Christianity would disappear altogether. Colonialism changed the way missionaries interacted with non-Western Christians, and racism made it even harder for them to be accepted in the West. Of course, within a few decades of William Carey's commitment to lifelong missionary service in India, the missionary impulse gave way to colonialism. As with William Carey, whose linguistic abilities were of great help to the British colonizers, most missionaries helped colonization in one way or another.

---

[62] Michael W. Goheen, "Toward a Missiology of Western Culture," *European Journal of Theology* 8, no. 2 (1999).

[63] See Anthony J. Gittins, "Reflections from the Edge: Mission-in-Reverse and Missiological Research," *Missiology* 21, no. 1 (1993).

With the help of the presence of British missionaries present in India, the British government declared their Indian Raj in 1858. The majority of sub-Saharan Africa was colonized in the 1890s. In most countries, the presence of the missionaries made colonization a little easier. Mongo Beti highlighted this aspect of the missionary influence when he painted the image of a frustrated Father Drumont, who, having reached the end of his twenty years of Catholic missionary work in Cameroon, declared to Monsieur Vidal, a new colonial administrator, "I can stay in this country along with you, associated with you, and thus *assist you to colonize it*, with dreadful consequences; *softening up the country ahead of you*, and *protecting your rear*—for that is how you envisage [the role of the missionary]."[64] He later added, "Or else, I can truly Christianize the country; in which case I'd better keep out of the way, as long as you are still here."[65] Mzee Jomo Kenyatta did not exclude the colonialists when he said, "When the missionaries came to Africa, they had the Bible and we had the land. They said, 'Let us pray.' We closed our eyes. When we opened them we had the Bible and they had the land."[66] Charles Domingo, a Mozambican who lived in Northern Malawi, commented in 1911:

> There is too much failure among all Europeans in Nyasaland. The three combined bodies—missionaries, government and companies or gainers of money—do form the same rule to look upon the native with mockery eyes. It sometimes startles us to see that the three combined bodies are from Europe, and along with them there is a title Christendom. . . . If we had power enough to communicate ourselves to Europe, we would advise them not to call themselves Christendom, but Europeandom. Therefore the life of the three combined bodies is altogether too cheaty,

---

[64] Beti, *Poor Christ of Bomba,* 153 (my emphasis).

[65] Ibid.

[66] This citation is often attributed to several African leaders like Desmond Tutu and Jomo Kenyatta. However, Nicholas Otieno suggests that it is the Mau Mau Fighters that made it popular in their anticolonial struggles in Kenya. See Nicholas Otieno and Hugh McCullum, *Journey of Hope: Towards a New Ecumenical Africa* (Geneva: WCC Publications, 2005), 7.

too thefty, too mockery. Instead of "Give," they say "Take away from."[67]

The end of colonialism meant two things for African Christianity. First, it exposed an obvious need to decolonize the African church, which needed to be a self-governing, self-propagating, self-supporting, and self-theologizing church. This was achieved gradually as the African church outgrew the influence of the Western missionaries. The second outcome of decolonization was the spread of African Christianity to the West and the rest of the world. The end of colonialism opened the door for the blessed reflex—or reverse mission as it is commonly known—to swing into action.

Reverse mission has been used to mean different things over the past three to four decades. Even though it has been used in relation to other religions, using it to discuss the reversal of the Christian missionary movement is our main interest here, especially because it enjoys the most popular use.[68] Within Christianity in recent missiological conversations, it has been used interchangeably with other terms like *mission in reverse* and *mission in return*. In a general sense, all these terms say the same thing: there has been a reversal in the direction of mission. In this century, Christianity has a strong presence on every continent, and every continent is both a mission-sending and a mission-receiving field. Missionaries are moving in all directions, from any continent to any other continent. Mission is omnidirectional, and the old Christian heartlands that once sent missionaries to the rest of the unevangelized world are now also receiving missionaries.

Reverse mission, in its truest sense, is a misnomer. First and foremost, mission remains mission, no matter where it originates. To say reverse mission, then, is to perpetuate the old assumptions that one geographic region is supposedly the originating center of all missionary endeavor and other regions are on the periph-

---

[67] A letter from Charles Domingo to Joseph Booth, 1911, quoted in Isichei, *History of Christianity*, 142.

[68] Afeosemime U. Adogame and Cordula Weisskoppel, *Religion in the Context of African Migration*, Bayreuth African Studies Series 75 (Bayreuth: Breitinger, 2005), 6.

ery, the receiving end. Incidentally, when colonial rule came to an end and the Western missionary movement unraveled, non-Western Christians began to wonder if the call to mission was solely for white people.[69] The explosion of world Christianity makes possible the movement of Christians from the rest of the world to the West. Indeed, this represents a change in the way mission has been carried out before. The church, no matter what part of the globe it is located in, is sent by the triune God to participate in God's mission in the world, and this sending can be local or foreign. It can be within the same continent or to another continent.

As has been discussed above, African immigrant Christians are not doing mission in the same way that Western missionaries did when they went to Africa. The circumstances of the contemporary African immigrant to the West differ greatly from those of the Western missionary of the nineteenth century. The fact that African immigrant Christianity is still largely locked up in African immigrant congregations, with very little in cross-cultural relations with Western Christianity (not to mention unchurched Westerners), challenges the prevalent definition of mission and thereby questions what exactly reverse mission means. Only a handful of African Christian leaders have been able to break the cultural barriers to do effective ministry among Africans that do not share their country of origin. Even fewer African leaders have been able to effectively reach out to white Westerners. Of course, most Western Christians have not realized the need for non-Western missionaries yet. For many, immigrant Christians are unwelcome. For others, immigrant Christians are here for other immigrant Christians and should not attempt to minister to local Christians.

We must conclude that the term *reverse mission* is not a very helpful term. However, in this book, it is preferable to concepts like mission in reverse and mission in return, since it is the most popular expression used for them all. In most places, it is simply replaced by "mission" or "Christian migration to the West" where

69   For instance, see Anderson, "Moratorium on Missionaries."

that qualification is needed. Despite the problematic nature of these terms, I have still found them useful for describing the missionary work that is the focus of this study—the movement of African Christians to the West.

African Missionary Work in the West

Although the entire enterprise of African Christianity and its missionary movement is a relatively new phenomenon, and the presence of African Christians in the West is undoubtedly a very recent development, this book would be remiss to leave the history of African religions in the "New World" unacknowledged. Certainly, there were many enslaved African Christians in the Americas in the eighteenth and nineteenth centuries. Many of these even became ministers who led the African American church in the segregated landscape of American Christianity. Quite a few of them chose to serve as missionaries overseas.

For instance, from North America, we have an impressive lineup of African American missionaries who went to serve in the West Indies, Latin America, and Africa.[70] Ten years before William Carey left England for India, an African American missionary by the name of George Liele left the United States for Jamaica, where he planted a church that grew to five hundred parishioners in ten years.[71] He is celebrated as the first black person to be ordained in North America. He is also celebrated as the first American Baptist missionary to serve overseas. One year after Liele went to Jamaica, in 1783, Moses Baker and George Gibbons moved to the West Indies to become missionaries.[72] In 1790 another African American minister by the name of Prince Williams left South Carolina for the Bahamas, where he planted

---

[70] See Vaughn J. Walston and Robert J. Stevens, *African-American Experience in World Mission: A Call beyond Community* (Pasadena, CA: William Carey Library, 2009), 24–29.

[71] Ibid., 49. For more about George Liele, see David Shannon, *George Liele's Life and Legacy: An Unsung Hero* (Macon, GA: Mercer University Press, 2013).

[72] Walston and Stevens, *African-American Experience*, 83.

a church.[73] Later, in 1792, David George led a group of twelve thousand freed Africans from Nova Scotia back to Africa.[74] He was their Christian leader and established a Christian community in the British colony of Sierra Leone. Another minister known simply as Brother Amos relocated from Nova Scotia to the Bahamas, where he planted a church.[75] Then, in 1821, the legendary Lott Carey left the United States for Liberia, where he worked as a missionary and a founder of the nation.[76]

Despite these trailblazers, most African missionary work in the West would emerge only in the twentieth century. The African missionary movement of the twentieth century was shaped by the migration of Africans from Africa to the West. The earliest known work was that of Thomas Kwame Brem-Wilson, a Ghanaian businessman and schoolmaster who was affected by the rise of Pentecostalism in California and started his own Sumner Road Chapel in South London in 1906.[77] After moving locations several times through the century, Sumner Road Chapel is now known as Sureway International Ministries and is located at Herne Hill in South London. Brem-Wilson led the church until 1929.[78]

In 1931, another African by the name of Daniels Ekarte (1896/7–1964), a Nigerian, opened the African Churches Mission and Training Center in Liverpool, England.[79] An extension of that church was later turned into an orphanage for black children on the south side of Liverpool. In the late 1960s, African immigrant churches began to pop up quickly on the European scene. Starting with the London church plants, Church of the

---

[73] Ibid., 49.

[74] Ibid.

[75] Ibid., 83.

[76] Ibid., 49–50. Also see Harvey J. Sindima, *Drums of Redemption: An Introduction to African Christianity,* Contributions to the Study of Religion (Westport, CT: Greenwood Press, 1994), 69.

[77] Israel O. Olofinjana, "The First African Pentecostal Church in Europe" (London), https://israelolofinjana.wordpress.com.

[78] Ibid.

[79] Jeanette Hardage, *Mary Slessor, Everybody's Mother: The Era and Impact of a Victorian Missionary* (Eugene, OR: Wipf & Stock, 2008), 295–99. Also see Israel O. Olofinjana, *Reverse in Ministry and Missions: Africans in the Dark Continent of Europe* (Milton Keynes, UK: Author House, 2010), 34.

Lord Aladura (1964), the Cherubim and Seraphim (1965), the Christ Apostolic Church (1974), many others were planted in Europe to cater to the religious and community needs of the many Africans who were migrating to Europe. By 1990 these African immigrant churches had spread all across Europe where many more Africans had settled. For instance, Gerrie ter Haar's research for *Halfway to Paradise,* carried out in the mid-1990s, explores Ghanaian communities that had been in the Netherlands for at least two decades.[80] Again, Afe Adogame's focus on the Celestial Church of Christ in Germany also suggests the presence of the church in Germany since the 1960s.[81]

As was the case with African immigrant churches in America in the 1990s, there is some consensus among scholars that most of the African immigrant churches in Europe came into existence simply because circumstances demanded it.[82] Most migration is for the purpose of finding a better living standard; missionary work is, for most, a secondary agenda. African immigrant churches emerged when African Christian leaders arose to take care of the spiritual needs of their fellow immigrants. Most immigrant churches were started because African migrants struggled with constant racial discrimination, cultural differences, and unfamiliar church styles in the Western churches.[83] The African immigrant congregation became the one place where they could be African without fear of being scrutinized by suspicious Western Christians or having to apologize for their Africanness.

The sense of a missionary calling among African Christians in the West is expressed in ways similar to those of African Christianity in Africa—all Christians are missionaries. There is minimal

---

[80] Gerrie ter Haar, *Halfway to Paradise: African Christians in Europe* (Cardiff: Cardiff Academic Press, 1998).

[81] Afeosemime U. Adogame, *Celestial Church of Christ: The Politics of Cultural Identity in a West African Prophetic-Charismatic Movement* (New York: Peter Lang, 1999).

[82] Kwadwo Konadu-Agyemang, Baffour K. Takyi, and John A. Arthur, *The New African Diaspora in North America: Trends, Community Building, and Adaptation* (Lanham, MD: Lexington Books, 2006), 122–26.

[83] Moses O. Biney, *From Africa to America: Religion and Adaptation among Ghanaian Immigrants in New York* (New York: New York University Press, 2011), 27.

gap between the clergy and the laity in African churches in the Diaspora. Many Africans who have started congregations in the Diaspora were not missionaries, in the professional sense, when they left Africa. Very few of them were even ministers in Africa. A significant number of them do not even have a theological education. They are Christian business executives, engineers, students, and asylum seekers, among other things, who simply believe that God can use them wherever they are located. This lack of proper distinction between lay Christians and missionaries among Africans makes it harder for Western Christians to understand and take African missionaries seriously. It adds to the factors that make missionary engagements between Africans and Western Christians difficult.

Nevertheless, since the 1980s, a few missionaries have been sent from Africa to the West, mainly at the request of Western denominations. This intentional sending of missionaries—already prepared and professionally qualified missionaries—from Africa to the West is a very recent phenomenon. Most of these are Roman Catholic and Anglican. In general, the missionary impact of African Christians in the West is still a matter of contention. After failing to reach Westerners with the gospel, many first generation immigrant missionaries believe that it is their children—the second generation of African immigrants, especially those who are brought up in the West—who will have the real missionary impact.

As for first generation immigrants, a study of the missionary activities of a majority of their churches suggests that only a few of them really carry out any form of cross-cultural missionary work that reaches out to people not homogeneous with themselves. Very few African immigrant churches have missionary efforts that go beyond their own cultural groups. Even those Pentecostal-charismatic churches that Hanciles suggests have a propensity for mission still find it difficult to reach people different from themselves.[84] Although many Africans claim that God

---

[84] Sunday Adelaja's The Embassy of the Blessed Kingdom of God for All Nations stands as a towering exception to this. However, its location in Kiev, Ukraine, suggests a radically different context from the Western European and North American context that it would allow for factors that make such a cross-cultural church possible.

sent them to the West as missionaries, fruitful methods for missional engagement are difficult to develop. Most of the missionaries sent from Africa have been sent to African congregations or communities already in place in the West.

African Christians in the West are preparing to be the primary missionary movement of the century. They have brought their African Christianity to continents that have long Christian histories—continents that sent missionaries to Africa some two hundred years ago. Their Christianity will look and feel different from Western Christianity, and they will redefine what it means to be missionary in this century. They will strengthen the non-Western missionary movement. Their presence in the West will invigorate Western Christianity in many ways. This is a significant development in Christianity and deserves proper attention. The following chapter explores some of the voices that have spoken on this subject.

Chapter Three

Mapping the Conversation

In order to piece together the historical narrative of the blessed reflex, we must pull together the various voices that have attended to the development of Africa's missionary movement in the Diaspora over the past forty years into one synchronized conversation. My goal is to map the historical developments that led to the academic awareness of the rise of the African missionary movement. The current developments in Christianity—the rise of non-Western missionary movements—are just the beginning of seismic shifts that will go on for generations around the world. We are witnessing the momentous beginnings of the impact of non-Western Christians in the West. They will certainly change the religious landscape of the world in some very significant ways.

As we go deeper into the twenty-first century, Western Christianity will become more diverse. Christians of color will soon begin to typify Christianity in places where Western Christianity has disappeared because of widespread secularization. Migration will continue to accelerate. Africa will be a major part of these world-changing movements of people, and African Christianity will be there to be part of the mix.

The scattered nature of the story so far calls for some consolidation of the few materials dedicated to this topic. At the moment, apart from the handful of books that have appeared in the past few years, there are only a few academic essays that try to explore these developments. It is difficult to locate even the basic facts about African missionaries in the West. Of course, the African missionary movement is a new phenomenon that has not even been fully recognized, even in Africa. It is an uncomfortable fact that at the time of this writing, it is unclear how many African immigrant congregations there are in the United States. There has been a general lack of interest in African Christianity once it leaves Africa. Even in Europe, where African immigrant congregations have been present for much longer, one will find only a few essays and even fewer books on the subject. It is the purpose of this chapter to appreciate and annotate some of these resources to make them accessible to those who may want to learn more about this topic of conversation.

We will look at the development of the conversation in three clusters. The first comprises some of the early voices to observe and predict the rise of African missionaries. The second cluster looks at the development in Europe, and the third focuses on the North American context. For the early voices in the conversation, this book makes use of materials from three main scholars: Andrew Walls, Anthony Gittins, and Roswith Gerloff. For the more recent European literature, we will engage the works of Afe Adogame, Grace Davie, Rebecca Catto, and Gerrie ter Haar. For the North American context, we will look at the works of Frieder Ludwig, Jehu Hanciles, and Jacob Olupona.

Europe

The conversation around African mission in the West, though it remains marginal, has been around in Europe since the 1970s. As it stands now, the most significant voices on the subject come from Scotland, Germany, and Holland. However, the geographical extent of their research covers all Europe and overflows into Africa. The European conversation provides context for whatever interest would appear on this subject in North America—which, incidentally started in the late 1990s and has produced a few monographs since 2005. We will start with the European scholars mostly because they raised their voices long before their American counterparts. Interestingly, the European conversation involves mainly white Europeans, whereas the North American conversation largely involves African scholars.

Andrew Walls

The role of Andrew Walls in this conversation deserves special attention. He recently retired from his position as the Director of the Center for the Study of Christianity in the Non-Western World at the University of Edinburgh but continues to teach at Liverpool Hope University in the United Kingdom. His interests in African Christianity have spanned a period of more than fifty years, starting in 1957 when he finished his studies at Cambridge and moved to Sierra Leone to "teach those in training for the ministry . . . church history."[1] The cross-cultural experience that he went through in Sierra Leone would shatter his theological confidence to the point that he felt he needed to be learning from the Africans (for whom Christianity was only in its second century). From Sierra Leone, he moved to Nigeria, where he continued to wonder at the growth of African Christianity. He left Nigeria, returning to Scotland, weeks before the 1966 Biafran civil war. He did, however, visit Africa at least once a year over the following forty years. He continues to teach at the Akrofi-Christaller Institute in Ghana, where he has taught every year since the 1960s.[2]

From the time he returned to Scotland, Walls has drawn students from around the world to study with him. More than a few have come from Africa. Walls has been involved in various roles in the development of many African scholars, most of whom have attended the University of Edinburgh where he taught for a long time. He is the founding editor of the *Journal of Religion in Africa,* which has been a major force in promoting Christian scholarship in Africa. He was involved in the founding of the *Journal of African Christian Thought* at the Akrofi-Christaller Institute. He has also been extensively involved in teaching and speaking all over the world. In an article about Walls, rightly titled "Historian Ahead of His Time," *Christianity Today* suggests that for most

---

[1] Andrew F. Walls, *The Missionary Movement in Christian History: Studies in the Transmission of Faith* (Maryknoll, NY: Orbis Books, 1996), xiii.

[2] His faculty profile at the Akrofi-Christaller Institute can be found at http://www.acighana.org.

North American Christians, Walls could be the most important person they do not know.[3]

The monumental contribution of Andrew Walls has been his ability to keep drawing the West's attention to the story of the growth of African Christianity within the wider context of exploding world Christianity. He has been a reflective commentator on the transition of Christianity from a Western religion to a global one. Walls went to Sierra Leone, in his words, believing that church history was full of lessons to be imparted to the younger churches from the accumulated wisdom of the older ones.[4] His transformation of mind took place when, as he says, he was "happily pontificating on the patchwork quilt of diverse fragments that constitutes second-century Christian literature" only to realize that he was "actually living in a second-century church."[5] This meant that he had to relearn the Christian story anew, paying attention to this new second-century church in Africa and what it had to say to the old traditions of Western Christianity. Over the ensuing years, Walls observed that the "labors of the missionary movement and the cross-cultural process in Christian history have borne fruit and catalyzed a shift in the center of gravity of Christianity that has immense implications for the theology of the future."[6]

Andrew Walls has, in his two major works, *The Missionary Movement in Christian History*[7] and *The Cross-Cultural Process in Christian History*,[8] anticipated that mission is approaching a point where non-Western Christians will be missionaries to the West. Indeed, Walls pays attention to the fact that the Christian heartlands are no longer in Western Europe and North America but are in South America, Africa, and Eastern Asia. Given the

---

[3] Tim Stafford, "Historian Ahead of His Time: Andrew Walls May Be the Most Important Person You Don't Know," *Christianity Today* (2007), http://www.christianitytoday.com.

[4] Walls, *Missionary Movement*, xiii.

[5] Ibid.

[6] Ibid., 9–15.

[7] Ibid.

[8] Andrew F. Walls, *The Cross-Cultural Process in Christian History: Studies in the Transmission and Appropriation of Faith* (Maryknoll, NY: Orbis Books, 2002).

migratory nature of Christianity (which forms the background to Walls's concepts of cross-cultural process in Christianity and the serial nature of the expansion of Christianity), non-Western Christians and missionaries will, for various purposes, start to find their ways to the West.

Walls foretold the blessed reflex before it started happening. He suggested the reoccurrence of "The Ephesian Moment"— the social coming together of two or more different cultures to experience Christ—in our times like it did in the days of early Christianity.[9] He said that the early church in Antioch experienced this Ephesian Moment, which resulted in the sending out of the first intentional missionaries. Now, with the migration of many foreign cultures to the West, there exists for the church an opportunity for another Ephesian Moment where Africans, Asians, Hispanics, and Caucasians will come together to experience Christ and enhance the missionary work of the church in the world.

Walls's most recent book, edited with Cathy Ross, *Mission in the Twenty-First Century*, adopts and explores the Anglican Church's Five Marks of Mission in this twenty-first century, namely:

1. To proclaim the Good News of the Kingdom.
2. To teach, baptize, and nurture new believers.
3. To respond to human need by loving service.
4. To seek to transform unjust structures of society.
5. To strive to safeguard the integrity of creation and sustain and renew the life of the earth.[10]

True to Walls's convictions that "mission must now be from all to all,"[11] this book is a collection of essays written by scholars

---

[9] Ibid., 78.

[10] Andrew F. Walls and Cathy Ross, eds., *Mission in the Twenty-First Century: Exploring the Five Marks of Global Mission* (Maryknoll, NY: Orbis Books, 2008). See John Clark and Eleanor Johnson, *Anglicans in Mission: A Transforming Journey: Report of Missio, the Mission Commission of the Anglican Communion, to the Anglican Consultative Council, Meeting in Edinburgh, Scotland, September 1999* (London: SPCK, 2000).

[11] Walls and Ross, *Mission in the Twenty-First Century*, xi.

from all corners of the globe. In a rather bold move, a majority of the authors are from the non-Western world, reflecting the potentiality of a global Christian conversation in which there is a fair representation of non-Western voices. Unlike some conversations on the mission of the church, which are context-specific, the material explored in this book is full of global perspectives. In her introduction to the book, Cathy Ross says, "We are confronted with the challenge of just whose religion is Christianity. . . . We must engage with living theology from the now many centers of Christianity around the world."[12]

Anthony Gittins

Another prominent contributor to the development of the concept of reverse mission is Anthony Gittins, a Roman Catholic priest and scholar. Currently, Gittins is professor emeritus of Christian Missions and Ministry at the Catholic Theological Union in Chicago.[13] Like Walls, Gittins is a British missionary who served in Sierra Leone. Gittins worked in Sierra Leone in the 1970s, and for over three decades he has been an outspoken proponent of reverse mission in Roman Catholic circles. He popularized the concept of mission-in-reverse in his *Bread for the Journey: The Mission of Transformation and the Transformation of Mission,* where he talks about mission-in-reverse as a process by which the missionary is converted by their experiences on the mission field.[14] In turn, this conversion of the missionary would lead to the conversion of the missionary's sending community. He discusses his own kind of conversion in an article entitled "Reflections from the Edge: Mission-In-Reverse and Missiological Research."[15] This conversion, he says, allows for mutuality and

---

[12] Ibid., xv.

[13] See Catholic Theological Union, "CTU Faculty Biography: Anthony Gittins, C.S.Sp.," http://www.ctu.edu.

[14] Anthony J. Gittins, *Bread for the Journey: The Mission of Transformation and the Transformation of Mission,* American Society of Missiology Series, no. 17 (Maryknoll, NY: Orbis Books, 1993).

[15] Anthony J. Gittins, "Reflections from the Edge: Mission-in-Reverse and Missiological Research." *Missiology* 21, no. 1 (1993): 21–29.

partnerships between Western missionaries and churches established elsewhere.

It is worth noting that Father Gittins did not talk about the migration of non-Western missionaries to the West. His interest is in the conversion of the missionary, which could possibly open doors for non-Western missionaries in the West. Nevertheless, his concept of "mission-in-reverse" has been at the forefront in missiological conversations within the Roman Catholic Church among those who are thinking about the role of non-Western Catholics in the West. As the years pass, the Roman Catholic Church in Europe and North America is experiencing a severe shortage of priests. Catholic scholars who wrote much later than Gittins have begun to see the necessity within the Roman Catholic Church of hiring priests from Africa, South America, and the Philippines to join the priesthood in North America and Europe.

James Okoye, a Nigerian Roman Catholic priest of the Spiritan order, who is now teaching and serving in Pittsburgh, made the following point in an article published in 2007:

> A 1999 CARA study found that 16 percent of priests in the US were foreign-born. Surveys of new ordinands found that in 2004, 31 percent of them were foreign-born; in 2005, the figure was 25 percent. In 2005, the Archdiocese of Chicago ordained 13 priests, only one of whom was native to Chicago and five of whom were East Africans being ordained for the Chicago Archdiocese.[16]

Similarly, although Virgilio Elizondo's *The Future Is Mestizo* does not use the language of reverse mission, it also sees a future in which Roman Catholic Christians from different parts of the world will work together in North America.[17] At the end of the first decade of the twenty-first century, there was a significant number of African and Hispanic Catholic priests serving in the West. The Roman Catholic Church in the United States has

---

[16] James Chukwuma Okoye, "'Third Church' Mission in the 'First World.'" *Spiritan Horizons* 2 (November 2007): 64.

[17] Virgilio P. Elizondo, *The Future Is Mestizo: Life Where Cultures Meet*, Meyer-Stone ed. (Oak Park, IL: Meyer-Stone Books, 1988).

been strongly buttressed by the presence and work of many non-Western priests, lay ministers, and parishioners alike.

Roswith Gerloff

Roswith Gerloff has been at the center of the British conversation around mission since the 1970s. Her publications cover a period of more than thirty years of research on the subject of African Christianity in Diaspora. Her first article on the Black Christian presence in Birmingham was published in 1975.[18] In general, at around that time, the presence of immigrant Christians was beginning to register on the national scales, and, therefore, research interests in the religious and cultural backgrounds and lives of immigrants began to blossom. A number of publications that appeared in the 1980s and 1990s focused first on Afro-Caribbean immigrants and then on West African immigrants, and also on the interactions between these groups.[19] However, the *missionary* implications of the immigrants in Britain did not draw attention in the academy until the mid-1990s, when sociologists of religion such as Grace Davie began to wonder about the changes in British Christianity in the second half of the twentieth century. Two major projects in the area of African Christian Diaspora took place in the United Kingdom in the 1990s. First, in 1997, the University of Leeds facilitated a consultation titled "The Significance of the African Christian Diaspora in Europe."[20] Then, in 1999,

---

[18]   Roswith Gerloff, "Black Christian Communities in Birmingham: The Problem of Basic Recognition," in *Religion in the Birmingham Area* (Birmingham, UK: University of Birmingham, 1975). See also Roswith Gerloff, Gisela Egler, and Paul Loffler, *Das Schwarze Lacheln Gottes: Afrikanische Diaspora als Herausforderung an Theologie und Kirche: Beitrage aus 30 Jahren Reflektierter Praxis* (Frankfurt am Main: Lembeck, 2005). See also Roswith Gerloff, "The African Diaspora and the Shaping of Christianity in Africa: Perspectives on Religion, Migration, Identity, and Collaboration," *Missionalia* 38, no. 2 (2010).

[19]   Frieder Ludwig and J. Kwabena Asamoah-Gyadu, *African Christian Presence in the West: New Immigrant Congregations and Transnational Networks in North America and Europe* (Trenton, NJ: Africa World Press, 2011), 7.

[20]   Out of this conference and some preliminary consultations came a journal publication; Roswith Gerloff, "The Significance of the African

Cambridge University held a conference under the name "Open Space: The African Christian Diaspora in Europe and the Quest for Human Community."[21] Roswith Gerloff was one of the organizers of both these conferences, and she continued to publish articles and to edit the books that came out of the conferences.

At the same time, Grace Davie's work continued to focus on the overwhelming secularization that seemed to sweep across the continent of Europe, especially toward the end of the twentieth century. In 1994, she published *Religion in Britain since 1945* in which she started to debunk the secularization theories of the 1960s.[22] There was a consensus among the British sociologists of religion that these secularization theories were misplaced. Davie later published *Europe—The Exceptional Case*.[23] In this book, Davie argues that Europe's fallout with religion is exceptional, since human beings are naturally religious. Humans are religious everywhere else apart from Europe. Peter Berger, one of the main proponents of the secularization theory, recently revisited much of his earlier work in the light of the apparent resurgence of religion in the world. In *The Desecularization of the World,* Berger confirms that the world today is "as furiously religious as it ever was."[24] Even secular sociologists such as John Micklethwait and Adrian Wooldridge, in *God Is Back*, acknowledge that God has made a comeback, especially the Christian God who has more followers in the majority world now than ever.[25] Davie observed,

---

Christian Diaspora in Europe: Selected Bibliography," *International Review of Mission* 89, no. 354 (2000).

[21] See Roswith Gerloff, "Open Space: The African Christian Diaspora in Europe and the Quest for Human Community," *International Review of Mission* 89, no. 354 (2000), and Ludwig and Asamoah-Gyadu, *African Christian Presence*, 8.

[22] Grace Davie, *Religion in Britain since 1945: Believing without Belonging*, Making Contemporary Britain (Cambridge, MA: Blackwell, 1994).

[23] Grace Davie, *Europe—The Exceptional Case: Parameters of Faith in the Modern World* (London: Darton Longman & Todd, 2002).

[24] Peter L. Berger, *The Desecularization of the World: Resurgent Religion and World Politics* (Grand Rapids, MI: W.B. Eerdmans, 1999), 2.

[25] John Micklethwait and Adrian Wooldridge, *God Is Back: How the Global Revival of Faith Is Changing the World* (New York: Penguin Press, 2009).

however, that even though Europeans were shunning religion in large numbers, immigrants from Asia, Africa, and Latin America did not seem to be affected. Whether they were Muslims, Christians, or belonged to other religions, they continued to be religious when they arrived in Europe. In Europe, the immigrants continued to organize themselves into congregations, mosques, and other religious communities.

Gerrie ter Haar

Gerrie ter Haar, from the Netherlands, has also done extensive research on African immigrant Christianity. In 1998 she published *Halfway to Paradise: African Christians in Europe* in which she explores the religious presence of Africans, especially Ghanaians, in the Netherlands.[26] *Halfway to Paradise* is based on extensive research that she conducted in the Netherlands and Ghana between 1992 and 1996, and therefore it described the situation as it was in the early 1990s. This may explain the groundbreaking status of *Halfway to Paradise* in the European conversation. It is expansive in its approach, digging into the history of Ghanaians in the Netherlands back to the 1960s. Most of the issues raised in this book have yet to be fully addressed even nearly twenty years after its publication.

Another major contribution from Haar is a book that came out of a collection of essays from a conference that she had organized at Leiden University in 1995, titled *Strangers and Sojourners: Religious Communities in Diaspora*.[27] She observed then that the historiography of African-initiated churches in Europe was in infancy—a statement as true today as it was then.[28] Since then, she has been one of the leading voices on African Diasporic Christianity. Her voice as an early European researcher on the subject still stands out. She has continued to write on African Christianity, both in Africa and in the Diaspora. Her 2009 work,

---

[26] Gerrie ter Haar, *Halfway to Paradise: African Christians in Europe* (Cardiff: Cardiff Academic Press, 1998).

[27] Gerrie ter Haar, *Strangers and Sojourners: Religious Communities in Diaspora* (Leuven: Peeters, 1998).

[28] Ibid., 3.

How God Became African: African Spirituality and Western Secular Thought, delves deeper into trying to understand African Christianity and its global presence.[29] This book emerged out of research that she carried out in Ghana in efforts to understand the Ghanaian immigrants in the Netherlands better. Her colleague from the Netherlands, Rijk van Dijk started *African Diaspora: A Journal for Transnational African in a Global World* in 2008.[30]

Afeosemime Adogame

Afeosemime Adogame is a Nigerian scholar now teaching at Edinburgh. He completed his PhD studies at Bayreuth University, and for his dissertation, Adogame studied the Celestial Church of Christ, a Nigerian church with congregations in several cities in Germany. Adogame's project highlighted an area that would draw a great deal of interest in the ensuing years. For instance, in February 2003, Bayreuth University organized a conference called "Religion in the Context of African Migration," which drew many scholars from Europe, Africa, and North America. Out of this conference, Adogame and Weisskoeppel published their book, *Religion in the Context of African Migration*.[31] Later on, in 2003, Adogame, Roswith Gerloff, and Klaus Hock organized a conference on immigration and religion in Berlin that produced *Christianity in Africa and the African Diaspora*.[32] Most of Adogame's works have focused on Europe. He has collaborated with most of

---

[29] Gerrie ter Haar, *How God Became African: African Spirituality and Western Secular Thought* (Philadelphia: University of Pennsylvania Press, 2009).

[30] Brill, "African Diaspora: A Journal of Transnational Africa in a Global World," http://www.brill.nl/african-diaspora. See also Rijk van Dijk, *Christian Fundamentalism in Sub-Saharan Africa: The Case of Pentecostalism* (Copenhagen: Centre of African Studies, University of Copenhagen, 2000). See also Mirjam de Bruijn, Rijk van Dijk, and D. Foeken, *Mobile Africa: Changing Patterns of Movement in Africa and Beyond*, African Dynamics (Boston: Brill, 2001).

[31] Afeosemime U. Adogame and Cordula Weissköppel, eds., *Religion in the Context of African Migration*. Bayreuth African Studies Series 75 (Bayreuth: Breitinger, 2005).

[32] Afeosemime U. Adogame, Roswith I. H. Gerloff, and Klaus Hock, *Christianity in Africa and the African Diaspora: The Appropriation of a Scattered Heritage*, Continuum Religious Studies (New York: Continuum, 2008).

the major European voices in the conversation. His other works include *African Traditions in the Study of Religion in Africa*[33] and *Religion Crossing Boundaries*.[34]

In Germany, a number academic conferences have focused on African immigrant Christianity.[35] Several institutions have established programs to work with African Christians and pastors, both to provide theological education but also to learn what they can offer to German Christianity. For instance, the Missions Academy at Hamburg University was involved in providing theological and missionary training to African church leaders in Germany.[36] Also, Claudia Währisch-Oblau mentions such efforts as that of the United Evangelical Church in Wüppertal, which has a "Church in Intercultural Context" program for training of African pastors and church leaders.[37] Bayreuth University is another German university that has contributed greatly to the study of African immigrant churches in Europe.

North America

The presence of African Christianity in North America has been mostly undocumented on the academic level until only

---

[33] Afeosemime U. Adogame, Ezra Chitando, and Bolaji Bateye, *African Traditions in the Study of Religion in Africa: Emerging Trends, Indigenous Spirituality and the Interface with Other World Religions*, Vitality of Indigenous Religions (Burlington, VT: Ashgate, 2010).

[34] Afeosemime U. Adogame and James V. Spickard, *Religion Crossing Boundaries: Transnational Religious and Social Dynamics in Africa and the New African Diaspora*, Religion and the Social Order (Boston: Brill, 2010).

[35] Benjamin Simon, *From Migrants to Missionaries: Christians of African Origin in Germany*, Studies in the Intercultural History of Christianity (New York: Peter Lang, 2010), i. For further exploration of this subject, also see Benjamin Simon, *Afrikanische Kirchen in Deutschland* (Frankfurt am Main: Lembeck, 2003).

[36] Universität Hamburg, "Institut Für Missions-, Ökumene-Und Religionswissenschaften," (Hamburg), http://www.theologie.uni-hamburg.de.

[37] See Claudia Währisch-Oblau, "From Reverse Mission to Common Mission . . . We Hope: Immigrant Protestant Churches and the 'Programme for Cooperation between German and Immigrant Congregations' of the United Evangelical Mission," *International Review of Mission* 89, no. 354 (2000): 467.

a few years ago. Most of the works that explore the religious
diversity emerging because of immigration are almost silent on
African Christianity. Both Stephen Warner's *Gatherings in Diaspora*[38] and *A Church of Our Own*[39] pay only flirting attention to
African immigrant Christianity in America. The same can be said
of Stephen Prothero's *A Nation of Religions*[40] and Helen Ebaugh's
Religion and the New Immigrants.[41] Part of the cause may be that
African migration to the United States accelerated only in the
1990s and therefore may have not really appeared on the radars
of academic researchers until after the turn of the century. In
addition, the African-born population in the United States hovers
around 0.5 percent of the national population. As such, it may be
too small a population to draw the attention it deserves. Nevertheless, the silence is unfortunate.

Three outstanding works have been published on the subject
of African Immigrant Christianity in the United States. Together,
these three books paint a faithful picture of the significance of
African Christianity in the Diaspora, both for the Diaspora and
for Africa. The first is an edited publication called *African Immigrant Religions in America* by Jacob Olupona and Regina Gemignani (2007),[42] followed by *Beyond Christendom: Globalization,
African Migration and the Transformation of the West* by Jehu Hanciles (2008).[43] The third, also an edited work, *African Christian
Presence in the West*, was edited by Frieder Ludwig and Kwabena

[38] R. Stephen Warner and Judith G. Wittner, *Gatherings in Diaspora:
Religious Communities and the New Immigration* (Philadelphia: Temple University Press, 1998).

[39] R. Stephen Warner, *A Church of Our Own: Disestablishment and Diversity in American Religion* (New Brunswick, NJ: Rutgers University Press,
2005).

[40] Stephen R. Prothero, *A Nation of Religions: The Politics of Pluralism
in Multireligious America* (Chapel Hill: University of North Carolina Press,
2006).

[41] Helen Rose F. Ebaugh and Janet Saltzman Chafetz, *Religion and the
New Immigrants: Continuities and Adaptations in Immigrant Congregations* (Walnut Creek, CA: AltaMira Press, 2000).

[42] Jacob Olupona and Regina Gemignani, *African Immigrant Religions in
America* (New York: New York University Press, 2007).

[43] Jehu Hanciles, *Beyond Christendom: Globalization, African Migration,
and the Transformation of the West* (Maryknoll, NY: Orbis Books, 2008).

Asamoah-Gyadu (2011).[44] Several other books have appeared that enhance the conversation in many ways. Among them is Moses Biney's *From Africa to America,* published in 2011.[45] It explores the issues surrounding the life of a Ghanaian Presbyterian church in New York. Mark Gornik's *Word Made Global: Stories of African Christianity in New York City,* also published in 2011, focuses on African Christianity in New York, as the subtitle states,.[46] Gornik has also contributes to the conversation in *To Live in Peace.*[47]

Jacob Olupona and Regina Gemignani

Jacob Olupona is a professor of African and African American Studies in the Faculty of Arts and Sciences at Harvard Divinity School.[48] Regina Gemignani is a gender consultant and research scientist at the World Bank. In their aforementioned book, Olupona and Gemignani bring to the forefront a conversation about the religious activities of African immigrants in North America. The book explores the growth of churches, mosques, and shrines established and led by African immigrants. It offers a multidisciplinary collection of thirteen essays from experts in African immigrant religions from a diverse array of fields, including history, theology, religious studies, political sciences, and anthropology. The book is divided into sections: "Historical and Theoretical Perspectives," "Reverse Mission: Faith, Practice, and Immigrant Journey," "Gender, Ethnicity, and Identity," and "Civic Engagement and Political Incorporation." The authors explore a wide range of issues, including transnational networks of Africans in the Diaspora, the religious cultures of Africans in the United States, and the impact of migration on religious commitment.

[44] Ludwig and Asamoah-Gyadu, *African Christian Presence.*

[45] Moses O. Biney, *From Africa to America: Religion and Adaptation among Ghanaian Immigrants in New York* (New York: New York University Press, 2011).

[46] Mark R. Gornik, *Word Made Global: Stories of African Christianity in New York City* (Grand Rapids, MI: Eerdmans, 2011).

[47] Mark R. Gornik, *To Live in Peace: Biblical Faith and the Changing Inner City* (Grand Rapids, MI: Eerdmans, 2002).

[48] Harvard Divinity School, "Faculty Biography: Jacob K. Olupona," http://www.hds.harvard.edu.

Central to their argument is the observation that since the late 1960s, the United States has been the chief destination of a new wave of African immigrants, who are already "making a significant social and cultural impact, especially through the proliferation of religious communities."[49]

Olupona and Gemignani raised awareness of the significant immigration of Africans to the United States since the Immigration Act of 1965, and set up the groundwork for the conversation that follows in the works of Hanciles and Ludwig. In their discussion of African immigrant religions, they focused on Christianity and Islam. For the discourse on immigrant Christianity, they placed an emphasis on African Initiated Churches, though this categorization is now outdated, since such churches can be either neo-Pentecostal (e.g., the Lighthouse Chapel) or traditionally African (e.g., the Kimbanguist church). The distinction between these two types of African immigrant churches is critical because it has serious implications for how they identify themselves and carry out their mission.

Jehu Hanciles

Jehu Hanciles, who was born in Sierra Leone, trained under Andrew Walls at the University of Edinburgh. He is the D.W. and Ruth Brooks Associate Professor of World Christianity at Emory University's Candler School of Theology. His research interests include the connections between globalization, migration, and religious expansion: specifically, the ways in which South-North migratory flows provide the structure and impetus for a full-fledged missionary movement from global Christianity's new heartlands in the non-Western world.[50]

Although Hanciles has published several works on mission, the book directly relevant to this book is *Beyond Christendom: Globalization, African Migration, and the Transformation of the West.*[51] Hanciles dedicated this work to Andrew Walls, who "taught [him]

---

[49] Olupona and Gemignani, *African Immigrant Religions*, 28.

[50] See Emory University, "Candler School of Theology Faculty Biography: Jehu J. Hanciles," http://www.candler.emory.edu.

[51] Hanciles, *Beyond Christendom*.

to see the world through African eyes." As the subtitle suggests, Hanciles explores the dynamics of globalization and migration, and how African migration to the West is transforming its religious landscape, especially in North America. This impressively researched book is divided into three sections.

In "Transforming the Margins," Hanciles lays down the framework for his dominant theme in the book, that in the context of the globalized world of the twenty-first century, the reversed migration patterns have brought many Christians from Africa—and the rest of the global south—to the West. A significant consequence of this is seen in the religious transformation that is being observed in the West. In the second section, "Migration and the New World Order," Hanciles explores the migratory nature of Christianity, and indeed, that of all Abrahamic religions, placing it in the migratory nature of the faith of the wandering Aramaean who is our common ancestor.[52] Here too Hanciles explores current global migration trends, noting the great increase in the number of people migrating from the Majority World to the West as well as African migrations both within and without Africa. He also takes a historical view of the transatlantic slave trade that moved huge numbers of Africans to the Americas as one of the foundational blocks to Africa's presence in the Americas. The third section, "Mobile Faiths," reflects on the spread of African religions, especially Christianity and Islam, to the West.

Unlike Olupona and Gemignani, who focus on African immigrant religions, Hanciles focuses on the impact of African immigrant Christianity in North America, dedicating only one chapter to Islam and none at all to other African religions. Immigrant congregations are, for him, communities of commitment, where every Christian migrant is a potential missionary.[53] In this vein, Hanciles discusses four types of African immigrant churches.[54] The first is the Abrahamic type, which includes those African immigrant churches that have their origin in the initiative of an individual African immigrant. Then he discusses the Macedonian type, which comprises congregations that come into existence

[52] Ibid., chap. 6.
[53] Ibid., 296.
[54] Ibid., 326.

through the missionary-sending initiatives of ministries or movements that are African-founded or African-based. The third category, the Jerusalem type, includes those congregations that are African-established or African-led with significant African membership, but are associated with Western mainline denominations. The fourth is the Samuel-Eli type. These are Western mainline denominations that attract significant numbers of African immigrants whose active involvement can generate evangelical vitality, contribute new expressions of spirituality, and influence worship styles.[55] Hanciles's study is predominantly about the first two types,[56] but it is the fourth type that is most pertinent here.

Hanciles finishes with a discussion of the missionary impact of African immigrant Christianity. He suggests that the secularization theory, in whatever form, falls apart in the face of the religious resurgence that is taking place in the world. Over 65 percent of Christians now live outside the West, and Christian migrants are revitalizing the religious life of America. Hanciles anticipates that this phenomenon will have a significant impact on mission and theological studies. He observes, however, that "for now, mission and theological studies remain largely hostage to the kind of world vision shaped by secular rationalism—in which Western models and initiatives are considered definitive."[57]

Frieder Ludwig and Kwabena Asamoah-Gyadu

Frieder Ludwig and Kwabena Asamoah-Gyadu coedited *African Christian Presence in the West,* a collection of essays that were presented at a conference held in March 2007 by the Global Mission Institute at Luther Seminary in Saint Paul, Minnesota. Ludwig is a German missiologist who, in 2008, left his position as director of the Global Mission Institute at Luther Seminary to head the Mission Seminary in Hermannsburg, Germany. He also lectures at the University of Göttingen in Germany. He has been involved with the African Christian community for some time and has spent time teaching in Tanzania and Nigeria.

---

[55] Ibid., 326–27.
[56] Ibid., 327.
[57] Ibid., 383.

Asamoah-Gyadu comes from Ghana. At the time of the conference, he was a guest scholar at Luther Seminary. His works focus on the contemporary trends in African Christianity, a subject that is attracting increased interest especially as it pertains to the growth and impact of the Pentecostal/charismatic movements in Africa. As a result, Asamoah-Gyadu's *African Charismatics*, which in itself is an excellent exploration of the development of charismatic Christianity in Africa, sets up a conversation that follows African Christianity into the Diaspora, since it is the charismatic expression of African Christianity that has attracted a great deal of attention in the past few years. His other works explore this specific field.

The main objective of the conference was "to discover what African immigrant churches are doing religiously in the United States, and what manner of religious institutions they are developing by and for themselves."[58] The book came out almost four years after the conference, and so Hanciles's groundbreaking *Beyond Christianity* was published first. Due to its timing, the conversations in *African Christian Presence* reflect earlier deliberations on the subject. The contributors include almost all the major scholars at work in the field, and the collection includes a wide denominational spectrum including Orthodox, Roman Catholic, Protestant mainline, and Pentecostal and charismatic churches. Certainly, it is a significant contribution to the conversation. It is divided into four parts: "The African Christian Presence in the West and Discourses on Migration"; "North American Case Studies"; "Comparisons and Interactions"; and "Migrant Theologies and Theologies of Migration."

It is worth noting that each of the scholars mentioned in this section, Andrew Walls included, presented papers at the Global Mission Institute conference at Luther Seminary. On the one hand, the organizers of the conference should be commended for inviting such a wide variety of conversational partners, even those from outside the United States. On the other hand, it is also quite noticeable that the field is new and has only a handful of scholars thinking about it. The fact that one conference can have almost

---

[58] Ludwig and Asamoah-Gyadu, *African Christian Presence*, preface.

all the main thinkers on a subject from both North America and Europe confirms the need for some more voices to join the conversation. In addition, owing to factors that will be discussed later, both the GMI conference and the papers collected from its presenters reflect the upper hand that West Africa has in matters of this academic field in comparison with the rest of Africa. Of course, there are immigrant Christians from South Africa, Zimbabwe, Kenya, Ethiopia, and many other African countries, but for one reason or another, their voices are yet to be heard in this discussion.

Mark Gornik

Mark Gornik's place in this conversation is unique. He is the founder and director of City Seminary in New York. He moved to Harlem in 1998 and was immediately struck by the presence of Africans in the area. With the influence of Andrew Walls in the background, Gornik became interested in exploring what kinds of Christianity were being practiced by Africans in the area. For the following ten years, he engaged in ethnographic research that took him to many of the African churches in New York. In his discussion with the Trans-Atlantic Roundtable of Religion and Race, Gornik spoke about visiting one African church after another, until he had compiled a list of 150 African immigrant congregations in New York.[59] He talked about the vibrant worship, the serious prayer, the dynamic and practical sermons, and the dancing that took place in these churches. His interactions with African immigrant Christianity in the City of New York led him to publish two books: *Word Made Global* and *To Live in Peace,* mentioned earlier. He carried out his research in three very different African immigrant churches to explore the pastoral, spiritual, and missional dynamics of African Christianity in New York City. His books are not informed in the way of a distant researcher who probes into a foreign culture to understand it and write a book about it; his ethnography was informed by becoming

---

[59] Trans-Atlantic Roundtable on Religion and Race, "Mark Gornik: African Christianity, a Gift for the Western Church," http://religionandrace.org.

embedded in the African communities with which he came into contact. In Gornik's own words:

> This story is also in part my story, because researching the African churches and writing *Word Made Global* trans-formed me. Through this work, not only did I come to really know New York City, but I also came to experience and be challenged by Christianity in the 21st century. My experience also profoundly shaped my understanding of urban ministry and theological education.[60]

Gornik is important in this conversation for two reasons. First, he is an American who actually took time to listen, to learn, and to try to understand the Africans in his neighborhood. His research is informed by going out of his way to visit the Africans to learn from them and about them. Second, both his research method-ology and his writing work to recognize the value of African Christianity and resist the urge to condemn it for its difference from American Christianity. Gornik is truly enthusiastic about African Christians in North America, and he seems excited about the African way of doing Christianity. He even anticipates what American Christianity will learn from the Africans.[61]

The Current State of the Conversation

I agree with Gerrie ter Haar, even almost twenty years after she published *Strangers and Sojourners*, that the conversation about Afri-can missionary movement to the West is still in its infancy. African Christianity is by far the least documented story of all Christiani-ties present in the West. Effectively, the story of African Christi-anity is undocumented. Compared with America, the European part of the conversation is certainly gaining more traction. The commitment of some universities like Bayreuth and Edinburgh to study world Christianity has begun to bear some fruits in terms of

---

[60] Eerdword, "Mark Gornik: Word Made Global: Stories of African Christianity in New York City," http://eerdword.wordpress.com.

[61] Covenant College, "Dr. Mark Gornik '84 to Present WIC Lectures," http://www.covenant.edu.

getting the African missionary movement story told in Europe. In addition, the presence of African Christians in Europe has drawn attention from various disciplines of study, including sociology, history, and philosophy. Of course, several other universities are beginning to see the significance of this movement. There are currently more collaborative multidisciplinary works involving African and Western scholars under development.

In Britain, African Christian leaders have written many popular books about their perceptions and experiences in the Diaspora. Earlier, their tone was condemning of Western Christianity. They called it dead and in need of a revival. They have said that whereas Africa used to be the "Dark Continent," it is Europe that is now the dark one, at least spiritually speaking.[62] Of late, however, there is a greater maturity in the way these books are engaging the British Christians. There is a somber realization that if they are to be effective missionaries in Britain, African Christians need to work with the British Christians the way they are now. This mission of Africans to Britain will not be successful if it continues to condemn and try to convert British Christianity.

Consequently, African Christian leaders in Britain are placing great emphasis on building cross-cultural bridges with Western Christianity. This is done with a great deal of missional intentionality and humility in their tone. Israel Olofinjana's book, *Reverse in Ministry and Mission: Africans in the Dark Continent of Europe*, published in 2010, begins to wrestle with the idea of mission in more cordial ways.[63] Adedibu Babatunde's *Coat of Many Colors* offers a comprehensive historical analysis of the Black Majority Churches in ways that promote collaborations among Christians from different parts of the world.[64]

---

[62] A classic example of this group of books is Wale Babatunde, *Great Britain Has Fallen: How to Restore Britain's Greatness as a Nation* (London: New Wine Press, 2002). In this book, Wale Babatunde threw down the gauntlet on Western Christianity saying African Christians (most of them are Pentecostal/charismatic) had little respect for Western Christianity. In his opinion, British Christianity was dead and needed to be revived.

[63] Israel O. Olofinjana, *Reverse in Ministry and Mission: Africans in the Dark Continent of Europe* (Milton Keynes, UK: Author House, 2010).

[64] Adedibu Babatunde, *Coat of Many Colors* (London: Wisdom Summit, 2012).

In the United States, the story is rather different. Unlike in Europe, where some universities and African immigrant churches have made efforts to bridge the gap and work together in thinking about mission in their context, the American conversation has been mostly confined to the academy. Even there, African Christianity in North America has been a field of interest mostly among African scholars rather than among Western scholars. The lineup of books about African immigrant Christians in North America is almost exclusively of African authorship. The two main books that deal with the subject in good depth are written by an African sociologist and an African historian. This means that there is still lacking a thorough treatment of the subject by a theologian or a missiologist. Currently, one would be hard-pressed to find even one book on the cross-cultural *experiences* of African Christians in the West. Even Western commentators of religion and immigration have only scantly mentioned Africa in their appraisals. It would be even more helpful for the conversation if an American theologian would publish on these subjects.

Nevertheless, one can find a great deal of promise for future conversation. There has been a surge in academic interests in the phenomenon of African Christianity in the West and all its implications. In the months between the fall of 2012 and the summer of 2014, at least ten academic conferences in different parts of the United States focused on African immigrant Christianity. Collaborations between the academy and African immigrant congregations have also increased. The work of Luther Seminary through its Global Mission Institute, for example, has led to the publication of Ludwig's *The African Christian Presence in the West*, which has been widely read and is global in its scope, and another that is very local in its approach, limiting its focus to the Twin Cities of Minneapolis and Saint Paul: *Mission and Migration: Fifty-Two African and Asian Congregations in Minnesota*.[65] Luther Seminary has also started an AGORA program that focuses on providing theological education to lay people from multicultural and eth-

---

[65] Dana K. Nelson and Frieder Ludwig, *Mission and Migration: Fifty-Two African and Asian Congregations in Minnesota*, Contemporary Issues in Mission and World Christianity (Minneapolis: Lutheran University Press, 2007).

nic-specific congregations.[66] This program is already proving to be a helpful avenue for connecting the seminary and the Ethiopian and Swahili-speaking congregations in the area. Contextual education courses in some of the seminaries in the Minneapolis-Saint Paul area bring African students into Western congregations while connecting African immigrant congregations.

As a result of all these efforts, many more Americans have become aware that African Christianity is likely to be a permanent part of America's religious landscape, and the phenomenon is of increasing interest in the United States. Generally speaking, this interest goes beyond any denominational barriers. Lutherans, Catholics, Presbyterians, Evangelicals, and other theological traditions are beginning to see and recognize the African Christians who live in their cities. It is very likely that as African Christianity continues to develop and contribute to American Christianity, much more scholarship in this field will appear.

There remains a great deal to be explored about African Christianity in the Diaspora. It appears now that the conversation is gaining momentum. Conferences and consultations on African Christianity in the West are taking place on both sides of the Atlantic. Out of these conferences, essays are collected and books are published that will enhance the conversation as a whole. Hopefully soon, Africans in Africa will join the conversation to raise awareness among potential missionaries before they migrate to the West. Nevertheless, we are still witnessing the birth of this great phenomenon. It is my hope that many more will join the conversation.

---

[66] Luther Seminary, "Agora at Luther Seminary" (St. Paul), https://www.luthersem.edu.

Chapter Four

African Immigrant Christianity
in the West

We are the first generation to witness the movement of African missionaries on this side of the Reformation, and most of the African immigrant congregations have come into existence in the past twenty years, many in the past ten. Regardless of its short time of existence, however, African Christianity is already making strong waves in the religious landscape of most Western cities and countries. Whether they are called Black Majority Churches or African immigrant churches, they are increasingly visible. Archbishop Onaiyekan of Abuja said in 2004, "The stream of Africans coming to Europe has become a river; even if the Church did not want to take notice of this fact before, it should now."[1] Indeed, even if it were for the sake of mission alone, African Christianity in the West ought not to be ignored any longer. This chapter explores some of the prominent characteristics of African Christianity in the West. My goal here is to attempt to explain African immigrant Christianity to some of those Western scholars, church leaders, and Christians who are either confused about or suspicious of its presence in the West.

Studying African Christianity
in the Postcolonial West

Studies on the subject of African Christianity in the West are usually located within the wider realms of the studies of the Black

---

[1] "The Church in the World: African Bishops Come to the Aid of Europe," *Tablet*, http://www.thetablet.co.uk.

Church in the United States and of Black Majority Churches in Britain. In North America, the Black Church is largely made up of African American Christians and has existed since the seventeenth century, when the institution of slavery brought black people from Africa to North America. Black Christianity in North America, therefore, predates the nineteenth-century arrival of Christianity in most of the continent of Africa.[2] In Britain, the Black Majority Churches are a more recent phenomenon, rising after World War II, and mostly comprising Afro-Caribbean Christians with a significantly increasing percentage of Africans in attendance.

All in all, the category of Black Christianity lumps together African American Christianity, Afro-Caribbean Christianity, and African immigrant Christianity in the Western context, where Africans are very small in numbers. As a result, African immigrant Christianity is usually studied in the shadows of the other two types of Black Christianity and therefore never gets the attention it deserves. David Daniels properly diagnosed this problem some years ago. He said, "For the religious experience of post-1965 African immigrants to become incorporated conceptually within the rubric of the Black Church, a re-conceptualization of the Black Church is required."[3] Indeed, until recently, there has been very little attention given to the distinctive type of African Christianity that has been brought from Africa to the West in the second half of the twentieth century. Western scholars seem to be more interested in Christianity in Africa and not African Christianity.

In recent years, however, a sizable collection of monographs exploring the African Diaspora in general, and African religions in Diaspora in particular, has emerged,[4] but most have been pub-

---

[2] Jacob Olupona and Regina Gemignani, *African Immigrant Religions in America* (New York: New York University Press, 2007), 47.

[3] David Daniels, "African Immigrant Religions in the United States and the Study of Black Church History," in *African Immigrant Religions,* ed. Olupona and Gemignani.

[4] See Paul Stoller, *Money Has No Smell: The Africanization of New York City* (Chicago: University of Chicago Press, 2002); Rogaia Mustafa Abusharaf, *Wanderings: Sudanese Migrants and Exiles in North America*, The

lished by African immigrants. An appreciative, if not sympathetic, Western perspective is yet to be heard. Major Western works such as Stephen Warner's *Gatherings in Diaspora*,[5] Helen Ebaugh's *Religion and the New Immigrants*,[6] and Karen Leonard's *Immigrant Faiths*[7] largely overlook the presence of African Christians in the North America. Unfortunately, Western studies of African diasporic religions usually focus on those religions of African origin that have been established in South America for centuries, like *Voodoo* in Haiti and *Candomble* and *Umbanda* in Brazil.[8]

Sometimes akin to studying an animal in the zoo, there are some Westerners who study these religions since they fit in the so-called less civilized categories, such as "animistic" and "primitive," and thereby arouse justifiable curiosity because they are largely unknown to many Westerners. Not so with African Christianity, as it is supposedly bringing back to the West something that was brought to Africa by Westerners. To some Westerners Africans are bringing back an inferior type of Christianity compared to the Western Christianity they believe they know well.

African Christianity in the West, just like the general population of African migrants in the West, has been received with a great deal of suspicion and sometimes outright discrimination.

Anthropology of Contemporary Issues (Ithaca, NY: Cornell University Press, 2002); Jacqueline Copeland-Carson, *Creating Africa in America: Translocal Identity in an Emerging World City*, Contemporary Ethnography (Philadelphia: University of Pennsylvania Press, 2004); and Wisdom Tettey and Korbla P. Puplampu, *The African Diaspora in Canada: Negotiating Identity and Belonging*, Africa: Missing Voices Series (Calgary, AB: University of Calgary Press, 2005).

[5] R. Stephen Warner and Judith G. Wittner, *Gatherings in Diaspora: Religious Communities and the New Immigration* (Philadelphia: Temple University Press, 1998).

[6] Helen Rose F. Ebaugh and Janet Saltzman Chafetz, *Religion and the New Immigrants: Continuities and Adaptations in Immigrant Congregations* (Walnut Creek, CA: AltaMira Press, 2000).

[7] Karen I. Leonard, *Immigrant Faiths: Transforming Religious Life in America* (Walnut Creek, CA: AltaMira Press, 2005).

[8] Gerrie ter Haar, *How God Became African: African Spirituality and Western Secular Thought* (Philadelphia: University of Pennsylvania Press, 2009). 88. Also see Leonard, *Immigrant Faiths*, 165–87.

This cold reception is more evident in Europe but also exists in subtle ways in North America. In *God's Continent*, Phil Jenkins observes that in Europe, a great deal of attention is given to Islam and other traditional religions, not African Christianity. He says, "In terms of the practice of religion itself, European media and officialdom have demonstrated rather greater tolerance toward Islam than immigrant Christianity, which is viewed as a peculiarly sinister faith not worthy of legal protections."[9] Jenkins goes further to suggest that the European media and policy makers are usually more suspicious and intolerant of African immigrant Christians, especially those of the Pentecostal tradition.[10]

In Britain, in response to heartrending news of exorcisms and witchcraft and child abuse cases among certain groups of African independent churches, the government has adopted a far stricter rule for African clergy and ministers entering the UK, "a draconian sanction introduced several months before any like restrictions were imposed on Muslim activists or imams preaching hatred and violence."[11] Such prejudices leave African Christianity, which is becoming more and more charismatic, perpetually at the margins, even in the academy.

Looking for a Home in a Strange Land

In one way or another, all Black Christianity in the West manifests cultural influences from the continent of Africa. Black Christianity, both in the form of Black Majority Churches in the United Kingdom and African American Christianity in the United States, has inherited cultural roots deeply steeped in African spirituality.

Once in Europe or North America, African Christians have tended to sort themselves out into several categories. One group usually joins African immigrant congregations, generally made up of ethnic groups from the same home country. The other group joins multicultural Western congregations, but some persons in

---

[9] Philip Jenkins, *God's Continent: Christianity, Islam, and Europe's Religious Crisis* (Oxford: Oxford University Press, 2007), 98.

[10] Ibid., 98–99.

[11] Ibid., 101.

this group will also visit or later join an African congregation. Moses Biney observes that there are several factors that precipitate the existence of African immigrant congregations. He says that the most outstanding factor is the adversity that immigrants have to face from all angles in their new places of residence. "Faced with harassment by government and discrimination by society," Biney says, "the immigrants' community becomes their most important source of help and existence. This is where [immigrant] religious congregations come in."[12]

Kwadwo Konadu-Agyemang has observed that the new African diasporic community has come to America with its own religious beliefs and ideals, sometimes importing leaders from Africa, and at other times, leaders have emerged out of the Diaspora.[13] Several research studies have also shown that the process of migration often results in the intensification of religiosity among immigrants.[14] Many of the active African Christians in the West might not have been as involved if they stayed in Africa. Even so, there are also many immigrants who have converted to Christianity after the process of immigration.[15] In addition, some members of African immigrant churches have not necessarily converted to Christianity but attend worship services in immigrant congregations for the social benefits of community. This is common especially in those African immigrant communities where social support is tied to religious structures. For instance, if a particular community in the Diaspora ties social significance to religious commitment, most new immigrants trying to find a sense of social belonging for themselves end up joining the church.

---

[12] Moses O. Biney, *From Africa to America: Religion and Adaptation among Ghanaian Immigrants in New York* (New York: New York University Press, 2011), 27.

[13] Kwadwo Konadu-Agyemang, Baffour K. Takyi, and John A. Arthur, *The New African Diaspora in North America: Trends, Community Building, and Adaptation* (Lanham, MD: Lexington Books, 2006), 121.

[14] Jehu Hanciles, *Beyond Christendom: Globalization, African Migration, and the Transformation of the West* (Maryknoll, NY: Orbis Books, 2008), 297. See also Ebaugh and Chafetz, *Religion and the New Immigrants*, 401.

[15] Stephen R. Prothero, *A Nation of Religions: The Politics of Pluralism in Multi-religious America* (Chapel Hill: University of North Carolina Press, 2006), 235.

The issue of race is usually mentioned as a main factor that determines whether Africans stay in Western congregations or not. Although it is often mentioned together with other factors, such as spirituality, it is a significant factor by itself. Africans who feel the pain of discrimination in white churches often resolve to go to an African church where they do not have to "apologize for being African"—in the words of one African immigrant Christian. It is worth mentioning here that many Africans who come straight from Africa have never really experienced white racism until they come to the United States.

Kwakye-Nuako adds that most of the immigrants first attend worship services in congregations affiliated with mainline denominations they belonged to in Africa. Later they break off to form their own churches because they feel that the established churches do not address their spiritual concerns and needs.[16] They consider the worship services in the established churches dead, lacking the energy and the enthusiasm that made their services exciting in Africa. Others cite lack of hospitality in established churches as the reason they leave to join African immigrant churches. Lack of hospitality, especially owing to Western individualism, particularly in the United States, is a significant challenge for most Africans. Having been accustomed to life in an open communal culture, adjusting to the individualistic life in the United States is usually a great struggle.

Four Streams of African Immigrant Christianity

African Christianity exists in four streams in the West. The largest group consists of Pentecostal and charismatic Christians. They have formed most of the African immigrant congregations in the West. The second consists of mainline African Christians who have joined mainline Western denominations or formed ethnic-specific congregations within mainline denominations. Most of the Africans in this group usually have strong ties with their Pentecostal/charismatic brothers and sisters. Many will actually belong to two congregations at one time, one mainline and

---

[16] Konadu-Agyemang, Takyi, and Arthur, *New African Diaspora*, 124.

another African immigrant or ethnic-specific community. The third belongs to the Roman Catholic tradition. These Christians will generally join the nearest Roman Catholic Church. However, even among them, the charismatic influences from Africa often lead them to visit African charismatic churches. The fourth stream is that of African Independent Churches. These are usually exclusive in their approach and outlook. They rarely make missional connections with others around them.

African Pentecostals in the West

One of the most important characteristics of African Christianity that Westerners need to understand is that it is generally charismatic in nature. It is fair to say that the landscape of African Christianity is dominated by the Pentecostals and their charismatic brothers and sisters, and increasingly so since the 1990s. However, the charismatization of African Christianity itself started with the first African Initiated Churches of the late 1800s. The trend began to explode in the early 1970s, and since then, the Pentecostal and charismatic movements have been at the center of the growth of Christianity in Africa. This growth is linked to a robust understanding of the spirit-world and the spirits' influence on everyday life in Africa. The charismatic kind of Christianity that opens itself to expressive manifestations of the presence and the power of the Holy Spirit connects easily with the spirit-centered culture of the Africans and their traditional religions.[17] At the moment of this writing, Pentecostals form around 30 percent of African Christianity, and they are still growing at a rapid rate.[18] When the charismatic Christians who do not belong to Pentecostal churches and other adherents are also considered, the entire Pentecostal and charismatic movement will account for 50 percent of Africa's Christians.[19]

---

[17] For more on this, see Harvey C. Kwiyani, "The Holy Spirit in African Theology," *Transformed* 1, no. 1 (2011).

[18] Todd M. Johnson, Kenneth R. Ross, and Sandra S. K. Lee, *Atlas of Global Christianity, 1910–2010* (Edinburgh: Edinburgh University Press, 2009), 110–11.

[19] Ibid.

After thirty years of such Pentecostal and charismatic influence, it is hard to find any African Christians today who have not been touched in one way or another by the movement. Even the staunch mainline pastors who want nothing to do with the "crazy Pentecostals" find themselves having to borrow from the Pentecostal way of doing things lest they lose all their members. One Nigerian Lutheran pastor lamented, "If you cannot beat the Pentecostals, just join them. Let people speak in tongues in your churches. Let them sing choruses."[20] Some scholars, such as Asamoah-Gyadu, have observed that charismatic Christianity is the religion of the young, educated, and upwardly mobile Christians in Africa.[21] African charismatic Christianity is an urban religion that is quickly becoming the religion of the middle class. These urban college-educated Africans come to the West for further education and end up in African immigrant congregations, oftentimes as leaders and pastors in such congregations. Unlike the Western context where charismatic Christianity is at the margins of the Christian population, African Pentecostals and charismatics enjoy extensive influence in the continent's religious landscape.

African Pentecostals and charismatics have embraced the missionary values of the worldwide Pentecostal movement. Their belief in the work of the Holy Spirit in both individuals and communities and that any individual can hear from God and follow the lead of the Spirit make it possible for them to multiply their churches around the world. Their theology assures them that any believer can be used by God to do missionary work, as long as they feel the calling to do so and possess the talents to carry out such an endeavor. In addition, the eschatological convictions

---

[20] Dr. Sekenwa Briska took time to explain to me about the impact of the Pentecostal and charismatic forms of Christianity on mainline Christianity in Nigeria. His words here do not reflect the opinions of the Lutheran Church in Nigeria. They do not even reflect his own opinion. They simply describe the attitude he had seen among other mainline denominations in Nigeria.

[21] J. Kwabena Asamoah-Gyadu, *African Charismatics: Current Developments within Independent Indigenous Pentecostalism in Ghana* (Boston: Brill, 2005), 201–12.

among many Pentecostals around the imminent rapture, tribula-
tion, judgment, and hell, make it imperative for them to reach
the world to save as many as possible. Many believe that we are
living on "borrowed time," a very critical time for every Christian
to join God's labor force and to save humankind from eternal
damnation. Margaret Poloma says, "It is their belief about being
in the 'last days' that has propelled them to untiring and sacrifi-
cial missionary endeavors—endeavors that have reaped even more
abundant harvest in the Third World than [in the West]."[22] They
usually eschew ecclesiastical bureaucracies in forming ministries,
and in doing so, they bring together missional entrepreneurism
and voluntarism—two key factors in their ministerial success.

This pentecostalization of Christianity in Africa has led to
the pentecostalization of African Diaspora Christianity. Almost
all scholars who have published on African Christianity in the
Diaspora have agreed that an overwhelming majority of African
immigrant congregations belong to the Pentecostal and charismatic tradition. Jehu Hanciles' study was carried out among
what he calls Pentecostal-type churches. Hanciles noted that
the study behind *Beyond Christendom* singles out African immigrant churches that are strongly missionary in outlook and function, and then adds, "The vast majority of churches that exhibit
this 'missionary' propensity are Pentecostal-charismatic-type
churches."[23] Afe Adogame confirms this observation in *Who
Is Afraid of the Holy Ghost?:* "African Pentecostal/charismatic
churches have taken to proselytizing in North America and
Europe. . . . [They have] systematically set out to evangelize the
world."[24] Jacob Olupona adds, "African Pentecostal and charismatic churches constitute the largest type of immigrant religious
group from Africa and are primarily evangelical, born-again Pentecostal sects that emphasize holiness, fervent prayer, charismatic

---

[22] Margaret M. Poloma, *The Assemblies of God at the Crossroads: Charisma
and Institutional Dilemmas* (Knoxville: University of Tennessee Press, 1989),
237.

[23] Hanciles, *Beyond Christendom*, 325.

[24] Afeosemime U. Adogame, *Who Is Afraid of the Holy Ghost?: Pentecostalism and Globalization in Africa and Beyond* (Trenton, NJ: Africa World Press,
2011), xvii–xviii.

revival, proximate salvation, speaking in tongues, baptism of the Holy Spirit, faith healing, visions, and divine revelations."[25] Ludwig and Asamoah-Gyadu support this observation.[26]

Even those scholars who have studied African mainline churches in the Diaspora have been quick to mention their charismatic tendencies. In some cases, these mainline churches look more charismatic than the ones who call themselves charismatic. For instance, Moses Biney's Presbyterian Church of Ghana in New York appears no different from the other two main Ghanaian churches in the Diaspora: the Church of Pentecost and the Lighthouse Chapel. In the same way, a Nigerian Episcopal church in Minneapolis is very similar to such Nigerian churches as the Deeper Life and the Redeemed Christian Church of God.

Again, after thirty years of constant Pentecostal and charismatic influence, there are many African Christians today who have no experience at all with mainline Christianity, especially those who converted after the 1980s. There is, indeed, a younger generation of Africans who have been raised in Pentecostal and charismatic churches who will find it confusing and less than exciting to sit through a scripted mainline church service. Mostly, it is these Africans who think of Western Christianity as dead. They are used to the expressive services that allow for more freedom and less structure. They will call the fifteen-minute sermon that is popular in mainline churches in the Midwest "an appetizer." The kind of Christianity that these Africans are looking for will not be found in a mainline church. They also find it difficult to settle down in an American Pentecostal church. The natural place for them will be among other Africans with whom they share more than just their faith.

Most of these African Christians are biblicist in their theology. God, for them, is not a distant figure who is only accessible on Sunday mornings. For most of them, a personal relationship with Jesus is the most important thing in life. Jesus relates with them on a daily basis throughout the week, and this constant awareness

---

[25] Olupona and Gemignani, *African Immigrant Religions*, 31.

[26] Frieder Ludwig and J. Kwabena Asamoah-Gyadu, *African Christian Presence in the West: New Immigrant Congregations and Transnational Networks in North America and Europe* (Trenton, NJ: Africa World Press, 2011), 7.

of Jesus' proximity means that they shape their lives in accordance with the Word of God. In their charismatic theology, there is no room for cessationism—they believe that apostles and prophets are especially anointed to "bring revelations hot and fresh from the throne-room of heaven." The pastors, commonly called "men of God," are God's prophetic vessels with a mandate to speak on God's behalf. For them, a *rhema*-word from God (a timely message from a passage of scripture) is more important than a three-point sermon. Prayer is a foundational practice that is encouraged as a way to involve God in their daily lives. Of course, many of these immigrants do not have an easy life. They might need God to intervene and fix their immigration status, or provide for their tuition fees, or even help them with building projects back in Africa. Consequently, most Africans pray with passion and fervor. Quite a few African congregations that I have seen in both Britain and the United Kingdom have prayer vigils on Friday nights.

The Case of the Redeemed Christian Church of God

The Redeemed Christian Church of God (RCCG) is a good example of a missionary-minded movement from Africa that is intentional about evangelizing the West.[27] It originally declared in its mission statement that it seeks to "plant churches within five minutes walking distance in every city and town of developing countries and within five minutes driving distance in every city and town of developed countries," adding that they would pursue this objective until every nation in the world is reached for Jesus Christ.[28] For the Western world, the RCCG has

---

[27] The RCCG is chosen for this discussion because of the extent of its global presence and the strength of its leadership structures. This story reflects the experiences of most of the African Christians who try to do missionary work in the West. Any African movement working in the West could tell the same story.

[28] See The Redeemed Christian Church of God, "Our Vision and Mission" (Lagos: RCCG Internet Outreach), http://rccg.org. See also Hanciles, *Beyond Christendom*, 354–57. For further exploration of the RCCG in North America, see Afeosemime U. Adogame, "Contesting the Ambivalences of Modernity in a Global Context: The Redeemed Christian Church of God, North America," *Studies in World Christianity* 10, no. 1 (2004).

modified this church-planting objective from planting a church within five minutes driving distance to "within 10 minutes driving distance."[29] Indeed, it has established churches in such places as India, Hong Kong, the Caribbean, and Russia. In the United States, the RCCG is among the fastest-growing immigrant denominations, claiming to have planted over three hundred branches in the past fifteen years.[30] The UK chapter of the RCCG is indeed planting churches at a very fast pace, having planted thirty-seven churches in 2005 alone, all of which are led by highly educated bivocational ministers.[31]

Nevertheless, even a vibrant, highly educated, and professional movement like this finds it hard to connect with the host cultures in Europe and North America. Their congregations are still largely made up of West Africans, especially Nigerians—a tendency that is typical of almost all African immigrant churches—people congregate according to their nationalities. For example, the RCCG churches in Minneapolis and Saint Paul, which I have visited occasionally, are mainly Nigerian in their attendance. Indeed, the RCCG has not been very successful in reaching even fellow Africans who come from other parts of the continent.

These examples suggest that optimism around the missionary impact of non-Western Christians in the West can be highly exaggerated. Apart from the impact they make through their presence, prayers, evangelism strategies, and more, their missionary presence has yet to blossom in many places. For most of the Africans, the immigrant church from their country of origin is usually the first choice when it comes to choosing a place of worship. Once they get established in these immigrant congregations, chances to interact with non-African Christians become rare. There may be too few bridges between the African immigrant Christians and their Western counterparts.[32]

[29] Adogame, "Contesting the Ambivalences," 32.

[30] RCCG North America, "Our Mission," (Greenville, TX: RCCG Internet Outreach), http://www.rccgna.org.

[31] See Alexander Campbell, "Mission 21: A Report in Church Planting in UK since 2000" (Sheffield, UK: Fresh Expressions, 2006). Later statistics could not be found, but my recent conversations with the Mission 21 Team suggested that RCCG has maintained the momentum.

[32] See Diana L. Eck, *A New Religious America: How a "Christian Coun-*

One hopeful story of cross-cultural mission in which an African from Nigeria has been exceedingly successful at attracting white Europeans is in Kiev, Ukraine. Sunday Adelaja founded the Blessed Embassy of the Kingdom of God in Kiev in 1993 as a Bible study group of seven members.[33] Today, the Blessed Embassy says that it has over 30,000 members across Kiev. Over 50 percent of the members are white, and quite a few of them are politically powerful and influential in Ukraine.[34] On any given Sunday, more than twenty worship services are held in various auditoriums around the city. In the past decade, over one hundred daughter congregations and satellite churches have been born in the region around Ukraine. They claim to have over two hundred churches in operation in the countries of the former Soviet Union, in the United States, in Germany, and in many other countries.[35]

African Mainline Christians in the Diaspora

In terms of numbers, mainline Africans trail behind their Pentecostal and charismatic brothers and sisters by a reasonably wide margin. Mainline Africans include all Africans who belong to mainline Western denominations that were brought to Africa by the missionaries: these denominations include Anglicans, Lutherans, Presbyterians, Methodists, and others. Unlike the African Pentecostals and charismatics who have maintained their independence and organized themselves into their own immigrant congregations, many mainline Africans have maintained their allegiance to their denominations and, in doing so, have avoided forming their own organizations. Even those who have formed

---

try" *Has Now Become the World's Most Religiously Diverse Nation* (New York: HarperSanFrancisco, 2001), 335–85.

[33] See J. Kwabena Asamoah-Gyadu, "African Initiated Christianity in Eastern Europe: Church of the 'Embassy of God' in Ukraine," *International Bulletin of Missionary Research* 30, no. 2 (2006).

[34] J. Kwabena Asamoah-Gyadu, "Spirit, Mission, and Transnational Influence: Nigerian-Led Pentecostalism in Eastern Europe," *PentecoStudies* 9, no. 1 (2010): 74–76.

[35] The Blessed Embassy of the Kingdom of God, "History" (Kiev), http://www.godembassy.com..

ethnically African congregations within the mainline traditions in the West must work with their Western denominational judicatories as well as their African denominational leaders in Africa. This affects their understanding of mission and ecclesiology.

When in the West, most of these mainline Africans are clustered according to their regions of origin; and this reflects the denominations of the missionaries who evangelized those regions. For instance, most African Lutherans will come from Ethiopia, Tanzania, Nigeria, and Liberia. A great number of African Methodists will come from Kenya, Ghana, and South Africa. African Presbyterians will generally come from South Africa, Malawi, Kenya, and Ghana. Furthermore, where missionaries from several different countries and denominations worked, denominational affiliations can also reflect ethnic/tribal lines. Kenyans in the city of Minneapolis are a good example. From my conversations with African immigrants in Minneapolis and Saint Paul, I learned that among the Kisii people of Central Kenya, Lutherans and Seventh-Day Adventists were the most effective missionaries. Therefore, the majority of Kenyan Lutherans and SDAs in Minneapolis are Kisii. The same applies for the Meru people, who were largely evangelized by the Methodists. My Ethiopian friends have told me that Ethiopians of Oromo heritage make up most of the Mekane Yesus Church in North America.

Since they started migrating to the West in large numbers in the 1980s, mainline Africans have approached religious practice in three distinctive ways. The first group has settled down in Western mainline congregations—mostly in those denominations that they belonged to in Africa. For most of these congregations, this has created an unexpected cultural diversity. Some congregations have taken this to be a good thing that God is doing in their midst; in other congregations, some would rather go back to the old days before the immigrants changed their neighborhoods. In general, the reception of the mainline African Christians in the West has not been as welcoming as one might have hoped.

From the few studies that have been carried out among mainline Christian immigrants from Africa, we have learned of some reasons for their staying in Western congregations.[36] First,

---

[36] For instance, Harvey C. Kwiyani, "Pneumatology, Mission, and Afri-

there is denominational loyalty. When mainline Africans migrate to the West, they will first try to find a congregation within their denomination. For instance, Presbyterian Africans will generally look for a Presbyterian church before trying anything else. Most of them love to continue with their denomination's familiar liturgy. For most immigrants, the massive change experienced in the process of migration is made bearable by the great sense of security of not changing denominations. In this day and age when denominations have sister synods around the world, most immigrants are generally aware of the Western counterpart of their denominations before they leave Africa.

Nevertheless, denominational loyalty only works when the immigrants feel accepted in the Western congregations that they choose to join. Many will stay in Western congregations because of the welcoming hospitality they feel in their first couple of visits. Where they feel unwelcome, they will not stay. They will keep looking, and if they do not find a congregation of their denomination that welcomes them, they will go to an African immigrant church. When asked why they stayed in Western congregations, Africans mention concepts like "feeling welcomed," "feeling appreciated," and "made to feel at home" during their early visits.[37] Conversely, those who indicate that they left a Western congregation usually mention lack of hospitality as the cause of their departure. Intercultural hospitality between the Western Christians and their African counterparts is a significant issue. Hanciles tells of the immigrants' strong desire to belong, which, sadly, is usually met with discrimination, rejection, marginalization, and prejudice.[38] He goes on to state, "The suggestion that the new immigrants will be compelled by impervious cultural forces to individually conform assumes that they are welcome in the first place."[39] Unfortunately, African immigrant Christians often feel they are not genuinely welcome in many Western churches. After two years of attending a Western congregation in

---

can Christians in Multicultural Congregations in North America" (PhD diss., Luther Seminary, 2012), 265–69.

[37] Ibid., 266.

[38] Hanciles, *Beyond Christendom*, 289.

[39] Ibid., 290.

Minneapolis, one Kenyan woman asked the congregation, "For how long shall we have to come here in order to be accepted as part of you? We are tired of being treated like visitors every Sunday for two years."

Some Africans stay in Western churches because they fit better in multicultural congregations and would have problems settling down in ethnic churches. For some, it is easier to connect in Western congregations than in an African immigrant church. Class is a major issue here. Several Africans told me that they believe that class is generally a stronger influence in congregational choice than race. Some Africans feel more at home in a multicultural congregation than in an African immigrant congregation. For instance, I met one Nigerian who has been in the United States for over thirty years who said that he has adapted culturally to such an extent that he feels out of place when he finds himself among other Nigerians. Indeed, there are many Westernized Africans who would have problems identifying well with other Africans.

Some stay because they want their children to grow up in a multicultural environment. Others stay because they could not find an African church in close proximity. For others still, it is the lack of an African congregation of their nationality that made them choose to go to a Western congregation. I met a Malawian woman in Minneapolis who spends most of her time with Kenyans, yet she goes to a Western church because she cannot find a Malawian church in Minneapolis. Others stay because of relationships they have formed with other cultures, through marriage or otherwise.

Finally, it is important to note that there is a tendency among many of these mainline Africans to belong to two congregations at the same time. One will be an African immigrant church and the other a multicultural Western church. For instance, it is common among the Swahili-speaking Lutherans in the Minneapolis–Saint Paul area to attend a Western Lutheran church on Sunday morning and then come together in the Swahili congregation later in the afternoon. The reasons behind this tendency also vary. Many are trying to expose their children to both Western culture, which they experience in school, and the African culture of which they need to be aware, in case they visit Africa some day. Others want to maintain a good social circle among Africans so they can still have a home away from home.

African Ethnic-specific Congregations in Mainline Denominations

Some Western pastors feel that introducing a foreign cultural group into their congregations is unnecessarily cumbersome. It demands too much energy and brings little gain. They find it easier to let the Africans organize their own immigrant congregations under the umbrella of their church's ministry. In doing so, they try to have strong partnerships with Africans while avoiding the messy process of creating a congregation of cultural heterogeneity. On the part of the Africans, because of matters such as language, some have voluntarily formed ethnic-specific congregations within their denominations or congregations. These cater mostly to those African immigrants who speak little or no English, or those who would simply love to hear the message and the liturgy in their mother tongue. Just like the Diasporic Pentecostals, most of these congregations are made up of people from the same countries. In Minneapolis, there is a Swahili-speaking Lutheran congregation of the Evangelical Lutheran Church in America which is made up mostly of Tanzanians but includes a few Kenyans. Most of the members of the Swahili congregation, which meets on Sunday afternoons, go to other churches on Sunday mornings. This is one example of the many mainline African immigrant congregations that are intentionally developed by Africans for other Africans. They live their congregational lives in between their home denominational judicatories in Africa and host judicatories in the West. Moses Biney's book *From Africa to America* talks about the experiences of one such Ghanaian Presbyterian church in New York.[40] The Ghanaian Methodist network in Britain also falls into this category. The Mekane Yesus network is a denomination of Ethiopian Lutherans that has spread across the world through their own Oromo-speaking congregations. The

---

[40] Biney, *From Africa to America*.

presence of the Mekane Yesus Church in Minnesota caters mostly to the Lutheran Ethiopians in the Twin Cities.

Unlike the Pentecostal and charismatic groups within African Christianity that encourage their members to plant independent or semi-independent churches in their somehow loosely connected networks, mainline African congregations maintain solid connections and authority over their denominations. Most of them will work with their "sending" synods and diocese in Africa while at the same time working with their juridical leaders in the Diaspora. These mainline immigrants think of themselves as missionaries in a very different way from the Pentecostal/charismatic immigrants. The sense of mission for the mainliners is usually subsumed under the denomination's understanding of mission. Unfortunately, for most of these denominations, mission is peripheral to their agenda, and it belongs to some specifically appointed professionals. Lacking the theological tools, the leadership, and even the missional community to work with, most mainline immigrants do not engage in mission at all. The Pentecostals, in contrast, have a general conviction that echoes God's words to Joshua; they believe that the promise, "Every place that the sole of your foot will tread upon I have given to you" (Josh. 1:3), applies to them too, even as individuals. As a result, they are usually very motivated to engage in mission.

In most circumstances, Western mainline denominations have been slow to think about how to cater to the spiritual needs of immigrants. Of course, it is true that Western Christianity, in general, has been very slow to recognize the rise of non-Western Christianity. Mainline denominations have rarely called for missionaries or pastors from overseas to help them negotiate the ministry that is needed for the immigrants. For so many reasons, there has been a lack of intentionality on the part of Western mainline denominations to engage immigrant Christians. There have been a few African immigrant leaders in the upper levels of some denominational hierarchies; however, such representation has been missing at the lower levels. Even then, most of these African Christian leaders came to the West to further their education and other such things, and have in one way or another found their ways to serving in mainline judicatories. As we stand today, most congregations that have a significant number of immigrants and minorities fail to make room for diversity in their leadership structures, without which it will be impossible to form good cross-cultural partnerships.

African Roman Catholics in the West

At the eighteenth General Congregation of the Assembly of the Synod of the Bishops for Africa in Rome in October 2009, the Synod Fathers concluded with a *nuntius* that recognized that "the Church in Africa thanks God for many of her sons and daughters who are missionaries on other continents."[41] Indeed, the synod recognized, "Many sons and daughters of Africa have left home to seek abode in other continents [where] many are doing well, contributing validly to the life of their new resident countries."[42] This may have been a rather late realization for the Roman Catholic Church (which is better than the blind eye that most Protestants have given the spread of African Christianity to the rest of the world), but it is still very hopeful news. The Vatican's positive response to the realization that "Africa has started moving, and the church is moving with her" opens up great possibilities for Roman Catholics of African origin in the global Roman Catholic Church.[43] It carries with it the potential to radically change the way the global Catholic Church carries out its mission in the world. The Synod of the Bishops' message included an exhortation for the global Catholic body to help the Africans with adequate pastoral care of the Church Family of God, wherever they are, adding, "'I was a stranger and you

---

[41] This was a continuation of the work that had been started by the Council of Bishops' Conferences of Europe (CCEE) and the Council of Bishops' Conferences of Africa and Madagascar (SECAM) in 2004. Synod of Bishops, "Message to the People of God of the Second Special Assembly for Africa of the Synod of Bishops," http://www.vatican.va.

[42] Ibid.

[43] Holy See Press Office, "Synodus Episcoporum Bulletin: II Ordinary Special Assembly for Africa of the Synod of Bishops, 4–25 October 2009," http://www.vatican.va.

made me welcome' (Matt. 25:35) is not only a parable about the end of the world but also a duty to be accomplished today."[44] These words—expressed from the Vatican—tell of a uniquely positive approach to the migration of African Catholics to the rest of the world.

The context of African immigrant Catholics in the West is thus different from that of Protestants. Two main factors account for this. The first is the centralized leadership system that makes the worldwide uniformity of the Catholic Church possible. The ecclesial system that emanates from the Vatican to the worldwide body of Roman Catholic Christians assures them that, at least at one level or another, they are doing similar things. The Catholic lectionary also means that on any given Sunday, a sermon preached in Maputo, Mozambique, will not be too different from the one preached in Caracas, Venezuela, or in Verona, Italy. There is a great deal of interdiocesan sharing of resources within the worldwide Roman Catholic structures. All Catholics in the world are accountable to the Bishop of Rome in a very regimented way. In this way, the Catholic body is somehow united in their conversations no matter where one comes from. Figuratively speaking, when African Catholics find themselves in Europe or North America, they have just moved from one room to another, but they remain in the same ecclesial mansion. The organizational structures that keep the house in order remain the same no matter where they are. Consequently, the immigrants have the privilege of systemic continuity. Although everything else is changing in the course of their migration process, the Catholic Church offers them a sense of stability. In most cases, the Protestant tradition lacks this continuity, especially among independent Pentecostals and charismatics.

Second, for almost half a century now, the Roman Catholic church in Europe and North America has found itself in the difficult position of needing to recruit priests from the rest of the world in order to survive. Although the Protestant churches are beginning to feel the pinch of declining seminary enroll-

---

[44] Synod of Bishops, "Message to the People of God of the Second Special Assembly for Africa of the Synod of Bishops."

ments, they have not reached the point of needing foreign help to fill their pulpits. As for the Roman Catholic Church, the once steady stream of young men being trained in the priesthood by American and European seminaries has slowed to a trickle. Consequently, more parishes are going without priests—over 3,389 in the United States in 2012, up from 549 in 1965.[45] To make up for the deficit, the Roman Catholic Church has had to rely on the ministry of foreign priests. According to Dean Hoge and Aniedi Okure, there were some 7,600 foreign-born priests serving in the United States in 1999 and again in 2004, representing 16 percent of all priests.[46] Thus, about one in every six priests working in America today is foreign-born. In addition, around 300 international priests arrive to work in the United States each year. Unlike the Irish, Italian, and Polish priests who joined the American priesthood in the twentieth century who came largely to serve immigrants from their countries, current foreign-born priests have little to nothing in common with the American populations they are serving.

The Roman Catholic weekly *The Tablet* observed in 2004 that Nigeria alone has about 7,000 seminarians (with 500 to be ordained in 2004), compared with Scotland's total of barely 30.[47] In the same year, there were 157 priests in training in France while there were only 18 ordinations in England and Wales in 2003.[48] Maïa de la Baume of the *New York Times* says in the article "In France, Foreign Aid in the Form of Priests" that "France had about 41,000 priests in the 1960s. Today, there are around 15,000, and about 10 percent of these are foreign-born."[49] She added

[45] CARA Services, "Frequently Requested Church Statistics," http://cara.georgetown.edu.

[46] Dean R. Hoge and Aniedi Okure, *International Priests in America: Challenges and Opportunities* (Collegeville, MN: Liturgical Press, 2006), 10–11.

[47] "The Church in the World: African Bishops Come to the Aid of Europe," *Tablet.*

[48] David Killingray, "African Missionary Activity at Home and Overseas," in *OCMS Public Lectures* (Oxford, 2005).

[49] Maïa de la Baume, "In France, Foreign Aid in the Form of Priests," *New York Times*, April 4, 2013.

that in France, about 800 priests die each year, and only 100 are ordained. In North American Roman Catholic seminaries today, about 1 in 3 of those studying for the priesthood are foreign-born, and not necessarily from Europe, like in the 1950s.[50] Most international seminary students today come from Latin America, the Philippines, and Nigeria.[51] Out of those foreign-born students, 84 percent plan to stay and work in the United States for some time after ordination. A survey of new Catholic ordinands indicates that 28 percent were foreign-born in 2003, 31 percent in 2004, and 27 percent in 2005.[52]

Furthermore, foreign-born priests are also needed because most of the growth in the Western Roman Catholic Church is happening among immigrant populations from the Philippines, Latin America, and Africa. According to the Society of Joseph, a community of priests that is dedicated to service among African Americans, there are about 300 priests of African descent who serve a growing population of 3 million to 4 million black Catholics in the United States.[53] A majority of these priests— approximately 200—come from Nigeria.[54] About 10 percent of the priests serving New York City come from West Africa. The National Association of African Catholics in the United States (NAACUS) was established in 2008 to work with the office of Cultural Diversity in the Church. NAACUS serves as an umbrella body for all African Catholics in the United States. According to its website, "It is dedicated to primarily serve African Catholics in the United States; it seeks to engage, support, nurture, build communities of African Catholics, and it will promote their spiritual wellbeing while liaising, coordinating and involving all Africans Catholics to maximize their charisms as a faith and worship Community in the United States."[55] Several

---

[50] Hoge and Okure, *International Priests in America*, 11.

[51] Ibid.

[52] The peak year for American missionaries going to the rest of the world was 1968, when there were 9,655 missionaries serving overseas, ordained and lay.

[53] Josephites, "Our Mission," http://www.josephites.org.

[54] Ibid.

[55] National Association of African Catholics in the United States

other national organizations also exist. For instance, the Nigerian Catholic Community in the United States of America was an outgrowth of the African/Caribbean Apostolate in the Office for the Pastoral Care of Migrants and Refugees (PCMR) under the auspices of the United States Conference of Catholic Bishops (USCCB) in Washington, DC, in 1996. It exists to provide central leadership to the many localized and tribalized Catholic communities around the United States.

At the congregational level, African Roman Catholic immigrants do not find it necessary to start their own congregations. Where there exists a group of Africans from the same country, or even the same tribe, they may celebrate the Mass in their vernacular languages once or twice a month. It is an extremely rare occasion to find an independent African immigrant Roman Catholic congregation. Unlike Latin Americans, most Africans speak English well enough not to need their own vernacular congregations, but even the Spanish-speaking congregations are rarely independent of the parochial leadership in their diocese. While researching this book, I became aware of a number of Roman Catholic congregations in several cities that had an Igbo Mass or a Swahili Mass twice a month. One Ghanaian priest from Chicago told me that he started a Twi Mass at the request of his bishop in order to facilitate a sense of solidarity among the Ghanaians in his parish. These vernacular Masses are held within the context of their regional Roman Catholic Church systems.

All in all, African Roman Catholics in the West generally assimilate into the wider Catholic body. Like mainline Protestant African immigrants, African Roman Catholics have very little written about them. Going through the major published books on African Christianity on the West (most of which were written by Protestant Christians), I was surprised to see so little attention given to the Roman Catholic branch of African immigrant Christianity. Only Ludwig and Asamoah-Gyadu dedicated a chapter to some connections between Roman Catholics in France and those in Burkina Faso.[56] However, the chapter did

---

(NAACUS), "A Welcoming Message from President Ntal Alimas," http://www.naacus.org.

[56] Ludwig and Asamoah-Gyadu, *African Christian Presence*, 289–302.

not even begin to explore the presence of Burkinabe Catholics in France. Since they continue to exist under the umbrella of the Roman Catholic Church after migration, they blend in to the wider Catholic communities in which they reside and do not form their own congregations.

African Initiated Churches (AICs)

African Initiated Churches are also known as African *Independent* Churches or African *Instituted* Churches. Whatever term is used to describe them, there is some persistent ambiguity in the terminology, since the words "initiated," "instituted," and "independent" can also be used to describe most of the Pentecostal and charismatic churches discussed earlier. However, the AICs referred to here are distinct. They are indigenous spiritual churches that are founded by African charismatic, prophetic, or visionary leaders. They are very spiritist in their practices, and they are built around their leaders' manifestation of spiritual power in terms of miracles such as healings and exorcisms. In the language of the missionaries of old, they are pseudo-Christian because they fuse biblical dogma, Christian beliefs and practices, and African spirit-centered cultural traditions. Even to date, most Western commentators label them as syncretic, or derogatorily label them as sects or cults, even though the AICs consider themselves part of the Christian church of God because of their commitment to Jesus Christ.[57]

Members are generally identifiable because of their dress code, usually a long white *sultana* robe accompanied by sandals or sometimes bare feet, and most of the men will wear a long white beard. Among the myriad AICs in Africa, the most popular are the Kimbanguists of Zaire/Congo who have established themselves in the French-speaking West (Belgium, France, Canada). There is also a sizable membership in Spain, Portugal, Germany,

---

[57] Olupona and Gemignani, *African Immigrant Religions*, 107. See Allan Anderson, *African Reformation: African Initiated Christianity in the 20th Century* (Trenton, NJ: Africa World Press, 2001). See Also Allan Anderson, *Moya: The Holy Spirit in an African Context*, Manualia Didactica 13 (Pretoria: University of South Africa, 1991).

and England. In the United States, they are found in some parts of New York City, Atlanta, and Houston. Another popular AIC is the Celestial Church of Christ (Nigeria) whose presence in Germany and the Netherlands Afe Adogame has documented well.[58] The Celestial Church (Nigeria) is also present in many states across the United States. Some AICs of the Aladura type from Nigeria have managed to transform themselves from being regarded as quasi-spiritual groups to being seen as vibrant Christian churches accepted in the World Council of Churches. A good example of this is the Redeemed Christian Church of God.

Most AICs are also known for their unwavering loyalty to their denomination's charismatic founders—loyalty that often seems to supersede their commitment to Jesus. For instance, in Jacob Olupona's *African Immigrant Religions*, Elias Bongmba talks about a Nigerian AIC called the Brotherhood of the Cross and the Star (BCS) that has established itself in Houston, Texas (also at Elephant and Castle in London), with branches in Germany, India, Trinidad, and Russia. The Brotherhood, as Bongmba calls it, was started by Father Olumba Olumba Obu in 1942. Father Olumba effectively led it until his death in 2002 or 2003.[59] His followers know him as God the Father incarnate and follow him with undivided loyalty.[60] According to Bongmba, "The title 'Father' defines his role as the cosmic leader and teacher of everything in heaven and earth, with no deputy or assistant."[61] In 2000, he appointed his son, Rowland, as his successor, calling him the Christ, King of Kings and Lord of Lords.[62] Walter Duru, the Brotherhood's media consultant, adds that the Brotherhood has "one universal leader, master, teacher and sustainer, leader,

---

[58] See Afeosemime U. Adogame, *Celestial Church of Christ: The Politics of Cultural Identity in a West African Prophetic-Charismatic Movement* (New York: Peter Lang, 1999).

[59] His death has been vehemently refused by his followers, such that there is until now no conclusive evidence that he is dead. However, most Nigerian sources say that he has not been seen since 2003.

[60] Olupona and Gemignani, *African Immigrant Religions*, 111.

[61] Ibid.

[62] Brotherhood of the Cross and the Star, "Christ Universal Spiritual School of Practical Christianity," http://www.ooo-bcs.org.

[and that is Father] Olumba Olumba Obu. His first begotten son, His Holiness Olumba Olumba Obu is the Chairman, Head of Administration and sole signatory of the Kingdom."[63]

With the migration of Africans to the West, African immigrant denominations of this nature are fast multiplying in Western cities. Most of these AICs in the Diaspora come from Nigeria, Congo, Zimbabwe, and South Africa and still have their mother churches (and headquarters) in those countries. Nigerian Aladura churches have opened congregations in London. Kimbanguism has almost half a million followers in Europe alone.[64] One of Europe's largest Congolese AICs is the Belgium-based New Jerusalem Church of God in Brussels. This New Jerusalem Movement has, in the past twenty years, multiplied its membership, especially among the French-speaking African immigrants in the United States and Canada. Many ethnic church federations can be found in both Europe and the United States. Phil Jenkins observes, "The Congolese-initiated Communauté des Églises d'Expressions Africaines de France (CEAF) claims thirty-five congregations across France while Greater Paris has 250 ethnic Protestant churches, chiefly black African."[65] London, Hamburg, Zurich, and many other European and North American cities have seen an exponential growth in the number of these AICs in the past twenty years.

In many respects, AICs find themselves at odds with Western Christianity. Both their theologies and their practices reflect a strong influence from the same African culture that the missionaries of the nineteenth century worked hard to evangelize. Consequently, most Western Christians (and Westerners at large)

---

[63] Walter Duru, "Brotherhood of the Cross and Star Press Release: Re-Olumba Olumba Obu No Longer God" (Accra: Modern Ghana).

[64] In 1969, the Kimbanguist Church was the first independent church ever to become a full member of the World Council of Churches. Today the Kimbanguist Church is home to 17 million Christians worldwide in DRC, Congo Brazzaville, Angola, Zambia, Burundi, Kenya, Belgium, France, USA, South Africa, etc. The Kimbanguist Church is also a member of the African Council of Churches and the South African Council of Churches.

[65] Philip Jenkins, "Godless Europe?," *International Bulletin of Missionary Research* 31, no. 3 (2007): 118.

are suspicious of their Christian standing. They are put off by the AICs' worship practices, most of which involve massive celebratory dancing with loud music. Their dress codes—the *sultanas* and the *kaftans*—present a serious cultural barrier that most Westerners find hard to negotiate. In addition, the obedience to the African charismatic leaders sounds more like an invitation to be indoctrinated, something that postmodern Westerners, with their anti-institutional mentality, tend to shy away from.

Bongmba observes that the Brotherhood is very intentional about their missionary enterprise in the world. "They are so globally focused in their outlook that they do not think of themselves as an African church."[66] In their work in Houston, Texas, the Brotherhood believes that the entire world is their parish, which they ought to serve faithfully as missionaries, irrespective of where they are. However, this missional mind-set does not always bear fruit because of the nature of the gospel that they preach and the manner in which they live out their faiths. Even though some of the AICs try to evangelize Western culture, their understanding of conversion makes it difficult for Westerners to engage. Their sect-like practices are a warning sign for most Westerners.[67] Their spirit-centered African-shaped gospel can also seem too far detached from Western Christianity and too intense for religiously suspicious Westerners. For instance, the demand to follow an African charismatic prophet in some extrabiblical practices of African culture presents a chasm that most Westerners can never jump. Worse, AICs in Europe have lately received bad press because of their exorcism practices, which have injured and killed several children. These things work to enforce the cult stigma that Westerners already associate with these Christian communities.

---

[66] Olupona and Gemignani, *African Immigrant Religions*, 111.

[67] Nevertheless, there are many *independent* African churches of the Pentecostal and charismatic type that have marginally made it to mainstream American Christianity. There are also some African movements like the Redeemed Christian Church of God that started out as the sect-like AICs that have transformed themselves to becoming mainstream charismatic movements.

How Much Longer?

The presence of African Christianity in the West has so far been a result of two factors, none of which are guaranteed to exist after the next few decades. The first is the current migration trends that have made it possible for Africans to find new homes in the West. Of course, it is not too far from reality to expect the trends to continue for another generation or two. However, we need to be cautious with our expectations. Global dynamics are changing rapidly. The West is becoming increasingly wary of migrating Africans. Restrictions against Africans are in place all over Europe. North America has relatively fewer African immigrants, but even there, African migration is on the wrong end of the immigration debate. Once African migration to the West peaks, growth of African Christianity in the West could peak as well.

Second, the spread of African Christianity to the West has been an outcome of the explosive growth of Christianity in Africa. The addition of 10 million new converts to Christianity each year in Africa has meant that most African immigrants are Christian. However, this growth of Christianity in Africa will peak soon, maybe in a generation or two. According to the World Religion Database, 48 percent of Africa's 1 billion inhabitants are Christian (495.8 million), and 60 percent of them live in sub-Saharan Africa. Forty-one percent of the African population are Muslim (423.5 million), of whom only 30 percent are south of the Sahara.[68] The remaining 11 percent of Africans are "other" or unaffiliated and are spread all over the continent. Further growth of Christianity will mean encroaching significantly into the Muslim strongholds, in addition to some of the lands that have strong affiliations with traditional religions. This will not be a small endeavor and will probably slow down the growth that we have seen since 1970. Following this, the export of African Christianity to the rest of the world will be slowed down as well.

That being said, this slowdown will not happen immediately. While we anticipate that change, and hope that it takes its time in coming, African Christians will continue to affect the global

---

[68] Pew Forum on Religion and Public Life, "The Future of the Global Muslim Population: Projections for 2010–2030," http://www.pewforum.org.

religious landscape. Since Western Christianity is still a white religion that remains largely segregated, the impact of world Christianity on the West will need careful and faithful attention. As suggested earlier, a majority of African Christians belongs to African immigrant churches. Although they live in culturally diversified cities, they attend segregated churches. On the one hand, this is a systemic problem that was present in the West before the Africans came on the scene. On the other hand, the immigrant congregation is a convenient survival tactic that would not be necessary under different circumstances. For this reason, Christianity should take advantage of this current cultural diversity to reinvigorate itself where it has been slowing down.

Thinking Forward

The spread of African Christianity to the West is an unexpected (and not always welcome in the West) phenomenon that has taken most of us by surprise. Its early days do not reflect any serious intentionality either on the part of Africans or Westerners. Indeed, its spread has been largely an unforeseen outcome of colonization, globalization, and neocolonization.

Even though the early missionaries of the 1800s hoped for a blessed reflex of foreign missionary work in the West, Western Christians have had very little to do with the rising presence of African Christians in the West. This makes the growth of African Christianity feel like a reflexive action that is taking place without anybody's control—maybe only God's. Quiet debates continue in many circles concerning whether this migration of non-Western Christians to the West is a good development.[69] Instead of debating what to do with these African Christians, Western Christians need to simply recognize that non-Western Christianity is here and here to stay. This is God's little surprise for us all. The question is, What is God doing with this development and how will Western Christians react to it? Will they embrace it as God's work? Or will they retreat into their prejudices about Africans and black people?

---

[69] See Hoge and Okure, *International Priests in America*, 24–68.

If the trends continue, Western Christianity will be in the minority in a few decades to come. Christianity will increasingly become a non-Western religion. It is already evident that Western Christianity will become darker in complexion as many Africans, Latin Americans, and Asians practice their Christianity in Western cities such as Atlanta, New York, London, Brussels, Lisbon, Madrid, and Rome. Consequently, as the West becomes more culturally diverse—moving toward multiculturalism kicking and screaming—so shall Western Christianity. This too is a work of the Spirit of God. Cultural diversity is always a great thing for Christianity. It looks risky, and most of the time it does not work out easily, but the freshness of life that it brings is worth the risk.

Chapter Five

Mission and African Migration

How is the rising African missionary movement to the West changing the religious landscape of Europe and North America? On many occasions I have heard people wonder if African immigrant Christians have any desire and capacity for organized missionary work when they arrive in Hamburg or Zurich or Helsinki. I argue here that indeed many African Christians in the Diaspora are missionary-minded, and some do have organized structures for their missionary work in the West. However, for various reasons, most African Christians find it hard to translate that missional-mindedness into any missionary effectiveness among Europeans and North Americans. I discuss some of the issues involved in this lack of missional effectiveness and explore some ways to deal with it.

Behold, a Worldwide Missionary Movement

The arrival of world Christianity has brought about the rise of a potentially worldwide missionary movement—a movement that will involve Christians of all races and from all continents serving as missionaries all over the world. Despite its weaknesses and shortcomings, it is good to acknowledge that the Western missionary movement of the nineteenth century initiated the ripples that would eventually cause a swell in the worldwide missionary movement. This is because in its DNA, Christianity is a missionary religion. At the center of Christianity's missionary philosophy is Jesus' exhortation to go into all the world and make disciples (Matt. 28:19). Every person who converts to Christianity is a potential missionary. Every Christian is called to be a missionary. To convert the world is to make missionaries of the entire world, nothing more, nothing less. Therefore, with Christianity now as a worldwide religion, present in every country and in all major languages around the world, we are seeing the unleashing of a worldwide missionary movement.

There was a time in the history of Christianity when mission was associated almost exclusively with the West—the Christendom of Western Europe and the Europeans' descendants in North America. The Great Commission was, for a long time, erroneously believed to have been valid only for the first-century apostles, but as time progressed and Christianity became identified with the geographical land of Europe, mission came to be identified with the spread of a Western religion and its civilization. Later, when Christianity began to spread around the world in the nineteenth and twentieth centuries, some believed that the missionary mandate was given to the white race only—that only white people could be missionaries. As recently as 1970, many Africans wondered if African Christians could be missionaries too.

Back in 1963, at the Congress for World Mission and Evangelism in Mexico City, it was agreed that mission is a six-continent affair.[1] In other words, they agreed in 1963 that mission is possible from all of the six continents and to all the six continents. In our world today, we must wrestle with the practicalities of this agreement. Even without the 1963 CWME agreement, a worldwide missionary movement would still come about, since it is impossible to convert a people or group and prevent them from being missionaries.

The rise of world Christianity makes a global multicultural and multiethnic missionary movement possible. This multiethnic missionary movement may be our only way forward, at least for the following two reasons. First, people from all nations, tribes, and tongues are converting to Christianity and, therefore, potentially heeding their missionary calling. They must be missionaries wherever God calls them. Second, it is a much-needed devel-

---

[1] See World Council of Churches, "CWME Meeting, Mexico City, Mexico, 1963," in *WCC Archives,* http://archives.oikoumene.org.

opment at a time when the global village continues to shrink and cultural diversity continues to grow. The distance between peoples of different ethnicities and cultural heritages is diminishing greatly. The recent technological advancements in travel and communications have accelerated the process of globalization. Cultural diversity is no longer just a localized phenomenon within specific cities in the West. It is a global phenomenon.

To engage in mission in most Western cities is also to cross cultures without leaving one's neighborhood. For instance, the Kenyans in the city of Minneapolis make it possible for Minnesotans to experience small portions of Kenyan cultures while in their homes in the United States. However, Skype, television, travel, and other technological avenues allow Minnesotans to connect with Kenyans in Kenya as well. And of course, travel from Minneapolis to Nairobi happens much faster and costs much less than it did a generation ago. Cross-cultural mission, then, is the way to reach people whether one wants to serve Kenyans in Kenya or Kenyans in Minnesota. If anything, for Minnesota Christians, missionary work in Kenya could work best if the Kenyans in Minnesota were more involved.

This worldwide missionary movement reflects the worldwide nature of the twenty-first-century Christian community. A culturally mixed world needs a culturally mixed missionary movement. The same gospel that invited Westerners to be missionaries in the world also invites Latin Americans, Africans, and Asians to be missionaries in the same world. This invitation is extended to all groups of people in the world as God invites all Christians— African, Asian, Latin American, North American, European, Australian—to participate in God's mission wherever they are in the world. To talk about African missionaries in the West makes sense, just as talking about Western missionaries in Africa did. The peoples of Africa can be, and indeed must be, missionaries wherever they find themselves, including in the West. If mission were simply the proclamation of God's good news to the world as the New Testament suggests, without getting entangled with the spread of one civilization around the world, the cultural superiority of one race over others, or its identification with affluence and imperial powers, all peoples of the earth would be able to proclaim the good news to any other peoples.

However, mission in our day and age involves much more than just the proclaiming of the gospel. Money, power, racism, classism, and many other factors determine whether one can be an effective missionary as well as where one can serve. So far as mission was tied to the spread of Western civilization, as was the missionary enterprise of the one hundred years between 1850 and 1950, it was closely attached to the imperialistic advances of the colonial powers. At the center of these colonial adventures was the underlying belief that the white race is superior to other races—a belief that undergirded the institution of slavery as well as the genocide of Native Americans. The doctrine of white supremacy, in its many forms, was the justifying philosophy that supported the West's urge to dominate and colonize other races.

On one end of the spectrum were the Europeans and North Americans who were believed to be civilized and evangelized. On the other end were the Africans, often thought to be uncivilized animists and barbarians.[2] Missionaries were moving from the centers of world political and economic powers to the periphery. Unfortunately, even though most of these supremacist sentiments were openly criticized by the anticolonialist and civil rights movements of the late twentieth century, they still drive how some Westerners view foreign-led missions. Segregation within Christianity is still alive and well in some places. Many white people do not consider black Christians capable of ministering to them. Of course, white Christians have little understanding of African Christianity, and generally what they do not understand they dismiss. Thus, I have heard many say, "What can the Africans say to us?"

In the past few years, I have seen several white Western Christians dismiss African Christianity as syncretistic, animistic, and superstitious, while calling African theology immature and backward. They show no efforts at all to see the possibility of

---

[2] For instance, at the beginning of white settlement of the Dutch people in South Africa, their missionaries were not allowed to evangelize Africans because "a person without a soul can not be saved." See Irving Hexham, *Understanding World Religions* (Grand Rapids, MI: Zondervan, 2011), chap. 6.

God's redemptive work in it. They see African missionaries only as economic refugees. Thus, any African missionary who desires to reach white Americans and other Westerners must be prepared to deal with discrimination from the wider Western culture and segregation within Christianity. A Roman Catholic missionary to the United States, Anthony Agbali, put it best:

> The West is mad that African priests are coming to their homeland. Is it surprising? In time past, in order to secure their domination over our lives, they came with the lovely theology of the universality of the Catholic Church. They even taught us in Catechism the meaning of baptism thus, "baptism makes us members of the Church, brothers and sisters with one another, and members of God's Family." They used books with such emotional titles like "Together in God's Family" to teach us the ways of the Lord. Why has all of a sudden our own in-road into the homelands of our brothers and sisters, members of God's Family, now become problematic? . . . We welcomed the "white missionaries" as priests and nuns in our midst, even when we least understood them. We thought that by coming to us they loved us, so we made it a point of duty to love them in return. Why can the same act of Charity, the great commandment as we were taught, not be reciprocal?[3]

Again, Andrew Walls's rule of palefaces continues unabated in the field of theology, but even more in the field of mission (and missiology).[4] Mission is still a dominantly Western field and has very little diversity.

Despite the presence of many non-Western missionary practitioners and scholars in the West, North American missiological conferences, for instance, still attract, and probably expect, a majority attendance of white Americans. Recent missiological conversations like those of the missional church and the emerging

---

[3] Anthony Agbali, "African Priests, African Catholicism, the West and Issues Emerging," http://www.utexas.edu.

[4] Andrew F. Walls, "Structural Problems in Mission Studies," *International Bulletin of Missionary Research* 15, no. 4 (1991): 152.

church seem oblivious to the presence of non-Western Christians and missionaries in the West. Both those conversations are very Western in their approach and membership base. I spoke to one of the original leaders of the missional church conversation a few years ago, and he was adamant that the conversation was intentionally Western—involving Western scholars and focusing on a Western problem. I wondered if these scholars realized that even the American context about which they were concerned is not a white context anymore but a multicultural one. Furthermore, I wondered if they would understand that foreign Christians living in the West consider the Western missional context their problem as well. To suggest to many Westerners that Africans are missionary partners in their Western communities is to force a radical paradigm shift on them. Nevertheless, these foreign missionaries would be great and resourceful partners with Western in mission—*in the West*. If anything, their social and cultural distance allows foreigners to critique Western culture and spot some missional opportunities that may not be readily visible to Western Christians. Realizing that foreign Christians could possibly understand the missionary needs of Western culture, Lesslie Newbigin said:

> We need their witness to correct ours, as indeed they need ours to correct theirs. At this moment our need is greater, for they have been far more aware of the danger of syncretism, of an illegitimate alliance with the false elements in their culture, than we have been. But . . . we imperatively need one another if we are to be faithful witnesses to Christ.[5]

Any claim to missional faithfulness in North America today ought to include Hispanic, African, and Asian voices in addition to the Caucasian voices that already dominate the conversation. A similar endeavor in England must include the voices of Africans, Afro-Caribbeans, Latin Americans, and Asians. This is the nature

---

[5] Lesslie Newbigin, *Foolishness to the Greeks: The Gospel and Western Culture* (Grand Rapids, MI: Eerdmans, 1986), 147.

of the context we live in. Twenty-first-century missions have to respond to the multicultural nature of the mission field.

Unfortunately, for most African Christians in the West, missional success is elusive. They face large barriers that they must overcome to make effective missional connections with Westerners. In this world of regiments and divisions, many Africans find themselves on the wrong side when it comes to class, race, and other measures of status. For instance, in the segregated context of North American Christianity, black African Christians are usually shocked to see that because of their skin color, they may never be fully accepted in some white churches. Even where they can become members, they may never be trusted in leadership positions. For the few that are so privileged, they have to cope with misunderstandings that arise out of their being Africans or foreigners.

Anthony Agbali adds, "Critics of African involvement in the Catholic Church in the USA argue that African priests are unwilling to work with the laity, they are misogynists, they have accents, they are here to make money and gain status, [and] white parishioners may be antithetical to black priests."[6] More often than not, I have heard Westerners complain about Africans' accents being too hard to understand. Much to their frustration, and those of their listeners, a great deal of what the Africans may want to share is lost in their accents. Unlike our grandparents in Africa who were patient with the missionaries when they spoke our languages with Western accents, some of our Western friends are not patient enough to continue to engage Africans even when the accents get in the way. However, without the racist sentiments that hide behind the concerns about accents, it should be possible for people to overcome those problems. Africans survived Western missionaries' accents when the missionaries ministered in Africa. Westerners can surely do the same. After all, the same Westerners who complain about accents in church are able to understand Africans when business opportunities demand it.

---

[6] Agbali, "African Priests, African Catholicism, the West and Issues Emerging."

The West Is a Mission Field

The recognition that the West was becoming post-Christian began in France in 1943, when Henri Godin and Yvan Daniel published *La France, Pays de Mission?*[7] The book described Europe as a secular continent. It was the first serious study to destroy the geographical myth of mission in which certain evangelized regions (the West) sent missionaries to other regions that were unevangelized. Godin and Daniel shocked the Christian world by their radical pronouncement that France had become a mission field,[8] a country of neopagans in the grip of atheism, secularism, unbelief, and superstition.[9] They suggested that the missionary-sending country now needed missionaries sent to it. This is not how mission had been previously understood. France had histori-cally been a pillar in Christendom, a nation that sent missionaries to the unevangelized parts of the world.

In this declaration, Godin and Daniel started a conversa-tion about a changing global context where the geographical divide between missionary-sending territories and missionary-receiving territories was beginning to disappear. These sentiments were picked up at the 1963 Commission on World Mission and Evangelism conference in Mexico City, where the geographical identification of mission was redefined to "mission in six conti-nents" (i.e. there are no established mission-sending and mission-receiving countries). Missionaries can now originate from any continent and work in any other continent. The great missionary movement is not over, but it has become omnidirectional—mis-sion to and within six continents—and its leadership is increas-ingly shaped and guided by Christian experiences from the non-Western world.[10]

---

[7] Henri Godin and Yvan Daniel, *La France, Pays de mission?*, Rencontres (Lyon: Éditions de l'Abeille, 1943). See also Maisie Ward and Henri Godin, *France Pagan? The Mission of Abbe Godin* (New York: Sheed and Ward, 1949).

[8] See David J. Bosch, *Transforming Mission: Paradigm Shifts in Theology of Mission*, American Society of Missiology Series (Maryknoll, NY: Orbis Books, 1991), 10.

[9] Ibid., 3.

[10] Peter Vethanagamony, "Mission from the Rest to the West," in *Mission after Christendom: Emergent Themes in Contemporary Mission,* ed. Ogbu Kalu,

One of the most influential scholars in the conversation about the Western mission field is the British theologian Lesslie Newbigin (1909–1998).[11] After his death, the *London Times* described him as "one of the foremost missionary statesmen of his generation . . . one of the most outstanding figures on the world Christian stage in the second half of the [twentieth] century."[12] Newbigin went to India in 1936 and served there as a missionary for thirty-eight years. For a large portion of that time, he served as a bishop in the South India Church. He served in a mission context that was resistant to Christianity, and this would open his eyes to the realities of missionary work. When he returned to England after nearly forty years in India, he was shocked to find that the Christian Britain that had sent him to India was now secular.[13] He was further shocked that most British Christians did not even realize that Britain was no longer Christian.

He would later say that the situation he met back in Britain was worse than that which he saw in India. In his autobiography, Newbigin describes the British situation in no uncertain terms. "It [the ministry] is much harder than anything I met in India. There is a cold contempt for the gospel [in England], which is harder to face than opposition."[14] He continued, "England is a pagan society, and the development of a truly missionary encounter with this very tough form of paganism is the greatest practical

---

Peter Vethanayagamony, and Edmund Chia (Louisville, KY: Westminster John Knox Press, 2010), 63.

[11] Geoffrey Wainwright, *Lesslie Newbigin: A Theological Life* (New York: Oxford University Press, 2000). For a summary introduction to Lesslie Newbigin, see Wilbert R. Shenk, "Lesslie Newbigin's Contribution to Mission Theology," *International Bulletin of Missionary Research* 24, no. 2 (2000). See also British and Foreign Bible Society, "A Tribute to Lesslie Newbigin (1909–1998)," in *The Bible in TransMission: A Forum for Change in Church and Culture* (Special Edition, 1998).

[12] "Obituary: The Right Rev. James Edward Lesslie Newbigin," *London Times,* January 31, 1998.

[13] Donald Leroy Stults, *Grasping Truth and Reality: Lesslie Newbigin's Theology of Mission to the Western World* (Cambridge, UK: James Clarke, 2009), 35–36.

[14] Lesslie Newbigin, *Unfinished Agenda: An Autobiography* (Geneva: WCC Publications, 1985), 249.

task facing the church."[15] Though public institutions and popular culture in Britain as well as in Europe and North America no longer made people culturally Christian, the British church still ran its ministries assuming that a stream of traditionally moral people who looked favorably upon Christianity would simply show up at services, eager to join and belong. Evangelization and mission were still thought of as activities that churches engage in and support in faraway unevangelized lands overseas. The church in the West had not adapted to the secular reality of its context. Newbigin, therefore, started to argue that the Western church had to become completely missionary in its own context if it were to be engaged with the non-Christian society surrounding it. It needed to develop a missiology for the Western postmodern culture just like it had done for other unevangelized cultures.

The secular England that he returned to in 1974 forced Newbigin out of his retirement. He would devote the ensuing twenty-four years of his life articulating a contextually relevant missionary theology for the West that would inspire theological conversations around the world. Although his mission theology for engaging Western culture has yet to be fully unpacked,[16] his books *Foolishness to the Greeks*[17] and *The Gospel in a Pluralistic Society*[18] received a warm acceptance among many scholars worldwide and thereby opened a wider audience to his theology of mission.

His exegesis of Western culture did not shy away from criticizing the influence of the Enlightenment and modernity on Western Christianity.[19] The themes in his theology of mission have drawn interest from many other mission scholars. In the early 1980s, Newbigin was involved with a British Council of Churches program, "The Gospel and Our Culture," which laid

---

[15] Ibid.

[16] For instance, it appears to me that Newbigin's theology of the Spirit (which was perhaps influenced by his experiences in India) has yet to find a place in Western theology. The Western interpreters of Newbigin have not engaged this aspect of his missional theology fully.

[17] Newbigin, *Foolishness*.

[18] Lesslie Newbigin, *The Gospel in a Pluralist Society* (Grand Rapids, MI: Eerdmans, 1989).

[19] See Lesslie Newbigin, *The Other Side of 1984: Questions for the Churches* (Geneva: World Council of Churches, 1983).

the foundation for the book *The Other Side of 1984*. Following this, the missiological conversation was picked up by a budding group of theologians and missiologists from North America who had been following Newbigin's writings from the early 1980s. They subsequently formed the Gospel and Our Culture Network (GOCN) in North America, which later changed its name to the Gospel and Culture Network. This network is the force behind the 1998 publication of *Missional Church*, a book that came out the year that Newbigin died. Newbigin's theological writings will certainly continue to inform missional theology worldwide deep into the twenty-first century. Newbigin is right. The Western context is a mission field—in most cases, a much harder mission field to evangelize than those cultures outside the West.

A Clash of Christianities

Globalization and migrations of Christians from different parts of the world to the West have created a phenomenon that I call a "clash of Christianities." The word "clash" may not necessarily describe what happens *after* the initial contact of Christianities from different parts of the world in the West, but it surely describes the initial encounter. Since Christianity is very contextual in its nature, Latin American Christianity, African Christianity, and Asian Christianity will be different from one another and also different from Western Christianity in many aspects. These differences play a significant role in the way the Christianities relate to each other in the context of Christian cultural diversity. Suspicion seems prevalent on both sides. The theological differences, cultural misunderstandings, and even their leadership styles can combine to make these Christianities seem mutually exclusive. In addition to these dividing factors, the history of colonialism and slavery and the attachment to capitalism and imperialism and the oppression it entails, as well as the stereotypical identification of Africa with poverty, disease, and political corruption, make it even harder for the Christianities to trust one another.

In most cases, especially in North America, Christianities of different ethnicities do not mix. This explains part of the reason for the high percentage of monoethnic churches in the United States. Donald McGavran's "homogeneous unit principle"—a theory that argues that (ethnic) homogeneity helps evangelism and mission, and thereby grows churches faster—contributed heavily to this segregation of American Christianity.[20] Sunday morning is still the most segregated hour in American life; American Christianity is more segregated than America's workplaces and schools. Most foreign Christians enter this milieu in oblivion. Once the reality of the racism and division begins to affect them, most immigrants will return to their own cultural camps. That way, they can keep the peace by staying within their homogeneous congregations and occasionally partner in their missional endeavors with other Christians outside their cultures. That is how the clash of Christianities is negotiated.

As a point of fact, ours is the first generation of Christians on this side of the Reformation to deal with this issue, especially within the geographical limits of the Western civilization. For the greater part of the past two millennia, Christianity has been a white man's religion with its heartlands in Europe and, later, white America. Even its spread around the world in the nineteenth century was tied closely to the migration of millions of Europeans to the rest of the world.[21] As late as 1950, Christianity was still a Western religion working hard to spread itself and its civilization around the world. Of course, we have to admit that there are still more Christians of Caucasian heritage than there are of any other race in the world. To add to that, the mission field that is the subject of our focus here—that of Europe and North America—has a higher proportion of Caucasians than any other race. However, being the first generation to think about

---

[20] Michael Horton, "The Ethnocentricity of the American Church Growth Movement," http://www.monergism.com. See also Donald Anderson McGavran, *Understanding Church Growth* (Grand Rapids, MI: Eerdmans, 1970). See also Donald Anderson McGavran, *The Bridges of God: A Study in the Strategy of Missions* (New York: Friendship Press, 1955). The main thrust of their message is that people like to become Christians without crossing racial, linguistic, or class barriers.

[21] Dudley Baines, *Emigration from Europe, 1815–1930*, New Studies in Economic and Social History (New York: Cambridge University Press, 1995), 21–30.

multicultural Christianity in the West does not let us off the hook easily; we must not be content to simply start the conversation.

In the early part of this century Curtiss DeYoung suggested that wherever possible, a congregation situated in a culturally diversified neighborhood must be multicultural.[22] I agree. Christian segregation is not only a sociological problem, it is above all, a theological problem. God's self-revelation to humankind does not depend on one's race. White privilege among Christians in the United States and apartheid among Christians in South Africa present to us a theological problem for one's treatment of the other, especially when the other is presumed to be lesser; this reflects one's understanding of God before whom there is neither white nor black. Racism is a social construct that taints our theology once we begin to use theology to explain and justify segregation. This was not just the case in South Africa during the apartheid era, it is also the case in North America.

Mission and the Immigrant Christian

The presence of non-Western Christians and missionaries in the West is inevitable. They will continue to increase for the next few decades. However, this growing presence of foreign Christians and missionaries in the West has a mixed impact on mission. On the one hand, it helps the work of missions by adding millions of new Christians and missionaries on the mission field, but it also changes the mission context itself. A majority of African immigrants arrive in Europe and North America with a great missionary zeal and spiritual vigor from their home countries where Christianity is growing by leaps and bounds. They arrive expecting Western Christianity to be as jubilant and celebratory as what they left in Africa, and they are usually disappointed. Nevertheless, the zeal and experience that they bring along is of great potential help to their missionary efforts. Overall, their presence in the West makes the Western missional context culturally diverse and, therefore, makes cross-cultural missional partnerships

---

[22] Curtiss Paul DeYoung, *United by Faith: The Multiracial Congregation as an Answer to the Problem of Race* (New York: Oxford University Press, 2003), chap. 1.

necessary. Unfortunately, such cross-cultural partnerships are difficult to make, but wherever they exist, the churches' missionary endeavors are greatly strengthened.

Jehu Hanciles is correct in suggesting that every immigrant Christian is a potential missionary.[23] Part of this comes out of the migratory nature of Christianity, and another part has to do with the type of Christianity that is coming from Africa. Since the first century, Christianity has spread through migration. When Christians migrate, they migrate with their religion, and wherever possible, they make efforts to share their religion with their new neighbors.

Many migrating Africans—especially the Pentecostal and charismatic Africans—come with a missionary mentality even though their work or study permits say they are immigrating for another reason. Since, a greater majority of African immigrants belong to the Pentecostal and charismatic groups, they are shaped by an evangelical type of theology that encourages them to try to bring others to the point of "accepting Christ into their hearts." They talk about their faith in the public sphere, bus depots, and market squares, just like they did back home. They belong to evangelical congregations that energize them for evangelism.

Most African immigrant Christians also lean toward a conservative interpretation of theology, since the Western conservative/liberal political and theological dichotomies do not apply to the African context. African conservatism comes from their commitment to a biblicist approach to the Scriptures, and it is not in any way a reaction to the rise of the liberals: such a thing has not been seen yet in African culture. As such, African Christians find the theological liberalism that shapes a great deal of Western mainline Christianity unpalatable. They stay out of the fiery debates that take place in Western Christianity, like those about gay and lesbian Christians, or those on abortion. For them, the culture is supposed to be shaped by religion just like it was in Africa. When they see the liberal tendencies of mainline American Christianity, they believe that it is shaped by the culture, and therefore, they conclude that Western Christianity is dead.

---

[23] Jehu Hanciles, *Beyond Christendom: Globalization, African Migration, and the Transformation of the West* (Maryknoll, NY: Orbis Books, 2008), 6.

At the same time, they are usually put off by the divisive and capitalistic tendencies among those who call themselves conservative Christians. Most African immigrant Christians shy away from the individualism and the prejudices that they see among the conservative Western Christians. Consequently, they end up finding their own ways to maintain community and encourage their faith in a biblicist Christianity with a robust theology of the role of the Spirit in their African immigrant congregations from where they try to evangelize the West.

Mission and the Immigrant Congregation

I have argued in the preceding chapters that African immigrant Christians and their congregations find it rather difficult to make missional connections with Western Christians. Jehu Hanciles makes similar observations in his *Beyond Christendom*.[24] European scholars such as Claudia Währisch-Oblau have also indicated that African immigrant congregations struggle in their missionary efforts in Europe.[25] Indeed, even though they talk about being missionaries to the West, most African immigrant congregations are engaged more in the spiritual care of fellow immigrants than they are trying to actually evangelize and convert the West. Generally speaking, African immigrant Christianity is isolated at the margins of the religious landscape of the West.

Although we acknowledge that the immigrant congregation is the safe place where African Christians can be the Africans they need to be in order to cope with life in the Diaspora, it is important to realize that the persistence of these monoethnic immigrant congregations has had a negative impact on the development of missional connections with Western Christians. Eventually, both Africans and Westerners need to overcome the strong

---

[24] Ibid., 365–73.

[25] For instance, see Claudia Währisch-Oblau, "From Reverse Mission to Common Mission . . . We Hope: Immigrant Protestant Churches and the 'Programme for Cooperation between German and Immigrant Congregations' of the United Evangelical Mission," *International Review of Mission* 89, no. 354 (2000): 475–76.

desire to remain within the secure realms of familiar territory and the suspicions and fear they have for the other—the different.

Oftentimes, mission is about people leaving their comfort zone to serve God in unfamiliar territory. Like the spread of early Christians from Jerusalem, this act of leaving one's comfort zones can sometimes be involuntary. For those Christians we read about in Acts, it took persecution to scatter them from their Jerusalem environment. It was after this involuntary dispersion that they began to share the gospel with the Gentiles. Of course, the African immigrant churches are necessary, but for some, they provide a situation like the Jerusalem church had in Acts; they need to be dislodged in order to be faithful to their missionary callings. Mission demands that for Africans to be effective missionaries to the West, they need to incarnate themselves in Western culture, and that may mean disbanding some of their immigrant congregations to serve as members in Western congregations. Mission from a distance is rarely effective.

This can also be said about Western Christianity. For the sake of the mission of God in the West, God will call some Western congregations to make way for foreign missionaries. Some leaders will be called to a ministry like that of Barnabas (in Acts) who opened the doors for Paul when the Apostles were suspicious and the Jerusalem Christians afraid. It was Barnabas who brought Saul back from Tarsus and made space for him at the forefront of Christian leadership to help establish a fledgling congregation at Antioch (Acts 11:25–26). This is one of the most critical acts in the development of mission in the early church. Once the Antioch church was established, it was Barnabas and Paul who were sent out as the first missionaries into Asia Minor. Thus, Barnabas gave Paul the legitimacy that he needed as an apostle not only before the Jerusalem and Antioch churches but also among the first churches in Asia Minor. Paul was an outsider—a foreigner, an enemy, and a persecutor—to the original group of Christians, who effectively led the early church in its missional obedience. Saul sent up many "red flags" for the early Christian community, and he needed Barnabas to make the way for him.

Some scholars have argued that the Jerusalem church was so reluctant to engage in cross-cultural mission that even after

God had dispersed them from Jerusalem, and had told Peter to evangelize the Gentiles (Acts 10), God had to bring in Saul. The cross-cultural partnerships needed for missional effectiveness in the West call for many "Barnabases."

In many ways, then, the missionary rhetoric that we hear is betrayed by the need for cultural security. African Christians want to reach out to Westerners, but they find it hard to make their congregational cultures open to Westerners. Many immigrant congregations are not even open to Africans from countries other than that of the dominant members of the church or their leaders. While there is a great passion and fervor in the way most Africans pray and minister, the impact can also be lost in translation. For instance, most Africans are used to worship services that take two to three hours. For many Westerners who are used to shorter worship services, this is a huge barrier. Most people begin to lose attention as the service draws to the one-hour mark. To connect with Westerners and enable them to attend their gatherings, African immigrant congregations need to shorten their services. They may have their extended services at home in their fellowships.

Both the quality and the length of their sermons also make a big difference. Most African immigrant pastors have little theological training, but they have extensive spiritual experience. When compared to Western sermons, African immigrant sermons can sound poorly prepared. Many African immigrant ministers preach their long sermons in a very African style—spiced with vernacular jokes and delivered with shouting and sweating. Most Westerners who appreciate shorter, well-prepared sermons delivered in a talk/presentation style find these African tendencies off-putting. Africans end up raising barriers to their own effectiveness—barriers that separate insiders from outsiders, consequently discouraging outsiders from joining their congregations. This happens even when a South African enters a Nigerian church.

All this is to say that African immigrant congregations have a great deal of adjusting to do to be able to be missionally effective in the West. They need to learn and understand Westerners—their culture and how they live—in order to establish good missional relationships. When Africans try to strike close friendships with Americans, expecting Westerners to behave like their African friends do, frustrations are inevitable.[26] For instance, African culture allows people to visit each other unannounced, but visiting a Western friend without appointment risks rejection if the Western friend has other things to do. While Africans desire a close friendship, Westerners may feel that the Africans are too overbearing.

For healthy missional relationships to form, both sides need to engage in serious social negotiations. It is because of these issues that most first-generation missionaries believe that it will be their children—second-generation immigrants—who are growing up in the West who will make the missional impact they are hoping for.

Beyond Mission by Presence Alone

Despite all this, I do often hear Western Christians say that African immigrant Christians are already having a great effect on Western Christianity simply by their presence in the West. Jehu Hanciles observes that African Christians have actually strengthened Western Christianity by their sheer numbers and commitment to church.[27] This is especially true for the city of London where, on any given Sunday, over 60 percent of church attendance is by foreigners, most of whom attend the Black Majority Churches. However, although it is true that their presence has some significant missional impact, to be satisfied simply with their presence is to undermine their missionary potential and to shortchange them of their calling.

When Westerners say that Africans are having a missionary impact in the West simply by their presence, it is often meant as an excuse to avoid the need to build relationships and form

---

[26] Most Africans borrow money from their friends when in need. This, they understand to be friendship, not to let your friends struggle when you can help. They are usually surprised that asking to borrow money from their white American friends spells out death for the friendship. In a multicultural ministry discussion that I attended in Minnesota, one American missionary to Africa looked at the African attendant and declared, "It does not matter how close we are as friends, when you ask me for money, we cannot be friends anymore." The Africans never returned to the subsequent conversations.

[27] Hanciles, *Beyond Christendom*, 282–302.

partnerships. In some cases, Africans and their Western counter-parts get together once in a while for prayers and other activities; however, they avoid getting into the messy relationships it takes to be partners. Mission by presence is just one part of what God has brought them to the West for. However, the essence of God's mission in the world is relationship. That is why God did not just charitably send help from heaven to save humankind but came down and "moved into the neighborhood" to build real relation-ships with people. In Jesus, God was the missionary who built relationships with humankind and depended on the hospitality of strangers to fulfill God's mission. In this divine relationship between God and humans, Jesus partook of human life on earth in order to bring us God's life. Jesus draws us into a relationship that transforms us into children—sons and daughter—of God. When he started his ministry, he called twelve men into new relationships as his disciples who learned from him for three and half years. Before his crucifixion, Jesus solidified these new rela-tionships with the new commandment: Love one another, for it is by love that the world will know that you are my disciples (John 13:34–35). The relationships formed in this short time would form the core of the church in Acts and mark the begin-ning of Christianity.

It is because of this trusting relationship that the writer of Hebrews assures us that Jesus understands what it is to be human. "For we do not have a high priest who is unable to sympa-thize with our weaknesses, but we have one who in every respect has been tested as we are, yet without sin" (Heb. 4:14–15). The church, both Western and otherwise, is called to the same task to establish missional relationships for the sake of the gospel. The Great Commission in Matthew's Gospel asks Christians to go, teach, and baptize the nations. This is only possible in the context of relationship building. Such relationships cannot be pretentious. To enter into such relationships with people is to let go of the white superiority and the black victim mentality that breed the suspicion that shapes most cross-cultural encounters.

Most relationships between Western Christians and their Afri-can counterparts do not go deep enough to challenge prejudices and power dynamics. Where there are collaborations happening, they are functionalistic in their approach. The partnerships usually occur around an event or a project. Both Westerners and Africans tread carefully not to offend one another during the partnership and when that time passes, they retreat to their camps, waiting for the next event to partner again. The partnerships become a poor substitute for relationships, giving both sides a way to check the "cross-cultural mission" box and yet continue in segregation. True relationships are rare.

Under normal circumstances, partnerships should come out of relationships, and not the other way round. It is fair to say that due to their cross-cultural nature, these relationships are harder to establish. However, they are indispensable for God's mission. They call for intentionality and hard work on both sides.

It is also unfortunately common to see Western congregations engage in missionary work in Africa while avoiding working with the Africans in their cities. I have seen many congregations in North America that send missionaries to Africa and yet have no connection with the African congregation that meets on their premises on Sunday afternoons. There is a church in Minneapolis that has a vibrant mission service in Ghana and yet knows nothing of the Ghanaian church that meets next door to them. I have often wondered whether cross-cultural mission, for them, falls in the category of charity, where they feel they have fulfilled the obligation without having to deal with the mess that comes with trying to build a relationship. I have complained to some of these friends, "If you cannot work with the Africans whom you see every Sunday on your premises, you have no business working with Africans whom you see for only two weeks a year in Accra." Needless to say, my complaint generally falls on deaf ears. The time and energy that is required to build relationships is too much for many.

The easy way out is to give of one's possessions—no relationships required. Paul seemed to think differently about this, saying: "If I give away all my possessions, and if I hand over my body so that I may boast, but do not have love, I gain nothing" (1 Cor. 13;3). We are primarily called to loving relationships. Mission is about relationships. Charity has to follow love, lest it become an empty ritual. A paradigm shift is needed for Western Christians and non-Western Christians to form these missional relationships.

Both camps need to rise above the dividing forces of racism and classism to move beyond charity and occasional partnerships to incarnational relationships.

The African Contribution

Perhaps some Western Christians wonder why this conversation about African Christianity in the West matters. When I taught a class at one of the seminaries in Minnesota, some students pushed back at me, arguing that the development of world Christianity was not of immediate interest to them. One woman declared, "What happens in Africa has little to do with my ministry here in rural Iowa where I serve as a pastor." Another one added, "Why should I be concerned about African Christians in my city, as if I will ever minister among them?" This is the very attitude that this conversation is trying to discourage, for two reasons. One, whatever happens in African Christianity affects the rest of the world. The Body of Christ is one. Two, these seminary students will serve the church in a multicultural world where Christians from other parts of the world will be in their congregations. Even in rural Iowa, there may come a day when immigrants will come to work in their agriculture industry. It will be too late for the pastors to complain, "Seminary did not prepare me for this."

As stressed earlier, immigrant Christians also bring gifts from God that can help invigorate Western Christianity. For the remainder of this chapter, I explore four of those contributions that African immigrant Christianity brings to the West.

Theological Renaissance

Andrew Walls once said that the representative Christianity in the twenty-first century will be largely charismatic and conservative, dominated by the voices of the southern hemisphere and Asia, suggesting that the representative theology of this century may as well be African.[28] More than twenty years after Walls made

---

[28] Andrew F. Walls, *The Cross-Cultural Process in Christian History: Studies in the Transmission and Appropriation of Faith* (Maryknoll, NY: Orbis Books, 2002), 85.

this observation, I have the privilege of hindsight to see that the representative theology of this century may be more non-Western in general, including Latin American and Asian theologies, and not just African. The worldwide spread of Christianity means the birth of world theologies.

Many theologies have risen in the world in the past generation that seek to harness Western theology and contextualize all theology for the twenty-first-century understanding of God and the Scriptures. For instance, feminist theology rightly argues for the recognition of the fact that Western theology is male-dominated, and in doing so, it is opening up space for women to have a theological voice. Liberation theology rose up in the face of oppression under the hierarchical religious structures in Latin America.[29] Black theology, a theological reflection of black people's understanding of God, has developed in the context of oppression, segregation, slavery, lynching, apartheid, disease, and poverty, both in North America and Africa.[30]

Western Christianity is two thousand years old, but now it is put into contact with—to listen to and learn from—foreign theologies from places that have had Christianity for several centuries. Western theology is thus forced to interact with the foreign theologies of the many non-Western theologies in its own backyard. This is the first time in several centuries this has happened on such a global scale. These contextual theologies that have emerged in the non-Western world have rejected the Western cultural baggage and theological hegemony that were exported with Western Christianity to the rest of the world. Harvey Sindima observes that a properly indigenized African theology realizes that more of the Western theological tradition has been generated by Western categories than by fidelity to the Scriptures, and therefore tries to return to the Scriptures to find its own

---

[29] Gustavo Gutiérrez, *A Theology of Liberation: History, Politics, and Salvation* (Maryknoll, NY: Orbis Books, 1973).

[30] See F. Eboussi Boulaga, *Christianity without Fetishes: An African Critique and Recapture of Christianity* (Maryknoll, NY: Orbis Books, 1984). See also James H. Cone, *The Cross and the Lynching Tree* (Maryknoll, NY: Orbis Books, 2011).

framework for a faithful local theology.[31] Such foreign theologies are now showing up in Western cities.

Furthermore, Walls suggests that the future of the Christian faith, its shape in the twenty-first and twenty-second centuries, is being decided by events that are now, or will be in the near future, taking place in Africa, Asia, and Latin America, leading him to conclude that new agendas for theology will appear outside the West.[32] But while non-Western Christianity continues to develop, there still remains an unjustifiable theological hegemony by the West over the world. Indeed, fifteen years after Walls critiqued the rule of palefaces in the academy, and thirtysomething years after Mbiti wrote about the provincial nature of theology, non-Western theology still faces an uphill struggle to be heard in the West.[33] Walls later said, "Western theological leadership of a predominantly non-Western church is an incongruity."[34] This will have to change. To quote Timothy Tennent, "We cannot afford to ignore the theological implications inherent in the demographic reality that Christianity is currently in a precipitous decline in the West and that the vast majority of Christians now live outside the West."[35] Indeed, the theological implications of the worldwide spread of Christianity in the twentieth century deserve a great deal of attention.[36]

Craig Ott identifies four problem areas for the encounter between Western Christianity and worldwide Christianity: the

---

[31] Harvey J. Sindima, *Drums of Redemption: An Introduction to African Christianity*, Contributions to the Study of Religion (Westport, CT: Greenwood Press, 1994), 163–64.

[32] Walls, *Cross-Cultural Process*, 85–86.

[33] John S. Mbiti, "Theological Impotence and the Universality of the Church," in *Mission Trends No. 3*, ed. Gerald H. Anderson and Thomas F. Stransky, Third World Theologies (Grand Rapids, MI: Eerdmans, 1976), 16–17.

[34] Andrew F. Walls, "Christian Scholarship in Africa in the Twenty-First Century," *Transformation* 19, no. 4 (2002): 221.

[35] Timothy C. Tennent, *Theology in the Context of World Christianity: How the Global Church Is Influencing the Way We Think about and Discuss Theology* (Grand Rapids, MI: Zondervan, 2007), 17.

[36] For a fuller argument on how globalization and theology relate, see Joerg Rieger, *Globalization and Theology*, Horizons in Theology (Nashville, TN: Abingdon, 2010).

West's "hegemony postulate"; the West's self-perception that it is "the center"; the perception of third world scholars as "purveyors of exotic, raw intellectual material to people in the North"; and the "dialogue of the deaf" between the West and the rest of the world.[37] Western theology continues to assume a central position in world theology even though it fails to deal with most non-Western theological questions. For instance, it struggles to fruitfully engage spiritually rich premodern cultures of Africa. Ali Mazrui was right to say that "Americans are brilliant communicators but bad listeners."[38] He could have easily generalized this to include all Westerners. There is still a serious theological communication breakdown between Africans and Western Christians, even in multicultural congregations where Americans and Africans attend worship together.

As we progress deeper into the twenty-first century, it is important that Christian theology become a field where Western and non-Western theologians can engage one another in mutually critiquing and edifying conversations that enrich each other. So far, theological tensions exist when African and Western Christians meet. Sometimes their reading of Scripture differs, and both groups become defensive. None of this is helpful. Both camps need to slow down and engage each other in thoughtful conversations, listening to what God may be saying through the other. Such conversations are good for the entire enterprise of theology—a field whose global voices desperately need to change from cacophony to polyphony, as they together celebrate the Spirit of God who speaks to Westerners just as well as non-Westerners.

Cross-cultural exposure is one of the best ways to expand one's horizons of knowledge. In Malawi, there is a proverb that states *kuphunzira sim'kalasi mokha, komanso kuyenda*, which means "travel and exposure are just as enlightening as formal (classroom) education." With this in mind, I believe that globalization and migration will have a significant impact on theology in the com-

---

[37] Craig Ott and Harold A. Netland, *Globalizing Theology: Belief and Practice in an Era of World Christianity* (Grand Rapids, MI: Baker, 2006), 46.

[38] Ali Al Amin Mazrui, *Cultural Forces in World Politics* (London: J. Currey, 1990), 116.

ing years. Theological cross-pollination will enrich not only such a world theology but also the contextual theologies that interact with one another as they bring resources together that would otherwise not be found in any one context.

Cultural diversity is a gift of the Spirit to the Western church —a gift that may be given back to the rest of the world in a generation or two when it becomes just as culturally diverse. It makes cross-cultural exposure possible without needing to travel to other continents. As such, it also makes theological cross-pollination possible.

Spirituality

Africans and Westerners approach their spiritualities in very different ways. Africans, by virtue of having lived in a spirit-oriented culture, find themselves very attentive and responsive to the spiritual atmosphere around them. As such, their Christianity will be intentionally holistic in its approach to theology and human life. First and foremost, African Christians will not only be interested in the work of the Spirit in the salvation of the human being. While salvation is an important work of the Spirit, for Africans, salvation is not just about the saving of the human spirit. It must include healing and deliverance, which are also central to Christianity. Indeed, within the African context, salvation is not only spiritual; it overflows to the needs of the whole human being.

Salvation is about humanizing the entire person and helping that person become more whole in every sense of the word. This includes spiritual wholeness, but it must also include emotional, physical, and even economic wholeness, among many things. For Africans, to be whole is to have life, and to be sick or needy is to have less life. As a matter of fact, any life-saving act in Africa could be easily attributed to the Spirit of God. Prayers and sacrifices are made for the harvests in the fields as well as for jobs and bank accounts. Fasting in order to receive a spouse is a common practice among Africans, for here too, to lack is to experience a failure in salvation. In many cases, to be free from need is to be well cared for by God, the spirits, and ancestors.

Furthermore, this holistic spirituality is not only an abstraction, but a matter of the mind and the heart. African spirituality involves the whole of the person's being, including whatever that person owns, which is usually understood as the extension of the person's being. Be it in celebration or in worship or any other religious activity, the participant's entire body and everything they possess engages in the process, singing, dancing, and more. When Africans come together for a religious service, they will bring an offering with them, maybe a goat, a chicken, a piece of cloth, or money.

When performing sacrifices to ancestors, or invoking the gods of the harvests, or when the rainmaker leads the community in intercession for the rains, people will participate with their entire beings. The African drum that is an invitation to dance is also used to invoke certain spirits. Certain ritualistic dances are spiritual, symbolically inviting the spirits to come and make the earth fruitful. When the spirits penetrate the material world, there are usually many bodily manifestations, such as people falling in trances, prophetic utterances and healings, glossolalia, and in rare cases, levitations.

This holistic spirituality from Africa is not afraid of charismatic gifts and the charisma they are associated with. African culture is open to spiritual enthusiasm, and, therefore, African Christianity and theology are more likely to engage and understand charismatic gifts. These are common in African culture, even where other religions apart from Christianity are involved. African religious history shows that charismatic expression is the spirit's gift to the community. Charismatic leaders, who abound in African culture, usually summon people together to fulfill a divinely inspired vision, or they motivate the community to the betterment of its life. Charismatic healers, diviners, marabous, and many others can be found almost everywhere in African history.

Mbona from Southern Malawi and Shaka Zulu from South Africa are some of the outstanding examples of charismatic leaders in pre-Christian Africa. Within indigenous Christianity, the prophetic healer—who incidentally replaces the secular diviners and marabous—is a person of great importance. In the African Independent Churches, William Wade Harris from Liberia and

Simon Kimbangu from Congo are some of the prime examples of charismatic leadership. An "anointed apostle" is the charismatic leader in the African Pentecostal churches, and Benson Idahosa of Nigeria and Ezekiel Guti of Zimbabwe are two legendary Christian examples of such leaders. Kwame Nkrumah and Nelson Mandela may be two other charismatic leaders who used their gifts on the continental political scene.

The African church itself embodies what some African theologians have called the "democratization of charisma."[39] Asamoah-Gyadu dedicates an entire chapter to this phenomenon, which he says puts into practice the New Testament theology of the priesthood of all believers in a church that is the "body of Christ."[40] "Here, each member is expected to function in his or her spiritual gift in order that 'the body' can function charismatically."[41] In addition, Asamoah-Gyadu notes that the definition of charismatic gifts in such a context is broadened. Citing James Dunn, he says, "Charisma is not restricted to particular sets of defined gifts, for whatever word or act mediates grace to the believing community is 'charisma.'"[42] Although the charismatic leader is important, the charismata are available to anyone who seeks them diligently enough.

In addition, an African spirituality, because of its understanding of the reality of the spirit world, must be intentional about the spiritual habits and practices of both the individual and the community. Since the Holy Spirit is at work in the individual member's life as well as that of the community, the habits that increase spiritual vitality will usually be encouraged. Prayer is the most visible of these. This may explain the reason behind the importance of prayer in African Pentecostal churches. They understand fervent prayers to be a way to tap into the spirit-world—that of the Triune God—"to move the hand that moves

---

[39] See J. Kwabena Asamoah-Gyadu, *African Charismatics: Current Developments within Independent Indigenous Pentecostalism in Ghana* (Boston: Brill, 2005). See also Allan Anderson, *African Reformation: African Initiated Christianity in the 20th Century* (Trenton, NJ: Africa World Press, 2001).

[40] Asamoah-Gyadu, *African Charismatics*, 130.

[41] Ibid.

[42] Ibid.

the world."[43] African prayer vigils often attract larger crowds than even normal worship services. Even in the Diaspora, African immigrant churches are usually known for their prayer meetings.

In the study mentioned earlier that I carried out with the help of Church Innovations Institute and Luther Seminary, I also discovered that this spirituality is quite a significant factor for Africans' choice of congregations to belong to.[44] Although spirituality is important, it follows hospitality in its order of importance, and so Africans will stay in a church that is hospitable even when they have no room to enjoy their spirituality. In such circumstances, they will usually also go to an immigrant congregation at a separate time to engage with an African spirituality. Where both hospitality and spirituality are missing, Africans will not stay. Congregations that have done well in engaging African immigrant Christians have adjusted their culture to accommodate this kind of spirituality to various extents in their services.

The cultural transition from modernity to postmodernity poses a great challenge to Western Christianity. In the postmodern world of people in their twenties and thirties, spirituality and spirit-talk are reemerging in Western culture. Postmodernity opens up the public sphere to spirituality in a way it may not to religion. It is not unusual anymore to hear of people who are "spiritual but not religious." Mysticism is becoming allowable, and in some cases it is actually encouraged.[45] Among most postmoderns, the secular agenda of the 1960s is empty and unattractive.

Such a shift from modernity to a culture that openly talks about spirituality and the reality of the spirit world makes possible new ways to talk about the Holy Spirit. As such, it could help the church engage in mission in new ways.[46] Sara Savage,

---

[43] This is a common motto among intercessory ministries in Africa.

[44] Harvey C. Kwiyani, "Pneumatology, Mission, and African Christians in Multicultural Congregations in North America." PhD diss., Luther Seminary, 2012.

[45] Stanley J. Grenz, *A Primer on Postmodernism* (Grand Rapids, MI: William B. Eerdmans, 1996).

[46] See Stuart Murray, *Church after Christendom* (Milton Keynes, UK: Paternoster, 2005). See also Kirsteen Kim, "The Potential of Pneumatology for Mission in Contemporary Europe," *International Review of Mission* 95, no. 378–79 (2006).

in a study by the Church of England, concluded that a typical postmodern person may actually engage in more spiritual practices than a typical Christian.[47] Nevertheless, Savage concluded that for their spiritual needs, most postmoderns would not consider a church as a place to go. The younger generation would rather turn to *kaballah* and other exotic traditions.[48] When asked to describe the church, the young generation in Britain said car-boot sales are better.[49]

However, the research was also quick to suggest that there is indeed immense spiritual hunger in the world.[50] Ruth Gledhill of the *London Times* observed that the only problem is that the church is not ready to meet it.[51] Could African Christianity enable Western churches to attract back to church those who have gone to mysticism? Or kaballah? Could postmodernity, then, open up ways to engage the Spirit in mission like we have seen happen in other parts of the world, including Africa?[52]

The Spirituality of Community

To those who can see it, the impact of individualism on the Western church is quite disheartening. Individualism pervades everything that the church does. Many worship services, for instance, are shaped to appeal to the consumer-minded individual who comes to church to receive religious goods.[53] At a recent

[47] The report from this research has been published in Sara Savage, *Making Sense of Generation Y: The World View of 15- to 25-Year-Olds* (London: Church House Publishing, 2006).

[48] Ibid., 3.

[49] Ibid., 15.

[50] Ibid., 16.

[51] Ruth Gledhill, "Church Seeks Spirituality of Youth . . . and Doesn't Like What It Finds," *Times Online* (2006), http://www.timesonline.co.uk. This newspaper article came out the day the said report was published.

[52] In thinking about this, I have found the works of the British missiologist Kirsteen Kim very helpful. For instance, see Kirsteen Kim, *Joining with the Spirit: Connecting World Church and Local Mission* (London: Epworth, 2009).

[53] Darrell Guder, *Missional Church: A Vision for the Sending of the Church in North America,* The Gospel and Our Culture Series (Grand Rapids, MI: Eerdmans, 1998).

ministers' conference in Duluth, Minnesota, I was surprised to note that all the songs were a conversation between God and the individual. A worship set of six songs included, "I will give you all my worship . . . for you alone are worthy of my praise," "Lord, I lift your name on high," "I am desperate for you," "I am giving you my heart," "I lift up my eyes," and "My redeemer lives." I was shocked at the lack of intentional awareness of the communal nature of worship. These individualistic tendencies can also be found in other ecclesial practices.

The African understanding of the spirit-world, in contrast, demands a communal understanding of spirituality. In Malawi, we have a proverb that says *chala chimodzi sichiswa nsabwe:* "A single thumb cannot kill a louse." Further, we say *kalikokha nkanyama, tili tiwiri ntianthu,* literally translated as "One that is alone is a beast, but them that are a pair are persons." For Africans, spirituality is best done in company. Be it in ancestral veneration, or a simple pouring out of a libation, there is always a way in which the community is represented and engaged.

Just as the Malawian philosophy *umunthu* says that one's personhood is constituted through other persons, one's spirituality is also constituted through the spirituality of others.[54] Any person with *umunthu* will pay attention to the spirituality of others as well as that of the community. Individual spirituality is never complete if it does not end in communal spirituality. Together with the community, one worships the god of the community, who is often the god of the ancestors. The entire spiritual experience is a public phenomenon. For instance, when a soothsayer enters a village, life stops for the whole village so that the community is able to hear what the spirits have to say. In those cultures where trances are a means of spiritual communication, when someone falls into a trance, the elders of the village are brought together to listen and mediate with the entire community. Individual spirituality has its telos—purpose and goal—in communal spirituality. Religion and the matters of faith still reign over the public arena.

---

[54] See Gerard Chigona, *Umunthu Theology: Path of Integral Human Liberation Rooted in Jesus of Nazareth* (Balaka, Malawi: Montfort, 2002). See also Kwiyani, "Pneumatology."

Looking at this the other way around, it is also quite true that the communality of African culture is a spiritual endeavor. The ancestors desire this to be. For example, it is common for the spirits of the ancestors to direct people to care for strangers or to feed the needy. In some cultures, when the life of a recently deceased person is celebrated, his or her spirit is "pacified" by a *sadaka*—a community meal for children in the community.

This ancestral orientation toward community is what makes the communal life a spiritual endeavor. To effectively engage in any religious activity, one needs company. For example, the arrival of a newborn into the community and the beginning of a new family by way of marriage are junctures in the community's life when, through rituals, the spirits are invoked. In some cultures, a strict set of ritualistic religious activities will shape the initiation rites by which children are accepted into the society. A community broken by death also has to go through rigorous ritual cleansing in order to restore itself.

Unity and connectedness, peace and harmony are the marks of a community that is in tune with its ancestors. These ancestors will not hesitate to intervene through dreams or divination when such harmony is destroyed. Jesus may have had something similar in mind when he said, "For where two or three are gathered together in my name, I am there in the midst of them" (Matt. 18:20).

Furthermore, this communal spirituality is not afraid to welcome the stranger. At its core, African Christian spirituality is particularly optimistic about engaging with the stranger. In fact, it is the possibility of the stranger being guided to this community by the ancestors, or the Spirit of God, or the possibility of the Spirit's hidden charisma in the stranger that is the Spirit's gift to the community that excites this kind of spirituality. In the presence of the stranger, Africans see the spirit's invitation into the experience of its deity.

As such, Christian community, be it in a congregation or a fellowship, is important for African Christians. Christian communities give them space to engage the Spirit communally and to listen and learn from other Christians. They also share and teach other Christians and recharge their spiritualities in readiness for the mission. If one has a song, or another has a psalm, this is the place to contribute. If one has a need, this is the place to receive help. Indeed, even congregations thrive in a community, and are thus more likely to help one another in many of their efforts since they believe that existence in isolation is never an option, spiritually speaking. African leaders discourage congregational individualism.

Mission and Evangelism

Richard Bliese, a missiologist and president of Luther Seminary, once made a joke that has stayed with me for years. It was about the times when Jesus told his disciples not to tell anyone about a miracle he had performed, or that he was the Messiah. Addressing students at Luther Seminary, Bliese said, "Jesus was talking to Lutherans, and we have obeyed that commandment really well. Lutherans do not tell anyone about Christ!"

Of course, Bliese was joking. Lutherans have always been very engaged in talking about their faith with others. However, the joke makes a point. It is hard for most Westerners to talk about their faith, especially to non-Christians. The joke also works for many Presbyterians, Methodists, Evangelicals, Mennonites, or Pentecostals. Evangelization is not one of the strengths of Western Christianity. Part of the problem is that for the past fifteen hundred years, the West was considered to be evangelized. To be a citizen of some Christian states, for instance, was also to be a Christian. Such contexts did not need any evangelism, since everyone was a Christian, at least in name. Evangelism was something the missionaries did in the unevangelized parts of the world. After hundreds of years of this, the Western church lost its understanding of evangelism. The overprofessionalization of the ministry in the West makes it even more difficult for nonordained Christians to engage in those duties reserved for the clergy, such as evangelism. It is only in the past few decades that the fall of Christendom has revealed this need to reevangelize the Western culture that is evidently post-Christian.[55]

---

[55] Murray, *Church after Christendom*. See also David Smith, *Mission after Christendom* (London: Darton Longman & Todd, 2003).

Following in the footsteps of Newbigin, a number of Western scholars and religious leaders have helped popularize the notion that the West must be evangelized.[56] In Great Britain, a massive evangelization campaign followed Newbigin's campaign to plant 10,000 churches in the 1990s.[57] In North America, missional conversations continue to imagine ways for Christians to be missionaries and evangelists in their own cities. For the Roman Catholic Church, in 2010 Pope Benedict XVI created the Pontifical Council for Promoting the New Evangelization in the Vatican with the purpose of reevangelizing the West and combating its secularization. Other denominations have also joined forces to evangelize and plant churches in the West. For instance, at their annual convention of 2012, the newly formed Lutheran Churches in Mission for Christ (LCMC) declared its vision to plant one thousand new churches in the next ten years—churches that must result from the LCMC's work of evangelization and not from Christians that defect from other denominations.

That said, most Western Christians have yet to understand what evangelism truly is. Of course, they know the work of the "Google Evangelist," who spreads Google's good news, but the connection between that evangelist and their own calling in God is not straightforward for many, even though they have a much better gospel to proclaim. Most congregations have mistaken church marketing for evangelism, and unfortunately, in this consumerist and individualistic society, church marketing works. Some congregations prefer ministers with more social and business skills that come with a master's in business administration to those who seek simply to serve missionally as witnesses and evangelists for Christ. Such congregations want their websites, brochures, and therapeutic sermon podcasts to do the job of inviting people to church where they will be enculturated into a comfortable community without being challenged by the sometimes uncomfortable message of Christ. As one friend told me, "It is easier to fill churches by marketing than evangelism." Although

[56] See Ross Hastings, *Missional God, Missional Church: Hope for Re-Evangelizing the West* (Downers Grove, IL: IVP Academic, 2012).
[57] See Newbigin, *Other Side of 1984.*

both church marketing and the MBA are good, they often get in the way of mission and should not replace evangelism. Church marketing ought to be a supplement to evangelism, and not the other way around.

This is where African immigrant Christians may be once again helpful. African Christianity has grown due to the efforts of millions of local Christians who engage in evangelism on a regular basis. As I argued in the first chapter, Africans practice the priesthood of all believers well. They have overcome the professionalization of the ministry that is usually seen in the West. They do not have a clergy/laity bifurcation, and neither do they have the sacred/secular division. Lay Christians in Africa are just as engaged and effective in evangelism as the clergy. As such, Africans are not shy about talking about their faith. Most African Christians understand themselves as evangelists and missionaries. Without the Western vocabulary that describes a missional lifestyle, Africans are living it out on a daily basis. Most Africans are shocked when they learn that the separation of church and state in the United States means that there are places where they are not allowed to talk about Christ. Even then, they are quick to recognize other avenues through which they may carry out their evangelism.

Multicultural Evangelism

Most Africans come from countries where cultural and religious pluralism are normative, and they have a worldview that supports communality and cultural diversity. For instance, in many African countries, tribal mixing is a normal daily occurrence. Tribal distinctions are usually strong enough to cause cross-cultural anxieties when one moves from one tribal land to another, but these anxieties do not force people to let go of their cultural identity. Generally, they will connect with other people from their tribe to form a foreign community in their tribal Diaspora, even in their own country.

Of course, Africa has the most displaced people in the world. For many reasons, people move from their tribal homes to other cultures on a constant basis. Most Africans also live in close proximity with people of other religions. Islam and other eastern religions, such as Bahai, have a strong presence in most African schools. By the time most Africans graduate from high school, they will have learned how to live amicably with people who are different from them. Some countries such as South Africa have significant racial diversity as well. In the film *Invictus,* where Morgan Freeman plays Nelson Mandela, excellent cross-cultural leadership skills by the veteran leader defused racial tensions that threatened to cause massive havoc in the country. Many Africans deal with such situations regularly and, in the process, acquire skills that could be put to good use in the Diaspora. The cross-cultural tensions that some Africans deal with give them a very good learning experience to draw on when faced with cultural pluralism in the West.

Furthermore, the daily life of the African in the Diaspora is a day-to-day cross-cultural experience that enables him or her to learn how to negotiate relationships across cultures and races. Even though they may end up in an immigrant congregation, they deal with Western culture everywhere else. Consequently, many African Christians understand multiculturalism and cross-cultural ministry to a fair extent. Many of them are fluent in crossing cultures. It is because of this that I believe that Africans have something to offer to the Western church in terms of multicultural evangelism. Many of them have the experience needed to reach out across cultural boundaries.

They may contribute effectively, if given a chance, to help destroy the segregation that characterizes Western Christianity. The multicultural mission field of the West needs a multicultural missionary community. As we move forward into this twenty-first century, Western Christians and African immigrant Christians ought to join hands with all the other Diasporic Christianities in the West to follow God in God's missionary work in a multicultural West. Learning from one another, we put the gift of cultural diversity that God has given us to good use—and that, I believe, is God's preferred future for the church.

There is a great missionary potential that comes with the arrival of African Christians in the West. They come with some tools that Western Christianity may need in order to be reinvigorated and to become relevant again in the West. However, as this chapter has explored, this missionary potential has not been maximized yet. Cross-cultural bridges between Africans and Westerners are only beginning to develop. As we go deeper into the century, and as many more Africans migrate to the West, the distance between the two cultures will diminish, and missional opportunities will be possible. The next chapter explores how these two Christianities can begin to work together to be faithful participants in God's mission in the world. It explores how we move beyond blessed reflex or reverse mission to being authentic partners in mission.

Chapter Six

Moving beyond the Blessed Reflex

The ultimate purpose of this book is to move our conversation forward from just talking about reverse mission to thinking about ways in which Africans and Westerners can actually work together in mission in the West and beyond. As I have suggested throughout, this is not an easy exercise. There are immense differences on both sides of the conversation: cultural, social, theological, among many others. There are many barriers that must be broken and many cross-cultural bridges that need to be built in order for the two groups to start working together effectively. In this chapter, I discuss the possibility of a multicultural missionary movement as God's preferred future for mission. I also explore some of the main challenges that non-Western Christians, particularly African Christians, face in their missional adventures in the West. I believe that naming problems for what they are is a good place to start when attempting to solve them. Therefore, I will name the main four challenges that I have recognized in the thirteen years I have worked with African Christians in the West. Following that, I will suggest some ways in which we can respond to these challenges and perhaps realize God's preferred future for this culturally diverse Western context.

A Multicultural Missionary Movement

According to research carried out by Stephen Warner in the early years of this century, over two-thirds of post-1965 immigrants to the United States are Christian.[1] Warner further noted,

[1] Stephen R. Prothero, *A Nation of Religions: The Politics of Pluralism*

"Because of the new [post-1965] immigration, American religious pluralism extends not only to denominational and ethnic diversity within American Christianity and to non-Christian alternatives but especially to increasing racial diversity within Christianity."[2] These immigrant Christians in the West "are expressing their Christianity in languages, customs, and independent churches that are barely recognizable [to], and often controversial for, European-ancestry Catholics and Protestants."[3] They give Western Christianity a multicolored global outlook. One of the potential consequences of the diversification of American Christianity will be, as discussed at length in earlier chapters here, its eventual de-Europeanization—when American Christianity and theology will reflect the global mosaic of the Christians who are living out their faith in the West.

In the meantime, there are still more areas of division between Western Christianity and non-Western Christianities in the West. There are very few avenues for collaboration between immigrant congregations and American congregations. Different theologies, experiences, and worldviews make it difficult for ethnically and culturally diverse Christians to mix. Often, the dynamics of power relations involved in cross-cultural relationships complicate collaboration between indigenous and immigrant Christians. Therefore, any multicultural conversation among Christians must understand that both race and class still matter. Both pose serious challenges to the formation of a multicultural missionary movement. Gibson Winter's *The Suburban Captivity of the Church* only began to explore the ecclesiological implications of race and class that continue to shape the landscape of American Christianity—and should have been at least a conversation starter.[4] Theories like the "homoge-

---

in *Multireligious America* (Chapel Hill: University of North Carolina Press, 2006), 234.

    [2] Ibid., 247.

    [3] Helen Rose F. Ebaugh and Janet Saltzman Chafetz, *Religion and the New Immigrants: Continuities and Adaptations in Immigrant Congregations* (Walnut Creek, CA: AltaMira Press, 2000), 14.

    [4] Gibson Winter, *The Suburban Captivity of the Churches: An Analysis of Protestant Responsibility in the Expanding Metropolis* (Garden City, NY: Doubleday, 1961).

neous unit principle" (the notion that it is easier for people to become Christians when they must cross few or no racial, linguistic, or class barriers) sacrifice mission at the altar of pragmatism, forgetting that the Incarnation and the Crucifixion were not the most practical way for God's mission in the world. Immigrant Christians are usually at a disadvantage when it comes to race and class.

Nevertheless, although it is not possible to overcome all dividing barriers among Christians, it is still possible for diverse Christians to work together across cultures for the sake of God's mission. This may be the call of the Spirit for this day and age, for Christians from around the world to work together and learn from one another. However, for us to get started on the journey to a multicultural missionary movement in the West, the entire Christian enterprise needs to wrestle with the dividing forces in the light of God's mission in the world. On the one hand, Western Christianity may have to adjust its speaking/teaching position to assume a learning/listening position, not only in relation to other Westerners, but also in relation to Latin Americans, Africans, and Asians. Unfortunately, many Westerners will close their churches before they listen to a foreigner.

On the other hand, non-Western Christians may have to step down from their pedestal from which they condemn Western Christianity as dead. They have to gather up courage to cordially engage and speak boldly to Western Christianity as they hear from the Spirit, realizing that it may take more than a few attempts before their Western counterparts listen. In addition, immigrant Christians also need to listen and learn from Westerners. The desire of the Spirit of God, the creator of cultural diversity, is that in unity, global Christians can help one another see and represent God better to the world at large. As is seen in the narrative of the birth of the church on the Day of Pentecost, the Spirit of God creates both the space and the occasion for cross-cultural engagement.

Among Malawians, whose concept of *umunthu* is used to negotiate cross-cultural relationships, a guest or stranger is usually invited to engage in a community's conversations as they try to figure out solutions to their problems. Malawians know the Chewa proverb, *mlendo ndi uyo abwera ndi kalumo kakuthwa*

("A stranger often comes better equipped [with a sharp pocket-knife] to help solve a community's long standing problems).")[5] A stranger's fresh pair of eyes may bring just the right perspective to illuminate solutions to a community's problems. It is thus wise to listen to and learn from strangers. Malawians believe that to welcome a stranger is not just to give them food and a place to sleep. It is to lend them an ear, and thereby give them a voice.[6]

In *Welcoming the Stranger*, Patrick Keifert articulates with eloquence the "missional" need for Christians and their congregations to be not only welcoming to, but also eager to learn from, the stranger.[7] Two ideas from Keifert's book are helpful here. The first is the reminder of the image of God as the host of Israel in all its dealings with the nations surrounding it.[8] Both Israel and the nations are guests hosted by God, and therefore, the people of Israel must treat the strangers among them with caution. The second lesson is the need for Christians to transcend the desire for intimacy in dealing with one another in order to be faithful to their calling to God's mission.

Keifert observed that hosting a stranger is usually a de-centering experience. However, moving away from the desire to connect with intimates, "[One] must approach the world of another's meaning with a willingness to learn, to be taught, to recognize the other precisely as other, not to reduce that one to an experience, a moment in my education or maturation."[9] Such hospital-

---

[5] Knives are extremely important multipurpose tools in that part of the world. The proverb talks about a sharp knife, even sharper than those of the local leaders, because it has to be able to do something that has not been done before. It is a pocketknife because it is hidden; you never know there is one until you ask.

[6] Luke 10 comes to mind here. It is a text that was used extensively in "Dwelling in the Word" in the process of this research. In Luke 10, Jesus sent the seventy disciples almost assuming that the hospitality that they would receive would enable them to speak—to share the Good News of the coming Kingdom—to the persons of peace who would accept them in their homes.

[7] Patrick R. Keifert, *Welcoming the Stranger: A Public Theology of Worship and Evangelism* (Minneapolis: Fortress Press, 1992), chap. 1.

[8] Ibid., chap. 4.

[9] Ibid., 79.

ity is good not only for the stranger but also for the host. Indeed, this kind of hospitality can be risky business, as Keifert observes that not all strangers are safe.[10] This is a call to humility and vulnerability. In his work with congregations, he teaches leaders the missional practice of listening to strangers "into free speech."

African Immigrant Christianity in the West: Some Challenges

The life of a non-Western missionary in the West is not easy. I am not suggesting that it should be easy, and neither am I suggesting that it is easier elsewhere. However, when compared to the rest of the world, the Western mission field is uniquely difficult in many aspects. Africans entering the West encounter distinct challenges that make it even harder for them to connect with Westerners, including the following four challenges: discrimination, theology, politics of immigration, and the tendency of many congregations to become more like social clubs than spiritual gatherings.

Discrimination

There are many identity markers that people in the West use to categorize other people, either to include them in their world or to exclude them. For most people, the check marks that need to be filled before they can belong are many. If you do not meet any of the requirements, you can be automatically marked as an outsider. You can never belong. In most cases, you have to be of the right color, subscribe to the right theology, wear the right clothes, speak with the right accent, have graduated from the right school, and know the right people before you can be considered for inclusion. This is almost normal in the segregated world of Western Christianity, where most African Christians naturally fall on the wrong side of most of these identifiers simply for being African and, sadly, for being black.

For most people in the West, even well-wishing Christian leaders, to be black is still to be suspicious. To be an African black is even worse. Afe Adogame once noted that in many Western

---

[10] Ibid., 8.

cities, a typical African on the street is first greeted with suspicion, perceived as a criminal, refugee, or a beggar until proved otherwise.[11] Unfortunately, a typical African Christian in a Western church is also greeted with suspicion, perceived as a potential criminal, refugee, or a beggar, and more often than not, he or she cannot prove otherwise. Many African Christians in the West have to face this reality every day in their lives and ministries.[12]

The topic of racial discrimination appears only as a side issue in most of the books discussing African Christian presence in the West, which may make sense if you are only interested in the historical facts of the phenomenon. Race relations within the Christian community is a sensitive subject, and it will become even more contentious as the distance between Christians from different parts of the world diminishes—as globalization intensifies—as we go deeper into the twenty-first century. In most of Western Christianity, to talk about race is to reopen scars from the past—something we do not need to talk about since "Christianity is working just fine as it is right now." In the United States, Christian churches are some of most segregated communities—with over 90 percent of congregations being monoethnic.[13]

---

[11] Afe Adogame, "African Instituted Churches in Europe," in *African Identities and World Christianity in the Twentieth Century: Proceedings of the Third International Munich-Freising Conference on the History of Christianity in the Non-Western World (September 15–17, 2004)*, ed. Klaus Koschorke (Wiesbaden: Harrassowitz, 2005), 233. See also Gerrie ter Haar, "The African Christian Presence in Europe: The Atlantic Difference," in *African Christian Presence in the West: New Immigrant Congregations and Transnational Networks in North America and Europe*. ed. Frieder Ludwig and J. Kwabena Asamoah-Gyadu, chap. 14 (Trenton, NJ: Africa World Press, 2011).

[12] When I planted a church in Minnesota, I was suspicious that there were some racist forces at play in the way my church plant was supported by the others in the area. Before long, I became aware of emails that were circulated among pastors in our network saying, "He is an African; trust him at your own risk." I ignored these antics until one day, one of the other pastors came to me and said, "Black people are not supposed to have spiritual oversight over white people." He even had the scriptures to prove it too!

[13] See Curtiss Paul DeYoung, *United by Faith: The Multiracial Congregation as an Answer to the Problem of Race* (New York: Oxford University Press, 2003). Yet we act as if that is the way things are supposed to be. The American church is more segregated than schools and offices. Yet, we don't

To imagine God's Spirit at work in this cultural diversity, and to imagine that God might be up to something in bringing Christians from around the world to Western cities, requires that we confront racial discrimination in all its forms. It is the single most significant factor in the missionary impact of non-Westerners—or minority Christians—in the West. The main problem, at least to me, is that racial discrimination seems to have been accepted as a reality against which we can do nothing. To call for racial reconciliation among Christians and congregations is to be a lone voice crying out in the wilderness, as one friend of mine said on his blog post, "Racial Discrimination in the Church: Are We Barking at a Mountain?"[14] I know of African immigrants who have wandered into white churches only to be told, "Your kind of church meets down the block." This is racism, and it is unwelcome in the body of Christ.

This segregation is not necessarily a new occurrence. It was there before African Christians thought of becoming missionaries to the West. It has been there as long as some white people have thought of themselves as superior to other races. Catejan Ihewulezi says that Christian racial discrimination is universal in most of Western Christianity, and it is rooted in the discriminatory laws of the past.[15] In his passionate work, *Beyond the Color of Skin*, he explores the role that mainline churches—both Roman Catholic and Protestants—played in the institutionalizing and sustaining of segregation in American Christianity, instead of speaking against it. Ihewulezi is a Nigerian priest who serves in the Catholic Church in the United States, and he speaks from his experience serving in Saint Louis, Missouri, for a couple of years. He raises his voice in chorus with other Nigerian and Ghana-

---

talk about race. It is a sacred cow. I have heard many ministers say, "If it ain't broke, don't fix it." I am often tempted to scream back, "Excuse me, mister, a segregated church is a broken church." In my opinion, Christian segregation is not just a social or cultural problem, it is a theological problem.

[14] Calvin Covington, "Racial Discrimination in the Church: Are We Barking at a Mountain?," in *FutureChurch* (Albany, NY, 2012).

[15] Cajetan N. Ihewulezi, *Beyond the Color of Skin: Encounters with Religions and Racial Injustice in America* (Charleston, SC: BookSurge, 2006), 13–44.

ian priests who worry about the racial discrimination that they face in their work within the Catholic Church. Dean Hoge adds, "International priests of darker skins, even after naturalization or incardination, or even American-born Asian priests are usually viewed by American Catholics as un-American, un-white, strange, 'international,' and foreign. They are considered as belonging to an inferior race and ethnicity and not acceptable to the 'in' group of American Catholics."[16] Another Nigerian, Father Bekeh Utietiang, says that African priests' "biggest frustration is a church that places no value in their genuine call to serve but see their priesthood or service in the West as merely for economic reasons."[17]

Roman Catholic immigrant priests can confidently speak against Catholic racism in America, because unlike Protestants their commitment to the Catholic Church prevents them from starting their own churches. Ihewulezi begins his *Beyond the Color of Skin* with a conversation he had with a Baptist ex-minister who told Ihewulezi that there are few Roman Catholic African Americans because most black people have an impression that the Catholic Church is racist.[18] However, the Baptist church to which the minister belonged was also a racist church; the only difference is that they solved the problem by splitting the denomination into two: a white Baptist denomination and a black Baptist one. Talking about the African American experience of racism in Christendom, the Baptist ex-minister added, "We have really been beaten down and marginalized economically, socially, politically, and even religiously, from the foundation of this country because of the color of our skin."[19]

Now, the black Baptist church to which he belonged was a "church of liberation" (from white oppression, I presume). Nevertheless, reading Ihewulezi, I realized that this is still the way we solve the race problem among Protestants. We have white churches and black churches, and in many subtle ways, we tell

[16] Dean R. Hoge and Aniedi Okure, *International Priests in America: Challenges and Opportunities* (Collegeville, MN: Liturgical Press, 2006), 135.
[17] Bekeh Utietiang, "The Challenge of African Priests in America" (Lagos: Gamji), http://www.gamji.com.
[18] Ihewulezi, *Beyond the Color of Skin*, 3.
[19] Ibid.

strangers, based on their skin, "Your kind of church meets elsewhere, not here." Unfortunately, most Africans are only vaguely aware of the depth of this problem when they come to the West. The discrimination that they face is shocking to most of them. It is a serious blow both to their faith and their identity. Since I began to understand the implications of the racism I saw in Western Christianity, I have always wondered how I might justify to my children my involvement in such a racist institution.

Since most Africans will have never experienced significant racial discrimination before, they find discrimination at the hands of fellow Christians very disorienting. While they may possibly fathom the discrimination they experience outside the church, it is the discrimination they experience within it that is much more shocking.

Furthermore, the relationships between African immigrants and African Americans are not any better. Hanciles observes, "After almost three decades of encounter and enforced interaction, the relationship between these two groups is fraught with tension and misunderstanding, even hostility."[20] The tension between these two groups is not racially motivated, for both of them are black. Hanciles outlines three possible reasons for the chasm between Africans and African Americans: (1) African Americans feel African immigrants do not understand and appreciate the effects of slavery and racism they have lived under for centuries; (2) African immigrants seem to play along with the economic system of America while African Americans are generally pessimistic about the "white man's system"; and (3) cultural differences.[21] In the case of Britain, the cultural differences between Africans and black people from the Caribbean would make relationships difficult.

---

[20] Jehu Hanciles, *Beyond Christendom: Globalization, African Migration, and the Transformation of the West* (Maryknoll, NY: Orbis Books, 2008), 320. In the process of researching and writing this book, I decided to "join" an African American church in Saint Paul, MN, for six months. People would be friendly until they heard my African accent, and then they would shut down. After six months, in spite of my effort to make friends in that church, I left the church having made not even one friend at all. This, I thought, was worse than some white churches would do.

[21] Ibid., 320–21.

I suspect that most Western Christians have not figured out yet how to deal with African Christians in the West. They know exactly what to do with Africans in Africa, and that is to go and build hospitals, schools, and churches. They go to Africa to do charity work even though, sometimes, it is not necessary. However, when it comes to the Africans in their Western cities, they would rather not connect: the potential demand for a relationship is too much of a threat. The Western individualistic mind-set that says, "We cannot be friends, but I will help you only with as minimal contact between us as possible"—which is why they would rather go to Africa—will continue to get in the way of real missional partnerships that are born out of real relationships.

Theology

African theology developed in a very spirit-oriented culture where the spirit and the material intertwine on a regular basis. Whereas Western theology continues a two-thousand-year heritage and has been influenced by science and reason during the Enlightenment and modernity, African theology is in some cases only several decades old and has been shaped in a spirit-filled religious culture that allows for minimal influence by science and reason. African scholars found ways to contextualize theology to make it African, mostly by rejecting a great deal of Western theology's attachment to reason and power. Certainly, a theology born among very religious and yet powerless people who are struggling with colonialism, poverty, and diseases tries to understand God in ways different from those articulated by the triumphalistic theologies of the West. The rise of African Independent Churches and, later, the rise of African Pentecostalism reflect the developmental journey of most of Africa's theologies, and their disjunction from Western theology.

The type of theology that informs most African immigrant Christians is viewed with suspicion in many Western circles. It does not render itself to easy categorization, for it eschews the Arminian-Calvinist dichotomy that is prevalent in Western theology. Most Africans do not even know what this dichotomy is about, and they do not feel any need to know it. Although

African theology has some remote access to Western theology, it is heavily shaped by the current African interpretation of the Scriptures without the mediation of those scholars and the two-thousand-year tradition that informs Western theology.

African theological fathers such as Tertullian, Athanasius, and Augustine are remotely acknowledged, and they do not carry as much weight as they do in Western theology. The chronological distance between these church fathers and contemporary Africans is too big to withstand the oral nature of African theology. In addition, since these fathers have been generally portrayed as Western theologians, it becomes difficult for Africans to identify with them. Part of the problem is the scarcity of theological education in a continent where even secular education is out of reach for most of its population. In most cases, the main interpreters will be the apostles and prophetic founders of their denominations, and even these will usually lack in theological education.

Generally speaking, African theology is oral theology and is passed around by word of mouth. Consequently, it attempts to preserve the immediate kernel of what is transmitted, interpreting the scriptural text just as it is while paying minimal attention to its surroundings. In most Western eyes, African immigrants are thus biblicist in their theology. Many will know the Bible inside out but will have little to no theological education. The Scriptures that seem to contradict one another are naturally problematic, but the interpretation that works for the moment is the interpretation that wins.

Second, African theology is spirit-centered. Since most African immigrant Christians in the West are Pentecostal or charismatic in their faith, their theology is "spirit-heavy" even though it does not align itself to the Western Pentecostal theology.[22] The

---

[22] The most obvious reason that I can give for this is that I feel charismatic Christianity is somehow native to African Christianity because of its spirit-centered culture. The Enlightenment-influenced anticharismatic Western theologies failed to de-charismatize African Christians. In addition, Pentecostal and charismatic Christianity is at the center of African Christianity. In Europe and North America, Pentecostalism is "foreign," since Western culture places very little emphasis on the spiritual world.

immediacy of the presence and the power of the Spirit that is accessible to them allows them to confidently thump the Bible and claim a direct connection to God. This, of course, is not a problem for Africans, since their Christianity is lived in a spiritually awakened context. Most of them will have experienced the spirit-world in many ways before converting to Christianity, and they find that their conversion brought the Spirit of God even closer in their daily walk. They struggle to find congregations that will be in tune with them theologically.

Noncharismatic theologies of the West are not attractive to African Pentecostal and charismatic immigrants. Conversely, most Westerners have no interest in African immigrants' Pentecostal or charismatic theology. As a result of these theological differences, Africans find it hard to identify theological acquaintances in the West. Furthermore, both African and Western theologies tend to become defensive whenever their theological traditions are criticized. As non-Western theologies become more vocal, and as non-Western theologians multiply in number, the theological hegemony of the West will be increasingly challenged. This slow dethroning of Western theology will be a painful experience, but a very necessary one. At the end of the day, world Christianity needs a decolonized theology as the future of Christianity lies in true theological relationships among Christians from different parts of the world. Theological cross-pollination is absolutely necessary in this new missional era.

Politics of Immigration

Immigration is always a highly sensitive political issue these days. Almost all Western countries currently have an ongoing discussion about how to deal with immigrants, many of whom come from Africa. The subject of black migration is, in itself, handled with great apprehension in Western politics. Unemployment looms large on both sides of the Atlantic Ocean, making it difficult for immigrants to find acceptance and hospitality. Anti-immigration sentiments can be heard every four or five years, when the time comes for political elections. These protestations are much louder in Europe than in North America, but African immigrants face similar prejudices on either side of the Atlantic. In Britain, for instance, the British National Party is an embodiment of an extreme racist anti-immigration commitment with a policy for zero migration.[23] European news channels often carry reports of would-be African immigrants who are intercepted in makeshift boats trying to cross the Mediterranean Sea into Spain, Italy, or Britain.[24] It is also all too common to hear about would-be immigrants who drown at sea as they attempt to enter Europe. Many risk walking hundreds of miles across deserts to reach places where such boats are found, paying their last dimes for a trip into the unknown. Even for those Africans who live in the West with all the required residency permits, random police monitoring, checks, and brutality are a constant part of life

These anti-immigration sentiments form a major part of the political agenda leading up to every election, be it in Germany, France, or the United States. The browning of the West—a result of the increase in the numbers of nonwhite people residing in Western nations—is a source of major concern for those who worry about the rising tide of the colored nations. As a result, the exercise of trying to secure a work permit for missionaries and church leaders from the Southern Hemisphere is a difficult one. Most Western countries are reluctant to recognize missionaries as "skilled professionals" worth granting a work permit to.

To get around some of these limitations, non-Western missionaries are forced to be bivocational professionals. For instance, numerous African missionaries lead congregations in the Diaspora in addition to working in a secular job to maintain a legal residency status. Many West African churches make use of medical doctors and engineers with legitimate work permits in their professional fields to plant and lead churches. Less skilled African missionaries in the West are usually admitted as students or asylum seekers.

---

[23] The BNP's website states that it intends to stop all migration to the UK except for exceptional cases. See BNP, "Immigration," http://www.bnp.org.uk.

[24] The BBC has a very insightful collection of documentaries on African illegal migration to Europe. For instance, see "Key Facts: African Migration to Europe," available at http://news.bbc.co.uk.

While Bongmba in *African Immigrant Religion* mentions congregations that are committed to making sure that their members do not find themselves on the wrong side of the immigration law, such congregations are not common.[25] Many Africans who attend immigrant congregations have overstayed their legal status and are thus illegally residing in their new countries. With a broken immigration system like that of the United States, it should not surprise anyone that many of its African-born residents are undocumented.[26] Pastors as well as members are often deported for illegal stays. One of the most popular prayer items at African prayer vigils is asking God to sort out most people's "papers" and thus help them normalize their stay in the West. This is a problem that spills over to many other aspects of the immigrant congregation's life. For instance, because of their residency status, many Africans (and other illegal immigrants) are suspicious of anyone who appears to have the power to get them deported, contributing to the insular nature of some communities. Nevertheless, times are changing. Many Western countries are beginning to rethink their foreign policies, especially regarding migration.

Identity

To their disadvantage, many immigrant congregations become small cultural enclaves where news and food from home are shared. At times they become gossip mills, where people update one another on the current affairs in their communities. "If you want to hear whose marriage is having problems, just go to church." When churches become such social gathering spaces for nursing homeland nostalgia, one does not necessarily have to be a Christian to belong. Any African who shares the culture will belong. Therefore, it is hard to really press for Christian morality

---

[25] Jacob Olupona and Regina Gemignani, *African Immigrant Religions in America* (New York: New York University Press, 2007), 115.

[26] Official statistics say there are 1.6 million African-born people living in the United States. However, it is likely that this figure understates the number of Africans living in the United States. U.S. Census Bureau, American Factfinder website, Table B05006: Place of Birth for the Foreign-Born Population in the United States, 2010 American Community Survey 1-Year Estimates, available at www.factfinder.census.gov.

and any sense of congregational responsibility from the participants. Where that happens, scandals of all kinds begin to follow
the congregations. In addition, lacking a consistent membership
base, these churches usually operate on low budgets and struggle
to find volunteers to get their work done.[27]

Many African immigrant congregations have a general
problem of identity; most are not sure whether to stay as cultural enclaves or to contextualize and become mission stations.
Although many African immigrant congregations and their leaders want to identify themselves as missionary places, for many of
the members, the church is the place where they can be themselves—a home away from home. My experience suggests that
they need both identities. There must be places where African
culture can still be accessed in the Diaspora, lest Africans forget
where they came from. Any Christian who wants to be an effective missionary must try as much as possible to identify with the
people he or she is trying to reach. An African trying to reach
Germans will have to culturally adjust to be acceptable among
Germans in ways that do not negate the gospel he is bringing. The same will be required of those Africans doing mission
among British people and Americans.

Most congregations seem to be stuck trying to decide which
one of the two identities to embrace. Earlier, I mentioned a Swahili-speaking congregation in Minneapolis. Attending their service felt more like one was in Tanzania and not America. I was
not surprised to see only Tanzanians and Kenyans. In contrast,
I visited an African congregation in North Saint Paul that had
nothing African about it. It could easily beat some Western congregations at being Western.

Mission after Reverse Mission

The worldwide missionary movement of this postcolonial
world of the twenty-first century will involve Christians from
many parts of the world working together. Mission after the

---

[27] This problem does not seem to affect some African immigrant
groups, like those of West Africa, who have enough committed Christian
members to offset the social group identity.

arrival of Africans in the West must be a common venture that involves Africans and Westerners serving God together. Christians in the West—a population that consists of people from many countries all over the world—will have to negotiate whatever challenges separate them in order to unite for the sake of God's mission. A multicultural missional context needs a multicultural missionary movement. The greatest challenge for this unity is the lack of relationships between Africans and Westerners, but this challenge can be overcome when the two groups of Christians become hospitable toward one another.

Hospitality

Most non-Western cultures are communal in their world-views. African culture is a good example. Africans are very relationship-oriented in their approach to life, ministry, and mission. Everything among them is communal. Individualism is a concept that does not make sense to many Africans. When they arrive in the West, most of them assume that Westerners will be just as relational and are disappointed to find out that the culture in Europe and America is different. People do not have as much time to socialize as much as the Africans would like. Unfortunately, for most Africans, the change in cultures is hard to negotiate, especially when they visit Western churches where they struggle to make friends. Often, those who try to build cross-cultural relationships with white Christians end up lonely. A pastor recently told me, "It is hard enough for an American to make friends here; how much harder would it be for an African who has to cross cultures to make friendships with Americans?" This is possible, however, with some missional intentionality and flexibility.

In a study I carried out with the Church Innovations Institute and Luther Seminary to explore the lives of African immigrant Christians in Western congregations, I discovered that the most important factor determining the stay of Africans in such congregations was their feeling of being welcomed and accepted. In other words, it all depends on relationships.[28] Where Africans are

---

[28] See Harvey C. Kwiyani, "Pneumatology, Mission, and African Christians in Multicultural Congregations in North America" (PhD diss., Luther

able to develop relationships with Westerners, they will stay and contribute to the life of the congregation in any way possible. Where they felt they were not welcome, they did not stay.

To them, the openness in a congregation to build relationships was considered to be a form of hospitality. Most Africans do not go to Western churches looking for help, financial or otherwise. They are only looking for friendships and relationships. Congregations that were hospitable enough to allow relationships with their African members attracted more Africans and, in the process, enjoyed their gifts—as Jesus said, he who receives a prophet in the name of the prophet receives the prophet's reward (Matt. 10:41).

When I pressed harder on how these congregations made themselves hospitable to Africans, I learned that there was a great deal of intentionality involved. One of the pastors I interviewed explained to me that the cultural diversity that I saw in his congregation was not an accident. It was a result of fifteen years of preaching to the congregation that we are all foreigners on earth with God as our host, meaning that we must play fair, for God—our host—is watching us all. He told me, "This congregation really believes that in cultural diversity, we see God better. They actually go out of their way to seek people of other cultures to help them understand themselves and God in a new light."

Another congregation was very committed to having Africans in leadership in various parts of their ministries, making sure that power was shared "equally" across racial lines. Several had actually let their African pastor take the senior pastor role, while the white American pastor was the assistant. Others had made intentionally inclusive decisions about their liturgy and had incorporated African songs in their worship services. Their worship teams were often pushed out of their comfort zones when they had to learn some Swahili and Zulu songs. The Africans also had their space for cultural gatherings and their night vigils. These vigils, I was told, were the reason they all described their cultural diversity as "the best thing that ever happened to us."

Seminary, 2012), 265. Church Innovations Institute is a missions research and consulting institute based in Saint Paul, MN.

This kind of hospitality is tricky, because for it to be successful, the guest has to actually feel welcome. The host is effectively bound to doing anything that will make the guests feel comfortable enough to be themselves. The goal is not to make the host invisible but to make the guest visible and, consequently, for both the host and the guest to be fully themselves while coexisting in the presence of God who is the ultimate host. Such hospitality cannot be extended without true commitment. Or, as Africans would put it, "This hospitality cannot be faked." It has to be intentional and authentic at the same time. It radically shifts the power dynamics to a point where both the host and the guest are equally powerful—or powerless, leaving room for God to be the powerful one in their midst.

In my interviews with a few African Christians who had left a Western mainline church to join an African immigrant church in Minnesota, they did not hesitate to tell me that they had started to feel invisible and unrecognized in the Western congregation. One woman told me, "We did not feel welcome anymore." They believed that hospitality that is forced is not hospitality at all, and where you don't feel welcome, it is best not to stay. True to their words, when I visited the congregation, I realized that there were no connections between Africans and Americans outside the Sunday morning service. Even after some Africans had left the congregation, there was no effort to build relationships with the few that remained. I was surprised that I could not get enough African immigrants for a focus group discussion because the American members (in leadership) did not know how to contact their African members.

Hospitality:
An African Immigrant's Understanding

Hospitality is also a concept that differs from one part of the world to another. What is seen as hospitable in one culture may be unacceptable, or even offensive, in another. For instance, among most Africans, hospitality is generally most expressed by offering the guest a meal—an offer that, in most cases, must not be refused no matter what time of day it is. Although an African may rejoice at such gestures, Westerners are usually perplexed. I have watched many of my Western friends in Africa wonder at this. "How could they give me all that food?" While the African thinks she is being hospitable, the Westerner feels pressured to eat something he does not want. The African host will find it offensive if the guest turns down her offer. Yet the Westerner sees very little hospitable about being expected—if not forced—to eat out of necessity. For hospitality to be possible, both the host and the guest must negotiate what works best for them in the context of the community, since a guest is usually regarded as a visitor to the community and not just the host family.

Among Malawians, hospitality is mostly concerned with humanizing the guest. Malawians believe that when you are hospitable to a stranger, you are saying to him, "You are just as human as I am." Therefore, in recognizing the stranger's humanity, the host is humanized too. A person's hospitality reflects his or her own humanity. To deprive the stranger of his or her humanity—by not being hospitable, for instance—is for the host to deprive himself his humanity too. Drawing from *umunthu*, both the host and the stranger need each other, if not for anything else, than just for the sake of their personhood. The guest must also understand that he or she must also be hospitable to the stranger that is his or her host. Hospitality, then, becomes a constant negotiation between two strangers playing host and guest to each other simultaneously. Thus, to be hospitable is to be flexible—and self-sacrificing—to meet the needs of the stranger. The comfort of the guest defines what successful hospitality looks like in any context. It is only in doing this that the guest can be liberated to be himself or herself among the hosts—to be comfortable enough to unpack the gifts that he or she has brought.

In Malawi, we have a proverb that says *mlendo ndi mame, sachedwa kusungunuka*: "A guest is just like morning dew, he or she will be gone before long." It is a very common proverb that is used to encourage hospitality among societies, assuring them that even though the guest may stay longer than hoped for, even if he or she may be more demanding than the community can handle, he or she will not stay forever. If he or she does not leave to return home, the guest will integrate into the society and therefore cease to be the stranger, becoming a host to other strangers. To Western Christians, this proverb might recommend being hospitable to immigrants, for they will not be forever immigrants. If they do not return home—which many immigrants will eventually do—many will overcome the challenges of being a foreigner in a few years, and they will also be able to contribute to society.

To be hospitable in this way may be a big challenge to many Westerners whose sense of hospitality is guided by a good sense of boundaries. I have heard so many Westerners warn one another that African Christians that visit their churches are only interested in scheming them out of their money. To the contrary, I have spoken to many African ministers who complained about being abused in Western congregations where they slave away for little or no pay at all. The South African theologian, Manas Buthelezi, has this to say:

> This means that the depth of Christian unity is to be prepared to be one with the other person after he or she has become a burden to us. . . . Similarly, to follow in Christ's footsteps means to be one even with the person who causes us pain, just as Christ has come to be symbolized by the cross that was a burden to him. [Taking up one's cross means] I should try to be one with [the other] in love, even if it is unilateral, unreciprocated love and to continue to minister to him even while he carves for himself a racist church.[29]

African hospitality believes that every conversation that wants to understand how to treat strangers must use the lens of Matthew 25:35, where Jesus said, "I was hungry and you gave me food, I was thirsty and you gave me drink, I was a stranger and you welcomed me." Hospitality here is directed toward the needy, the hungry, the thirsty, the wanderer, conditions that generally characterize immigrants, especially those who arrived recently. James adds, "If a brother or a sister is naked, and lacks daily food, and

---

[29] Manas Buthelezi, "Church Unity and Human Divisions of Racism," in *The Debate on Status Confessionis: Studies in Christian Political Theology,* ed. Eckehart Lorenz (Geneva: Department of Studies, Lutheran World Federation, 1983), 19.

one of you say to them, 'Go in peace; keep warm and eat your fill,' and yet you do not supply their bodily needs, what is the good of that?" (James 2:15–16).

God's Preferred Future:
A Multicultural Missionary Movement

The German missiologist Claudia Währisch-Oblau has suggested that all Christians in Europe need to move beyond the concept of reverse mission to start talking about cross-cultural collaboration in mission.[30] African and European Christians need to start working together in order to be relevant for mission in the multicultural cities that they inhabit. The subject of multicultural Christianity is new to most of us. Our theologies, missiologies, and ecclesiologies have yet to catch up with the reality of the culturally diverse world that we see in many of our Western cities. The gap between immigrant Christianity and local Western Christianity is worrisome. As long as this gap is sustained, the church will continue to talk about reverse mission—even though this Christian migration to the West is doing little in terms of reaching Westerners. One of the participants commented that even among Western Christians themselves, there are divisions that seem insurmountable. This is no justification for the marginalization of immigrant Christianity, or any Christianity. As long as immigrant Christianity is kept separate, Western Christianity will continue to set the agenda and dominate the conversations. There will be little possibility for partnerships in which all the parties involved are on an equal footing.

Instead of talking about reverse mission, it would be more relevant for the church to start talking about being collaborators in mission. This would mean that Western and immigrant Christians would work together in their missional endeavors. This would force them to talk to one another, asking for help where neces-

---

[30] Claudia Währisch-Oblau, "From Reverse Mission to Common Mission . . . We Hope: Immigrant Protestant Churches and the 'Programme for Cooperation between German and Immigrant Congregations' of the United Evangelical Mission," *International Review of Mission* 89, no. 354 (2000): 475–76.

sary. The immigrant Christians need help from local Christians so they can understand how to reach multicultural Western contexts with the gospel. The West needs the spiritual reinforcements that immigrant Christians bring to the West. However, it may take a long time before Western Christianity begins to believe that it *must* collaborate with immigrant Christians. Even Western theological education, which should lead the course in engaging non-Western scholars, lags behind. One would be hard-pressed to find non-Western professors in many Western seminaries.

Learning Multicultural Mission

Mission after reverse mission requires us to change the way we understand ourselves and the way we understand God's mission in the world. In our current context where we are all only beginning to figure out this multicultural missionary enterprise, there are several ways we can make our learning process easier.

New Theological Tools

The entire Christian church needs to develop new theological language that looks at faith, race, and mission in healthy ways that encourage cross-racial missional partnerships. Consequently, Christianity needs to rethink its theology as far as race is concerned. We need a theology that will intentionally discredit the racial prejudices that prevail in the church today. We need a theology today that sees cultural diversity as the gift of the Spirit that it is. In Christ, race should not matter. In Christ, difference should not be seen as threatening.

Cross-cultural Leadership Models

Leaders on both sides of the conversation need to model cross-cultural partnerships for their followers. They need to show their people what it looks like to respectfully recognize and work with people who look different from them. Western leaders need to go out of their way to make their "home ground" conducive for the "away" team to engage at play. The also need to show their people what vulnerabilities playing "away" will entail, and how that is not necessarily a good reason to avoid working with strangers. As with everything in life, there is a great deal of risk in welcoming a stranger, but mission is always a risk. Without risk, there would be no Christianity at all. God took major risks to save humankind: for instance, in the Incarnation, the crucifixion, and trusting the twelve disciples. We engage in mission not because it is safe, but because God started it, and then asked for our obedience in following God's example in missional risk-taking.

Both groups of leaders need to tone down their exclusionary rhetoric and begin to respect the other group, even when they disagree with them on some issues. For Westerners, calling African Christianity superstitious and suspicious will only continue to marginalize the help that God has sent them to evangelize the West. For Africans, continuing to label Western Christianity as dead will end up discrediting their missional intentions. If Africans want to be able to reach out to the West, they will surely need the help of Western Christians.

The Ministry of Barnabas

We need people with the heart of Barnabas (Acts 9:27) who are courageous enough to risk opening doors for Christians outside their own culture to engage missionally with the West. African Christians need leaders who will trust Western leaders and thereby give them credibility among other Africans. We also need Western leaders who will open doors for African leaders in Western Christianity. There is also a need for intentionality in recruiting people with some cross-cultural fluency to serve as interpreters. This risk will pay off sometimes. More often than not, this risk will result in painful heartbreaks. However, it is a necessary risk if cross-cultural partnerships will be possible, as we are the first generation to attempt this.

Commitment to Mutual Learning

Good leaders in this multicultural missionary movement will have to stay committed to learning about and from one another.

They may be able to create space where race and justice can be talked about without shame, guilt, or condemnation. The more we learn about one another, the better our chances of successfully partnering for mission. Mutual love and respect is the only way forward. Both sides need to listen to one another. There are countless lessons that African Christians can learn from Western Christians, and likewise, there are countless lessons Western Christians can learn from African Christians.

After everything has been said and done, Western Christianity (and this time I use the term to encompass all Christianities currently present in the West) needs to move beyond reverse mission to begin to embrace the culturally diverse missionary movement it has at its disposal and to engage the culturally diverse context in which it finds itself. If European and North American Christianities want to be faithful to God's mission in the twenty-first-century world, they have to do better at their relationships with non-Western Christianities. In the same way, if world Christianity is going to truthfully partner with God in God's mission, it has to negotiate the multicultural reality in a more amicable way. Many other sectors of society have had to adjust to be able to function in an increasingly multicultural situation; cultural diversity should not be feared as much as it is in Christianity. God's hand is at work in the migrations of the world, and the cultural diversity that ensues is purposeful. May the church jump on board, God has already gone ahead of us.

Chapter Seven

Final Reflections

The bottom line of my argument in this book is that in this multicultural world where we live, Christians ought to be constantly reminded that we are all foreigners—immigrants, sojourners, and strangers—on a common mission in Christ. Faithfulness to *missio Dei* means rising above the dividing forces to work together as a multicultural missionary movement in God's world. God is our host, and we are all foreigners. The Apostle Paul reminds us that in this God, there is neither Hebrew nor Greek, neither male nor female. In our twenty-first-century world, there is also neither black nor white, neither European nor African, and neither Hispanic nor Asian. God is the host, and everything we are or own belongs to this Father of our Lord, Jesus Christ. Even in this growing cultural diversity in the world, God's hand is at work. The sooner we embrace it, the better. It is good for the church's self-identity as well as its sense of mission.

You Were Once Strangers

To the dismay of many anti-immigration Westerners, cultural diversity will continue to grow in Western cities, and it will involve the migration of more non-Westerners to the West. Christian churches need to rethink their engagement with these strangers, the immigrants and the foreigners. The entire Christian enterprise needs to rethink its corporate identity in a multicultural world. If it helps, the Bible is clear about how to deal with strangers:

> You shall love the stranger, for you were once strangers in
> the land of Egypt. (Deut. 10:19)

> The alien who resides with you shall be to you as the
> citizen among you; you shall love the alien as yourself, for
> you were aliens in the land of Egypt: I am the Lord your
> God. (Lev. 19:34)

In shaping the story of the nation of Israel, God was very intentional in teaching them hospitality to the stranger. The lesson
was experiential, beginning with Abraham's leaving of his father's
land through the birth of the nation of Israel in the womb of a
foreign nation—Egypt. It appears God wanted this experience
to stay engraved in the collective memory of the nation forever.
They should never forget that they "were once strangers in the
land of Egypt." After all, to follow the God of the patriarchs is
to follow the God of wanderers. God's self-identification as the
God of Abraham, Isaac, and Jacob is telling the world of God's
relationship to three generations of wanderers who lived "looking for a city whose builder and maker is God" (Heb. 11:8–16).
God is identifying Godself, here, as the God of the immigrant. In
many unambiguous ways, God taught Israelites of the importance
of making space for and taking care of the strangers in their communities.

The writer of Hebrews picks up on this and further encourages readers to show hospitality to strangers. The author exhorts
readers: "Do not neglect to show hospitality to strangers, for by
doing that some have entertained angels without knowing it"
(Heb. 13: 2). It is Abraham who once again embodies this story
to us. When God visited Abraham in Genesis 18, it was in the
form of three strangers, and even though Abraham did not know
who they were, he was hospitable to the strangers and compelled
them to share a meal with him before proceeding with their
journey. This blind encounter with the three strangers is one of
the most significant moments in Abraham's life. Similar incidents
of hospitality occur in the lives of many other Israelites in contexts where the strangers were not necessarily safe. For most Israelites, the stranger was a threat who might bring their foreign
gods into Israel. However, God instructs the Israelites to welcome, protect, share with, and identify with the stranger because
of the shared experience of having been strangers themselves.

We live today in a very individualistic Western culture that has lulled us into forgetting what it means to be a stranger, and worse, how to be a host. Cultural homogeneity in our circles of acquaintances prevents us from having real opportunities to interact with strangers. This culture encourages its people not to trust the stranger at all. Of course, some strangers are dangerous. However, the Bible invites us not only to be hospitable to strangers but also to get out of our familiar zones to depend on the hospitality of another: to be strangers to the strangers that we meet. What we would normally think of as a host meeting a stranger is really a meeting of two strangers.

There is an invitation here for us to continuously move back and forth between being a host and a stranger. In a way, God told Israel, "Do not forget what it means to be a stranger." God's visitation to us might be actually in the form of a stranger as well. In modern-day culture, Jesus would have sparked a great controversy when he described his judgment toward the stubborn and selfish people of his day:

> "You that are accursed, depart from me into the eternal fire prepared for the devil and his angels; for I was hungry and you gave me no food, I was thirsty and you gave me nothing to drink, I was a stranger and you did not welcome me, naked and you did not give me clothing, sick and in prison and you did not visit me." Then they also will answer, "Lord, when was it that we saw you hungry or thirsty or a stranger or naked or sick or in prison, and did not take care of you?" Then he will answer them, "Truly I tell you, just as you did not do it to one of the least of these, you did not do it to me." And these will go away into eternal punishment, but the righteous into eternal life. (Matt. 25: 41–46)

Generally speaking, people who are open to strangers are those that have once experienced being a stranger in their lives. In pleading for openness to strangers, God is calling for a multicultural community of strangers who consider God their host. For most Westerners, encounters with strangers will be in the form of something I would call "cross-cultural migration." The strangers in this situation are not necessarily Africans or Asians. They are fellow Americans, but of a different cultural outlook. This may be a result of different economic class backgrounds. A welcoming Christian community should reflect the demographics of its society in more ways than just skin color. Poor, rich, educated, uneducated, young, old—all should be able stay together in the same Christian community. Difference ought not be a threat to the faithful. It is usually an invitation to encounter a stranger, a transaction that takes place in the presence of the Lord.

My Experience in My First Years

When I arrived in America in 2007 and joined the American branch of a church movement I had worked with in Europe, I had no inclination at all that my being a black African—a true embodiment of the stranger in a denomination that is over 90 percent white in the United States—would make me an unwelcome guest among some of the brothers and sisters with whom I shared my denominational alliance.[1] In fact, until I crossed the Atlantic to come and live in Minnesota, I had never really experienced racial discrimination from other Christians, even though I had spent seven years working with white Christians in seven European countries.[2] My gifts and abilities had always connected me with the right people who valued what I brought to the ministry and did not care at all what my skin looked like. Consequently, I did not have any clue of what it means to be treated differently because you are black among suspicious and somewhat insecure white people.

---

[1]   I had worked with the same organization on three continents. In reflection, now, I see that it has not been able to cross the racial barrier, even in Africa. Part of the reason may be that it is a white-led movement in Africa as well, being led primarily by white South Africans.

[2]   I am not suggesting that Europeans are not racist, and, of course, I realize that Africans might be just as racist. I know many Africans who will say that racism is just as rampant in Europe as it is in the United States, and some will say they have not experienced any such discrimination at all.

I wrongly presumed that my history with this organization, my ministry, missionary experience, and now my education would be something that local leaders would be interested in. Not that I needed the platform. I had worked hard in Europe for seven straight years, and I was now working on my doctoral studies, so a break would be timely. However, I did not expect that I would be treated differently because I am a black African who should not be trusted at all. I came to America very eager to learn from and contribute as much as I could to a denomination that I had grown to love. I believed that my foreign perspective would contribute positively to a predominantly white denomination that was trying to break racial barriers.

I was dead wrong. Within a few months of planting a church in Saint Paul, the organizational support network that I had counted on suddenly evaporated. They had been warned, "Watch out, he is an African." The rat race that followed for the ensuing five years would reshape everything I knew about American Christianity.

I was lucky to be given a license to plant a church in Minnesota. It was this single event that would uncover all the racist sentiments that I suspected were there. Of course, I got the license on the belief that I would plant an *immigrant* church that should have attracted Africans and not white people. When some leaders realized that the new church was attracting mostly white Americans, they put out disclaimers telling others, "He is an African; trust him at your own risk." This, coming from people whose recommendation would make or break my ministry, did more than just isolate me from the support group that I needed to get the new church running well. It hurt my life in ways that I could have never imagined.

At first, I thought some of the leaders had problems with my theology or something about the way in which I conducted my ministry, but I never heard any complaints to that effect. Neither did I ever get any complaint about anything else. As time went on, the disclaimers multiplied and got louder. They changed from "trust at owner's risk" to "we do not know him at all." Numerous attempts to connect with the wider organizational network would prove futile, as many of them had been warned about "that

African." Even the local church-planting coach had no interest in talking to me. Once, after I had called him numerous times, his secretary called me back to say, "Mike [not real name] will call you when he wants to talk to you." Several attempts to seek intervention only complicated the problem. It was the all-too-familiar scenario of a black man complaining about mistreatment at the hands of a white man to other white men—who happened to be the perpetrator's good friends. Justice was always out of reach. Three years later, when I left the church plant, the local area leader emailed me saying, "Thank you for being a part of our network." No apologies, no explanations, not even an interest to inquire what had happened. For a few weeks I wondered if there was some form of elation in their community—the African has finally left the house.

As I have walked my journey in missions for a long time now, I have come to know many other Africans, Latin Americans, and Asians who may share similar stories; some of them have worse treatment than this one. After leaving that organization, I met a black South African who had sought a ministry position in his denomination in Minnesota for a long time, and though he often found himself among the final two applicants, he always came short. He had learned that the problem was his being an African. He told me, "Here in America, it all boils down to power. Very rarely will you find white people that can allow a person of color to have spiritual authority over them." I had heard this before, and my experience was not too dissimilar. Unfortunately, many people tie the concept of power to race, believing that being of a certain race makes them more or less powerful than others. When this outlook is imported into Christianity, it becomes easy to theologically justify evils like racism and apartheid.

Power, Race, and Mission

With 65 percent of world Christians now living in the global south and Asia, twenty-first-century Christianity could easily pass for a non-Western religion. As we move deeper into the century, it will become more evident that Christianity is not a white man's religion anymore. In this day and age, Latin Americans,

Africans, and Asians can confidently claim Christianity as their religion just as much as Westerners can. In a couple of decades, no one will think of it as an oxymoron for one to be African and Christian. Of course, in a few decades, even Western Christianity will be largely nonwhite in its ethnicity.[3] The impact of this rise of non-Western Christianity at a time when Western Christianity is losing most of its members has yet to register in most theological and missiological conversations—and both these fields are still very Western.

The problem on our hands is that of the relationship between power, race, and *missio Dei*. The tie between power and race has created a world where one race of people believes that it is better than and superior to all other races. Bob Marley once sang, "Until the philosophy which holds one race superior and another inferior is finally and permanently discredited and abandoned, everywhere is war."[4] Of course, he used the word "war" in a figurative way, standing for all the chaos that follows when one group of people begins to believe it is better than others. The tribal wars that continue to devastate Africa are usually a result of such belief that one group of people is superior to other groups. The history of the late twentieth century reminds us of South Africa's apartheid, the Rwandan genocide, and the Sudan-Darfur conflict—all of which have their origins in ethnic conflicts. For instance, the word "cockroach" took a totally new meaning in my mind when I watched the film *Hotel Rwanda,* where it was used to describe a tribe of people believed to be of lesser humanity.

This tie between race and power (and economics) has had a huge impact on the world. It has created a global village in which people try to dominate one another based on race and ethnicity. As Samuel Huntington showed in *The Clash of Civilizations,* the Caucasian peoples—and their Western civilization—have in the past few centuries dominated the rest of the world, but now that dominance is waning.[5] Huntington explored the implications of

---

[3] Jehu Hanciles, *Beyond Christendom: Globalization, African Migration, and the Transformation of the West* (Maryknoll, NY: Orbis Books, 2008), 293.

[4] Robert Nesta Marley, *War* (Kingston, Jamaica: Island Records, 1976).

[5] Samuel P. Huntington, *The Clash of Civilizations and the Remaking of World Order* (New York: Touchstone, 1997), 50–53, also 81–101. See also

the rise of non-Western civilization, especially on global politics and economy, as the balance of civilizations shifts and the West fades. However, even though Thomas Friedman argues that technology has flattened the world in terms of innovation, neocolonialism continues to threaten to maintain Western superiority in the world.[6] The hierarchy of civilizations—even that of the races—still guides most world political and economic dynamics. Of course, the rise of the BRICS nations (Brazil, Russia, India, China, and South Africa) will shift these geopolitical and economic balances. Nevertheless, I believe that it will take several generations before we are able to overcome the concept of racial and civilizational hierarchies.

It is my belief that just as the non-Western civilizations will shift the power balances in politics and economy, they will also shift the balance in world religions. The rise of non-Western civilizations will bring along the rise of non-Western religious expressions. In the case of Christianity, we should expect that the rise of non-Western Christianities will have a greater impact on world Christianity. Unfortunately, in the eyes of many Africans, Christianity was the religion of the colonizers and therefore the religion of the oppressors. The problem facing Christianity is that among most of its Western adherents, Western superiority is alive and well. Indeed, a great deal of Western Christianity still believes that it is, in many ways, better than and superior to those Christianities that have emerged in other parts of the world.

Especially in North America, but also quite visible in Europe, white privilege makes it rare to see foreigners in positions of spiritual authority in Western congregations and other church bodies. Cajetan Ihewulezi tells many stories of Western Catholic Christians who would rather not receive communion from or

---

Francis Fukuyama, *The End of History and the Last Man* (New York: Free Press, 1992).

[6] Thomas L. Friedman, *The World Is Flat: A Brief History of the Twenty-First Century*, 1st updated and expanded ed. (New York: Farrar, Straus and Giroux, 2006). If anything, I have argued elsewhere that the world is terraced and not flat as Friedman suggests in his book. His scanty treatment of Africa makes me wonder if he considers Africa as a player on the global economic and technology scene.

listen to a sermon given by, not to mention sit under the leadership of, a person of color.[7] Western Christianity is used to teaching the rest of world about Christianity. Even where the Western
superiority complex has been discredited, it is rare to find Westerners who have developed healthy working relationships with
non-Westerners.

Fortunately, the God of the mission does not regard race as a
prerequisite for engagement. The same God that uses Westerners
also uses Latin Americans, Africans, and Asians, no matter where
they are. God uses non-Western Christians even when they are
in the West. In addition, God can use these world Christians to
minister to Western Christians. If anything, we can learn from
Paul who said:

> But God chose what is foolish in the world to shame the
> wise; God chose what is weak in the world to shame the
> strong; God chose what is low and despised in the world,
> things that are not, to reduce to nothing things that are,
> so that no one might boast in the presence of God. He is
> the source of your life in Christ Jesus, who became for us
> wisdom from God, and righteousness and sanctification
> and redemption, in order that, as it is written, "Let the one
> who boasts, boast in the Lord." (1 Cor. 1:27–31)

In this generation, just like the Corinthians Paul was addressing in
his first epistle, God is using the low and despised to speak prophetically to Western Christianity. God's mission is global, and
Christ is a foreigner in every culture, and no culture has a corner
on Christianity. The sense of power that is tied to race flies in the
face of a God who views all human beings as equal. The mission of
God—*missio Dei*—should not be tied to any particular race or geographical location. Most Western Christians will have to go through
a significant paradigm shift to be able to see non-Westerners as
missionaries whom God can use to invigorate Western Christianity.
Non-Western Christians will need to have the confidence to keep

---

[7] Cajetan N. Ihewulezi, *Beyond the Color of Skin: Encounters with Religions and Racial Injustice in America* (Charleston, SC: BookSurge, 2006).

on praying, preaching, and speaking prophetically to the West despite discrimination and marginalization. God has brought them to the West for a reason, and Western Christianity needs their voice right now.

God's Preferred Future for Mission

The mission of God in the world has not changed from what it was a century or two ago, but the context of the world that the missionary seeks to engage has changed drastically. I find it exciting, however, that the missionary movement that will reach the world in this century will be composed of Christians from all parts of the world. We will see a great number of missionaries from Latin America, Africa, and Asia moving around the world. Although many of them will serve in their own geographical regions, some will migrate across oceans to serve in foreign continents.

I have suggested that this worldwide missionary movement is already in motion, and an important piece of its development is the rise of non-Western Christian missionaries serving in Western countries. For instance, the presence of Latin American Christians—both Catholics and Pentecostals—in the United States and Canada has had a significant impact on the strength of these denominations in North America. Similarly, the presence of Asians—mostly from South Korea—in London accounts for a significant portion of all church attendance in a city where more foreigners than locals attend church every Sunday. In addition, the growing presence of African Christians in Europe and North America will become more noticeable as they increase in numbers and in their missional activities.

Like most foreign-born Christians in the West, Africans are finding it difficult to be effective missionaries. They are even finding it hard to find Western congregations that they may call home. There are many reasons for these problems—racism, classism, theological differences, cross-cultural incompetence, and more. Moving forward, the entire Christian body in the West will need to work together to overcome these challenges in order to make it possible for Christians from different parts of the world to work together for God's mission in the world.

The gifts of African Christianity have so far been confined within African communities because there are still very few avenues for collaboration between Africans and Westerners. Most Western churches have also not been able—or keen—to share their gifts with African immigrant congregations for such reasons as racial distrust, among others. For the Christian churches to be able to be effective in their missionary endeavors, they will need to work together across races and cultures. This will be necessary for two reasons. One: the Spirit of God loves cultural diversity. Two: the multicultural context of the Western world will require a culturally diverse missionary movement to proclaim to it the gospel of salvation.

It is my belief, therefore, that in this context, God is inviting the church to a higher level of unity for the sake of God's mission. The God of the mission is no respecter of race. The blessed reflex is a proper outcome of the spread of Christianity around the world. In the cultural diversity that characterizes many parts of the Western world, this new reality of mission is only the beginning of a greater work of the Spirit of God—one that will involve Christians from all parts of the world for the purpose of God's mission. God's Spirit has propelled the nations into each other's arms so that they can embrace each other to fulfill God's mission on earth. One of Jesus' final remarks to his disciples was, "Love one another, for it is by love that the world will know that you are my disciples." This exhortation is fitting today for the many races of Christians around the world: love one another across cultures. *Missio Dei* depends on it.

Bibliography

Abusharaf, Rogaia Mustafa. *Wanderings: Sudanese Migrants and Exiles in North America*. Anthropology of Contemporary Issues. Ithaca, NY: Cornell University Press, 2002.

Adepoju, Aderanti, and Network of Migration Research on Africa. *International Migration within, to, and from Africa in a Globalised World*. Accra, Ghana: Sub-Saharan Publishers, 2010.

Adogame, Afeosemime U. "African Instituted Churches in Europe." In *African Identities and World Christianity in the Twentieth Century: Proceedings of the Third International Munich-Freising Conference on the History of Christianity in the Non-Western World (September 15–17, 2004)*, edited by Klaus Koschorke. Wiesbaden: Harrassowitz, 2005.

———. *Celestial Church of Christ: The Politics of Cultural Identity in a West African Prophetic-Charismatic Movement*. New York: Peter Lang, 1999.

———. "Contesting the Ambivalences of Modernity in a Global Context: The Redeemed Christian Church of God, North America." *Studies in World Christianity* 10, no. 1 (2004): 25–48.

———. *Who Is Afraid of the Holy Ghost?: Pentecostalism and Globalization in Africa and Beyond*. Trenton, NJ: Africa World Press, 2011.

Adogame, Afeosemime U., Ezra Chitando, and Bolaji Bateye. *African Traditions in the Study of Religion in Africa: Emerging Trends, Indigenous Spirituality and the Interface with Other World Religions*. Vitality of Indigenous Religions. Burlington, VT: Ashgate, 2010.

Adogame, Afeosemime U., Roswith I. H. Gerloff, and Klaus Hock. *Christianity in Africa and the African Diaspora: The Appropriation of a Scattered Heritage.* Continuum Religious Studies. New York: Continuum, 2008.

Adogame, Afeosemime U., and James V. Spickard. *Religion Crossing Boundaries: Transnational Religious and Social Dynamics in Africa and the New African Diaspora.* Religion and the Social Order. Boston: Brill, 2010.

Adogame, Afeosemime U., and Cordula Weissköppel. *Religion in the Context of African Migration.* Bayreuth African Studies Series 75. Bayreuth: Breitinger, 2005.

Agbali, Anthony. "African Priests, African Catholicism, the West and Issues Emerging." Detroit. http://www.utexas.edu.

Anderson, Allan. *African Reformation: African Initiated Christianity in the 20th Century.* Trenton, NJ: Africa World Press, 2001.

———. *Moya: The Holy Spirit in an African Context.* Manualia Didactica 13. Pretoria: University of South Africa, 1991.

Anderson, Gerald H. "A Moratorium on Missionaries." Chicago: Christian Century. http://www.religion-online.org.

Asamoah-Gyadu, J. Kwabena. *African Charismatics: Current Developments within Independent Indigenous Pentecostalism in Ghana.* Boston: Brill, 2005.

———. "African Initiated Christianity in Eastern Europe: Church of the 'Embassy of God' in Ukraine." *International Bulletin of Missionary Research* 30, no. 2 (2006): 73–75.

———. "Spirit, Mission, and Transnational Influence: Nigerian-Led Pentecostalism in Eastern Europe." *PentecoStudies* 9, no. 1 (2010): 74–96.

Augustine. *Confessions.* Edited by Henry Chadwick. New York: Oxford University Press, 1992.

———. *The Confessions, The City of God, On Christian Doctrine.* Edited by Marcus Dods, J. F. Shaw, and E. B. Pusey. Great Books of the Western World 18. London: Encyclopaedia Britannica, 1952.

Babatunde, Adedibu. *Coat of Many Colors.* London: Wisdom Summit, 2012.

Babatunde, Wale. *Great Britain Has Fallen: How to Restore Britain's Greatness as a Nation.* London: New Wine Press, 2002.

Baines, Dudley. *Emigration from Europe, 1815–1930*. New Studies in Economic and Social History. New York: Cambridge University Press, 1995.

Balia, Daryl M., and Kirsteen Kim. *Edinburgh 2010: Witnessing to Christ Today*. Eugene, OR: Wipf & Stock, 2010.

Barrett, David B., George Thomas Kurian, and Todd M. Johnson. *World Christian Encyclopedia: A Comparative Survey of Churches and Religions in the Modern World*. 2nd ed. New York: Oxford University Press, 2001.

Barth, Karl. *Church Dogmatics*. Vol. 4.1: *The Doctrine of Reconciliation*. Edinburgh: T&T Clark International, 1956.

Baur, John. *2000 Years of Christianity in Africa: An African Church History*. 2nd rev. ed. Nairobi, Kenya: Paulines, 1998.

Berger, Peter L. *The Desecularization of the World: Resurgent Religion and World Politics*. Grand Rapids, MI: W.B. Eermands, 1999.

Beti, Mongo. *The Poor Christ of Bomba*. Long Grove, IL: Waveland, 1971.

Biney, Moses O. *From Africa to America: Religion and Adaptation among Ghanaian Immigrants in New York*. New York: New York University Press, 2011.

Blessed Embassy of the Kingdom of God. "History." Kiev. http://www.godembassy.com.

Bosch, David J. *Transforming Mission: Paradigm Shifts in Theology of Mission*. American Society of Missiology Series. Maryknoll, NY: Orbis Books, 1991.

Boxer, Charles R. *The Church Militant and Iberian Expansion, 1440–1770*. Baltimore: Johns Hopkins University Press, 1978.

Bright, John. *A History of Israel*. Louisville, KY: Westminster John Knox, 2000.

Brill. "African Diaspora: A Journal of Transnational Africa in a Global World." http://www.brill.nl.

British and Foreign Bible Society. "A Tribute to Lesslie Newbigin (1909–1998)." In *The Bible in TransMission: A Forum for Change in Church and Culture*. Special Edition, 1998.

Brotherhood of the Cross and the Star. "Christ Universal Spiritual School of Practical Christianity." http://www.ooo-bcs.org.

Bruijn, Mirjam de, Rijk van Dijk, and D. Foeken. *Mobile Africa:*

Changing Patterns of Movement in Africa and Beyond. African Dynamics. Boston: Brill, 2001.

Butcher, E. L. *The Story of the Church of Egypt: Being an Outline of the History of the Egyptians under Their Successive Masters from the Roman Conquest until Now.* New York: AMS, 1975.

Buthelezi, Manas. "Church Unity and Human Divisions of Racism." In *The Debate on Status Confessionis: Studies in Christian Political Theology,* edited by Eckehart Lorenz. Geneva: Department of Studies, Lutheran World Federation, 1983.

Campbell, Alexander. "Mission 21: A Report in Church Planting in UK since 2000." Sheffield, UK: Fresh Expressions, 2006.

CARA Services. "Frequently Requested Church Statistics." http://cara.georgetown.edu.

Cardoza-Orlandi, Carlos F. *Mission: An Essential Guide.* Nashville, TN: Abingdon Press, 2002.

Catholic Theological Union. "CTU Faculty Biography: Anthony Gittins, C.S.Sp." http://www.ctu.edu.

Catto, Rebecca. "From the Rest to the West: Exploring Reversal in Christian Mission in Twenty-First Century Britain." PhD diss., University of Exeter, 2010.

Chigona, Gerard. *Umunthu Theology: Path of Integral Human Liberation Rooted in Jesus of Nazareth.* Balaka, Malawi: Montfort, 2002.

"The Church in the World: African Bishops Come to the Aid of Europe." *Tablet.* http://www.thetablet.co.uk.

Clark, John, and Eleanor Johnson. *Anglicans in Mission: A Transforming Journey: Report of Missio, the Mission Commission of the Anglican Communion, to the Anglican Consultative Council, Meeting in Edinburgh, Scotland, September 1999.* London: SPCK, 2000.

Cone, James H. *The Cross and the Lynching Tree.* Maryknoll, NY: Orbis Books, 2011.

Copeland-Carson, Jacqueline. *Creating Africa in America: Translocal Identity in an Emerging World City.* Contemporary Ethnography. Philadelphia: University of Pennsylvania Press, 2004.

Covenant College. "Dr. Mark Gornik '84 to Present WIC Lectures." http://www.covenant.edu.

Covington, Calvin. "Racial Discrimination in the Church: Are We Barking at a Mountain?" In *FutureChurch.* Albany, NY, 2012.

Cuffe, Jenny. "African Dream of a Better Life." BBC News Online, June 16, 2007.

Cyprian, and M. Bâevenot. *The Lapsed: The Unity of the Catholic Church.* Ancient Christian Writers, no. 25. London: Newman Press, 1957.

Daniels, David. "African Immigrant Religions in the United States and the Study of Black Church History." In *African Immigrant Religions in America,* edited by Jacob Olupona and Regina Gemignani. New York: New York University Press, 2007,

Darch, John H. *Missionary Imperialists?: Missionaries, Government and the Growth of the British Empire in the Tropics, 1860–1885.* Colorado Springs: Paternoster, 2009.

Davie, Grace. *Europe—The Exceptional Case: Parameters of Faith in the Modern World.* London: Darton Longman & Todd, 2002.

———. *Religion in Britain since 1945: Believing without Belonging.* Making Contemporary Britain. Cambridge, MA: Blackwell, 1994.

de la Baume, Maïa. "In France, Foreign Aid in the Form of Priests." *New York Times,* April 4, 2013, 4.

DeYoung, Curtiss Paul. *United by Faith: The Multiracial Congregation as an Answer to the Problem of Race.* New York: Oxford University Press, 2003.

Dijk, Richard van. "Young Puritan Preachers in Post-Independent Malawi." *Africa* 62, no. 2 (1992): 159–81.

Dijk, Rijk van. *Christian Fundamentalism in Sub-Saharan Africa: The Case of Pentecostalism.* Copenhagen: Centre of African Studies, University of Copenhagen, 2000.

Dunn, Geoffrey D. *Tertullian.* New York: Routledge, 2004.

Duru, Walter. "Brotherhood of the Cross and Star Press Release: Re-Olumba Olumba Obu No Longer God." Accra: Modern Ghana.

Ebaugh, Helen Rose F., and Janet Saltzman Chafetz. *Religion and the New Immigrants: Continuities and Adaptations in Immigrant Congregations.* Walnut Creek, CA: AltaMira Press, 2000.

Eboussi Boulaga, F. *Christianity without Fetishes: An African Critique and Recapture of Christianity.* Maryknoll, NY: Orbis Books, 1984.

Eck, Diana L. *A New Religious America: How a "Christian Country" Has Now Become the World's Most Religiously Diverse Nation.* New York: HarperSanFrancisco, 2001.

Eerdword. "Mark Gornik: Word Made Global: Stories of African Christianity in New York City." http://eerdword.wordpress.com.

Elizondo, Virgilio P. *The Future Is Mestizo: Life Where Cultures Meet.* Meyer-Stone ed. Oak Park, IL: Meyer-Stone Books, 1988.

Emory University. "Candler School of Theology Faculty Biography: Jehu J. Hanciles." http://www.candler.emory.edu.

Etambala, Zana Aziza. "Congolese Children at the Congo House in Colwyn Bay (North Wales, Great Britain) at the End of the 19th Century." *Afrika Focus* 3, no. 3–4 (1987): 237–85.

Eusebius. *Eusebius: The Church History.* Edited by Paul L. Maier. Grand Rapids, MI: Kregel Publications, 2007.

Friedman, Thomas L. *The World Is Flat: A Brief History of the Twenty-First Century.* 1st updated and expanded ed. New York: Farrar, Straus and Giroux, 2006.

Fukuyama, Francis. *The End of History and the Last Man.* New York: Free Press, 1992.

George, Timothy. *Faithful Witness: The Life and Mission of William Carey.* Birmingham, AL: New Hope, 1991.

Gerloff, Roswith. "The African Diaspora and the Shaping of Christianity in Africa: Perspectives on Religion, Migration, Identity, and Collaboration." *Missionalia* 38, no. 2 (2010): 307–20.

———. "Black Christian Communities in Birmingham: The Problem of Basic Recognition." In *Religion in the Birmingham Area*, 61–84. Birmingham, UK: University of Birmingham, 1975.

———. "Open Space: The African Christian Diaspora in Europe and the Quest for Human Community." *International Review of Mission* 89, no. 354 (2000): entire issue.

———. *A Plea for British Black Theologies: The Black Church Movement in Britain in Its Transatlantic Cultural and Theological Interaction with Special References to the Pentecostal Oneness (Apostolic) and Sabbatarian Movements.* Studien zur Interkulturellen Geschichte des Christentums. Frankfurt am Main: P. Lang, 1992.

―――. "The Significance of the African Christian Diaspora in Europe: Selected Bibliography." *International Review of Mission* 89, no. 354 (2000): 281–290.

Gerloff, Roswith, Gisela Egler, and Paul Loffler. *Das Schwarze Lacheln Gottes: Afrikanische Diaspora als Herausforderung an Theologie und Kirche: Beitrage aus 30 Jahren Reflektierter Praxis.* Frankfurt am Main: Lembeck, 2005.

Gifford, Paul. *African Christianity: Its Public Role.* Bloomington: Indiana University Press, 1998.

―――. *The Christian Churches and the Democratisation of Africa.* New York: Brill, 1995.

―――. *Ghana's New Christianity: Pentecostalism in a Globalizing African Economy.* Bloomington: Indiana University Press, 2004.

Gittins, Anthony J. *Bread for the Journey: The Mission of Transformation and the Transformation of Mission.* American Society of Missiology Series, no. 17. Maryknoll, NY: Orbis Books, 1993.

―――. "Reflections from the Edge: Mission-in-Reverse and Missiological Research." *Missiology* 21, no. 1 (1993): 21–29.

Gledhill, Ruth. "Church Seeks Spirituality of Youth . . . and Doesn't Like What It Finds." *Times Online* (2006). http://www.timesonline.co.uk.

Godin, Henri, and Yvan Daniel. *La France, Pays de mission?* Rencontres. Lyon: Éditions de l'Abeille, 1943.

Goheen, Michael W. "Toward a Missiology of Western Culture." *European Journal of Theology* 8, no. 2 (1999): 155–68.

González, Justo L. *The Story of Christianity.* Vol. 1: *The Early Church to the Reformation.* New York: HarperCollins, 2010.

Gornik, Mark R. *To Live in Peace: Biblical Faith and the Changing Inner City.* Grand Rapids, MI: Eerdmans, 2002.

―――. *Word Made Global: Stories of African Christianity in New York City.* Grand Rapids, MI: Eerdmans, 2011.

Green, Jeffrey. "009: Colwyn Bay's African Institute: 1889–1912." London. http://www.jeffreygreen.co.uk.

Grenz, Stanley J. *A Primer on Postmodernism*. Grand Rapids, MI: William B. Eerdmans, 1996.

Groody, Daniel G. "Crossing the Divide: Foundations of a Theology of Migration and Refugees." *Theological Studies* 70, no. 3 (2009): 638–67.

Guder, Darrell. *Missional Church: A Vision for the Sending of the Church in North America*. The Gospel and Our Culture Series. Grand Rapids, MI: Eerdmans, 1998.

Gutiérrez, Gustavo. *A Theology of Liberation: History, Politics, and Salvation*. Maryknoll, NY: Orbis Books, 1973.

Haar, Gerrie ter. "The African Christian Presence in Europe: The Atlantic Difference." In *African Christian Presence in the West: New Immigrant Congregations and Transnational Networks in North America and Europe*. edited by Frieder Ludwig and J. Kwabena Asamoah-Gyadu, chap. 14. Trenton, NJ: Africa World Press, 2011.

———. *Halfway to Paradise: African Christians in Europe*. Cardiff: Cardiff Academic Press, 1998.

———. *How God Became African: African Spirituality and Western Secular Thought*. Philadelphia: University of Pennsylvania Press, 2009.

———. *Strangers and Sojourners: Religious Communities in Diaspora*. Leuven: Peeters, 1998.

Hanciles, Jehu. *Beyond Christendom: Globalization, African Migration, and the Transformation of the West*. Maryknoll, NY: Orbis Books, 2008.

Hardage, Jeannette. *Mary Slessor, Everybody's Mother: The Era and Impact of a Victorian Missionary*. Eugene, OR: Wipf & Stock, 2008.

Harvard Divinity School. "Faculty Biography: Jacob K. Olupona." http://www.hds.harvard.edu.

Hastings, Adrian. *The Church in Africa: 1450–1950*. The Oxford History of the Christian Church. Oxford: Oxford University Press, 1994.

———. *A History of African Christianity, 1950–1975*. African Studies Series 26. Cambridge: Cambridge University Press, 1979.

Hastings, Ross. *Missional God, Missional Church: Hope for Re-Evangelizing the West*. Downers Grove, IL: IVP Academic, 2012.

Hexham, Irving. *Understanding World Religions*. Grand Rapids, MI: Zondervan, 2011.

Hinchliff, Peter Bingham. *Cyprian of Carthage and the Unity of the Christian Church*. London: G. Chapman, 1974.

Hoekendijk, Johannes Christiaan, and Erich Walter Pollmann. *Kirche und Volk in der Deutschen Missionswissenschaft*. Munich: Kaiser, 1967.

Hoge, Dean R., and Aniedi Okure. *International Priests in America: Challenges and Opportunities*. Collegeville, MN: Liturgical Press, 2006.

Holy See Press Office. "Synodus Episcoporum Bulletin: Ii Ordinary Special Assembly for Africa of the Synod of Bishops, 4–25 October 2009." Vatican. http://www.vatican.va.

Horton, Michael. "The Ethnocentricity of the American Church Growth Movement." http://www.monergism.com.

Hughes, William. *Dark Africa and the Way Out: Or a Scheme for Civilizing and Evangelizing the Dark Continent*. New York: Negro Universities Press, 1969.

Hume, Susan. "Contemporary African Migration to the United States: Are We Paying Attention?" In *Association of American Geographers*. Los Angeles, 2002.

Huntington, Samuel P. *The Clash of Civilizations and the Remaking of World Order*. New York: Touchstone, 1997.

Ihewulezi, Cajetan N. *Beyond the Color of Skin: Encounters with Religions and Racial Injustice in America*. Charleston, SC: BookSurge, 2006.

Isichei, Elizabeth. *A History of Christianity in Africa: From Antiquity to the Present*. Grand Rapids, MI: Eerdmans, 1995.

Jack, J. W., and Robert Laws. *Daybreak in Livingstonia: The Story of the Livingstonia-Mission, British Central Africa*. New York: Negro Universities Press, 1969.

Jenkins, Philip. "Godless Europe?" *International Bulletin of Missionary Research* 31, no. 3 (2007): 115–18.

————. *God's Continent: Christianity, Islam, and Europe's Religious Crisis*. Oxford: Oxford University Press, 2007.

————. *The Lost History of Christianity: The Thousand-Year Golden Age of the Church in the Middle East, Africa, and Asia, and How It Died.* New York: HarperOne, 2008.

————. *The Next Christendom: The Coming of Global Christianity.* 3rd ed. New York: Oxford University Press, 2011.

Johnson, Todd M., Kenneth R. Ross, and Sandra S. K. Lee. *Atlas of Global Christianity, 1910–2010.* Edinburgh: Edinburgh University Press, 2009.

Josephites. "Our Mission." http://www.josephites.org.

Kalu, Ogbu. *African Christianity: An African Story.* Trenton, NJ: Africa World Press, 2007.

————. "The Anatomy of Reverse Flow in African Christianity: Pentecostalism and Immigrant African Christianity." In *African Christian Presence in the West: New Immigrant Congregations and Transnational Networks in North America and Europe*, edited by Frieder Ludwig and J. Kwabena Asamoah-Gyadu. Trenton, NJ: Africa World Press, 2011.

Kalu, Ogbu, Peter Vethanayagamony, and Edmund Chia. *Mission after Christendom: Emergent Themes in Contemporary Mission.* Louisville, KY: Westminster John Knox Press, 2010.

Kane, J. Herbert. *A Concise History of the Christian World Mission: A Panoramic View of Missions from Pentecost to the Present.* Grand Rapids, MI: Baker, 1982.

Keifert, Patrick R. *Welcoming the Stranger: A Public Theology of Worship and Evangelism.* Minneapolis: Fortress Press, 1992.

Kendall, R. Elliott. *The End of an Era: Africa and the Missionary.* London: SPCK, 1978.

————. "On the Sending of Missionaries: A Call for Restraint." *International Review of Mission* 64, no. 253 (1975): 62–66.

Keswick Week, 1897.

Killingray, David. "African Missionary Activity at Home and Overseas." In *OCMS Public Lectures.* Oxford, 2005.

Kim, Kirsteen. *Joining with the Spirit: Connecting World Church and Local Mission.* London: Epworth, 2009.

————. "The Potential of Pneumatology for Mission in Contemporary Europe." *International Review of Mission* 95, no. 378–79 (2006): 334–40.

Konadu-Agyemang, Kwadwo, Baffour K. Takyi, and John A. Arthur. *The New African Diaspora in North America: Trends, Community Building, and Adaptation.* Lanham, MD: Lexington Books, 2006.

Koschorke, Klaus. *African Identities and World Christianity in the Twentieth Century: Proceedings of the Third International Munich-Freising Conference on the History of Christianity in the Non-Western World (September 15–17, 2004).* Wiesbaden: Harrassowitz, 2005.

Kwiyani, Harvey C. "The Holy Spirit in African Theology." *Transformed* 1, no. 1 (2011).

———. "Pneumatology, Mission, and African Christians in Multicultural Congregations in North America." PhD diss., Luther Seminary, 2012.

Latourette, Kenneth Scott. *A History of the Expansion of Christianity.* New York: Harper, 1937.

Leonard, Karen I. *Immigrant Faiths: Transforming Religious Life in America.* Walnut Creek, CA: AltaMira Press, 2005.

Livingstone, William P. *The Life of Robert Laws of Livingstonia: A Narrative of Missionary Adventure and Achievement.* New York: George H. Doran, 1923.

Lockhart, Kirbey Blair. *Zambia Shall Be Saved: The Nevers Mumba Story.* Lusaka, Zambia: Lockhart, 2001.

Ludwig, Frieder, and J. Kwabena Asamoah-Gyadu. *African Christian Presence in the West: New Immigrant Congregations and Transnational Networks in North America and Europe.* Trenton, NJ: Africa World Press, 2011.

Luther Seminary. "Agora at Luther Seminary." St. Paul. https://www.luthersem.edu.

Macintosh, Andrew Alexander. *A Critical and Exegetical Commentary on Hosea.* Edinburgh: T&T Clark, 1997.

Marley, Robert Nesta. *War.* Kingston, Jamaica: Island Records, 1976.

Mazrui, Ali Al Amin. *Cultural Forces in World Politics.* London: J. Currey, 1990.

Mbiti, John S. *African Religions and Philosophy.* Garden City, NY: Anchor Books, 1970.

————. "Theological Impotence and the Universality of the Church." In *Mission Trends No. 3*, edited by Gerald H. Anderson and Thomas F. Stransky, 6–18. Grand Rapids, MI: Eerdmans, 1976.

McGavran, Donald Anderson. *The Bridges of God: A Study in the Strategy of Missions*. New York: Friendship Press, 1955.

————. *Understanding Church Growth*. Grand Rapids, MI: Eerdmans, 1970.

Meinardus, Otto Friedrich August. *Two Thousand Years of Coptic Christianity*. Cairo: American University in Cairo Press, 1999.

Micklethwait, John, and Adrian Wooldridge. *God Is Back: How the Global Revival of Faith Is Changing the World*. New York: Penguin Press, 2009.

Mott, John R. *The Evangelization of the World in This Generation*. New York: Student Volunteer Movement for Foreign Missions, 1900.

Murray, Stuart. *Church after Christendom*. Milton Keynes, UK: Paternoster, 2005.

Nacpil, Emerito P. "Mission but Not Missionaries." *International Review of Mission* 60, no. 239 (1971): 356–62.

Nasr, Amir. *St. Mark the Apostle and the School of Alexandria*. Cairo: Bishopric of Youth, 1993.

National Association of African Catholics in the United States (NAACUS). "A Welcoming Message from President Ntal Alimas." http://www.naacus.org.

Neill, Stephen, and Owen Chadwick. *A History of Christian Missions*. The Pelican History of the Church. New York: Penguin Books, 1986.

Nelson, Dana K., and Frieder Ludwig. *Mission and Migration: Fifty-Two African and Asian Congregations in Minnesota*. Contemporary Issues in Mission and World Christianity. Minneapolis: Lutheran University Press, 2007.

Newbigin, Lesslie. *Foolishness to the Greeks: The Gospel and Western Culture*. Grand Rapids, MI: Eerdmans, 1986.

————. *The Gospel in a Pluralist Society*. Grand Rapids, MI: Eerdmans, 1989.

————. *The Other Side of 1984: Questions for the Churches.* Geneva: World Council of Churches, 1983.

————. *Unfinished Agenda: An Autobiography.* Geneva: WCC Publications, 1985.

Norman, Andrew. *Robert Mugabe and the Betrayal of Zimbabwe.* Jefferson, NC: McFarland, 2004.

Oden, Thomas C. *The African Memory of Mark: Reassessing Early Church Tradition.* Downers Grove, IL: IVP Academic, 2011.

————. *How Africa Shaped the Christian Mind: Rediscovering the African Seedbed of Western Christianity.* Downers Grove, IL.: IVP Books, 2007.

Okoye, James Chukwuma. "'Third Church' Mission in the 'First World.'" *Spiritan Horizons* 2 (November 2007): 63–70.

Olofinjana, Israel O. "The First African Pentecostal Church in Europe." London. https://israelolofinjana.wordpress.com.

————. *Reverse in Ministry and Missions: Africans in the Dark Continent of Europe.* Milton Keynes, UK: Author House, 2010.

Olson, Roger E. *The Story of Christian Theology: Twenty Centuries of Tradition and Reform.* Downers Grove, IL: InterVarsity Press, 1999.

Olupona, Jacob, and Regina Gemignani. *African Immigrant Religions in America.* New York: New York University Press, 2007.

Origen. *Contra Celsum.* Edited by Henry Chadwick. Cambridge: Cambridge University Press, 1953.

Osborn, Eric Francis. *Tertullian, First Theologian of the West.* New York: Cambridge University Press, 1997.

Otieno, Nicholas, and Hugh McCullum. *Journey of Hope: Towards a New Ecumenical Africa.* Geneva: WCC Publications, 2005.

Ott, Craig, and Harold A. Netland. *Globalizing Theology: Belief and Practice in an Era of World Christianity.* Grand Rapids, MI: Baker, 2006.

Pew Forum on Religion and Public Life. "The Future of the Global Muslim Population: Projections for 2010–2030." http://www.pewforum.org.

Phiri, D. D. *John Chilembwe.* Malawians to Remember. Lilongwe: Longman Malawi, 1976.

————. *Let Us Die for Africa: An African Perspective on the Life and Death of John Chilembwe of Nyasaland.* Exp. ed. Blantyre, Malawi: Central Africana, 1999.

Pohl, Christine D. "Biblical Issues in Mission and Migration." *Missiology* 31, no. 1 (2003): 3–15.

Poloma, Margaret M. *The Assemblies of God at the Crossroads: Charisma and Institutional Dilemmas.* Knoxville: University of Tennessee Press, 1989.

Proprio, Apostolic Letter in the Form of Motu. "Ubicumque et Semper" of the Supreme Pontiff Benedict Xvi Establishing the Pontifical Council for Promoting New Evangelization." Vatican City. http://www.vatican.va.

Prothero, Stephen R. *A Nation of Religions: The Politics of Pluralism in Multireligious America.* Chapel Hill: University of North Carolina Press, 2006.

Ranger, Terence, and Timothy Samuel Shah. *Evangelical Christianity and Democracy in Africa.* Evangelical Christianity and Democracy in the Global South. New York: Oxford University Press, 2008.

Ransford, Oliver. *David Livingstone: The Dark Interior.* London: J. Murray, 1978.

Rieger, Joerg. *Globalization and Theology.* Horizons in Theology. Nashville, TN: Abingdon, 2010.

Robert, Dana Lee. *Christian Mission: How Christianity Became a World Religion.* Malden, MA: Wiley-Blackwell, 2009.

Roetzel, Calvin J. *The World That Shaped the New Testament.* Rev. ed. Louisville, KY: Westminster John Knox Press, 2002.

Ross, Kenneth R. "'Blessed Reflex': Mission as God's Spiral of Renewal." *International Bulletin of Missionary Research* 27, no. 4 (2003): 162–68.

Sanneh, Lamin O. *Disciples of All Nations: Pillars of World Christianity.* Oxford Studies in World Christianity. New York: Oxford University Press, 2008.

————. *Translating the Message: The Missionary Impact on Culture.* American Society of Missiology Series. Maryknoll, NY: Orbis Books, 1989.

Savage, Sara. *Making Sense of Generation Y: The World View of 15- to 25-Year-Olds.* London: Church House Publishing, 2006.

Schroeder, Roger. *What Is the Mission of the Church?: A Guide for Catholics*. Maryknoll, NY: Orbis Books, 2008.

Severus of Al'Ashmunein. *History of the Patriarchs of the Coptic Church of Alexandria: Saint Mark to Theonas (300 AD)*. Paris: P. FAGES, v. g. http://www.tertullian.org.

Shannon, David. *George Liele's Life and Legacy: An Unsung Hero*. Macon, GA: Mercer University Press, 2013.

Shenk, Wilbert R. "Lesslie Newbigin's Contribution to Mission Theology." *International Bulletin of Missionary Research* 24, no. 2 (2000): 59

———. "Recasting Theology of Mission: Impulses from the Non-Western World." *International Bulletin of Missionary Research* 25, no. 3 (2001): 98–107.

Shepperson, George, and Thomas Price. *Independent African: John Chilembwe and the Origins, Setting, and Significance of the Nyasaland Native Rising of 1915*. Edinburgh University Publications: History, Philosophy, and Economics, Edinburgh: University Press, 1958.

Simon, Benjamin. *Afrikanische Kirchen in Deutschland*. Frankfurt am Main: Lembeck, 2003.

———. *From Migrants to Missionaries: Christians of African Origin in Germany*. Studies in the Intercultural History of Christianity. New York: Peter Lang, 2010.

Sindima, Harvey J. *Drums of Redemption: An Introduction to African Christianity*. Contributions to the Study of Religion. Westport, CT: Greenwood Press, 1994.

Smith, David. *Mission after Christendom*. London: Darton Longman & Todd, 2003.

Smith, William. *A Dictionary of Greek and Roman Biography and Mythology, "Lucanus, Terentius."* London: J. Murray, 1876.

Stafford, Tim. "Historian Ahead of His Time: Andrew Walls May Be the Most Important Person You Don't Know." *Christianity Today* (2007). http://www.christianitytoday.com.

Stanley, Brian. *The World Missionary Conference, Edinburgh 1910*. Grand Rapids, MI: Eerdmans, 2009.

Stanley, Henry M. *Through the Dark Continent; or, The Sources of the Nile around the Great Lakes of Equatorial Africa, and Down the Livingstone River to the Atlantic Ocean.* 2 vols. New York: Harper, 1878.

Stoller, Paul. *Money Has No Smell: The Africanization of New York City.* Chicago: University of Chicago Press, 2002.

Stults, Donald Leroy. *Grasping Truth and Reality: Lesslie Newbigin's Theology of Mission to the Western World.* Cambridge, UK: James Clarke, 2009.

Sundkler, Bengt, and Christopher Steed. *A History of the Church in Africa.* Studia Missionalia Upsaliensia 74. New York: Cambridge University Press, 2000.

Synod of Bishops. "Message to the People of God of the Second Special Assembly for Africa of the Synod of Bishops." Vatican. http://www.vatican.va.

Tengatenga, James. *The Umca in Malawi: A History of the Anglican Church, 1861–2010.* Zomba, Malawi: Kachere Series, 2010.

Tennent, Timothy C. *Invitation to World Missions: A Trinitarian Missiology for the Twenty-First Century.* Grand Rapids, MI: Kregel Publications, 2010.

————. *Theology in the Context of World Christianity: How the Global Church Is Influencing the Way We Think about and Discuss Theology.* Grand Rapids, MI: Zondervan, 2007.

Tettey, Wisdom, and Korbla P. Puplampu. *The African Diaspora in Canada: Negotiating Identity and Belonging.* Africa: Missing Voices Series. Calgary, AB: University of Calgary Press, 2005.

Tornasi, Silvano "The Prophetic Mission of the Churches: Theological Perspectives." In *The Prophetic Mission of the Church in Response to Forced Displacement of Peoples: Report of the Ecumenical Consultation, Addis Ababa, November 6–11, 1995,* ed. World Council of Churches, 36–43. Geneva: World Council of Churches, 1996.

Trans-Atlantic Roundtable on Religion and Race. "Mark Gornik: African Christianity, a Gift for the Western Church." http://religionandrace.org.

Uka, Emele Mba. *Missionaries Go Home?: A Sociological Interpretation of an African Response to Christian Missions.* New York: Lang, 1989.

Utietiang, Bekeh. "The Challenge of African Priests in America." Lagos: Gamji. http://www.gamji.com.

Van Rheenen, Gailyn. *Missions: Biblical Foundations and Contemporary Strategies*. Grand Rapids, MI: Zondervan, 1996.

Vethanagamony, Peter. "Mission from the Rest to the West." In *Mission after Christendom: Emergent Themes in Contemporary Mission,* edited by Ogbu Kalu, Peter Vethanayagamony, and Edmund Chia. Louisville, KY: Westminster John Knox Press, 2010.

Währisch-Oblau, Claudia. "From Reverse Mission to Common Mission . . . We Hope: Immigrant Protestant Churches and the 'Programme for Cooperation between German and Immigrant Congregations' of the United Evangelical Mission." *International Review of Mission* 89, no. 354 (2000): 467–83.

Wainwright, Geoffrey. *Lesslie Newbigin: A Theological Life*. New York: Oxford University Press, 2000.

Walls, Andrew F. "Christian Scholarship in Africa in the Twenty-First Century." *Transformation* 19, no. 4 (2002): 217–28.

———. *The Cross-Cultural Process in Christian History: Studies in the Transmission and Appropriation of Faith*. Maryknoll, NY: Orbis Books, 2002.

———. "Mission and Migration: The Diaspora Factor in Christian History." *Journal of African Christian Thought* 5, no. 2 (2002): 3–11.

———. *The Missionary Movement in Christian History: Studies in the Transmission of Faith*. Maryknoll, NY: Orbis Books, 1996.

———. "Structural Problems in Mission Studies." *International Bulletin of Missionary Research* 15, no. 4 (1991): 146–55.

———. "Towards a Theology of Mission." In *African Christian Presence in the West: New Immigrant Congregations and Transnational Networks in North America and Europe*, edited by Frieder Ludwig and J. Kwabena Asamoah-Gyadu, 407–17. Trenton, NJ: Africa World Press, 2011.

Walls, Andrew F., and Cathy Ross. *Mission in the Twenty-First Century: Exploring the Five Marks of Global Mission*. Maryknoll, NY: Orbis Books, 2008.

Walston, Vaughn J., and Robert J. Stevens. *African-American Experience in World Mission: A Call beyond Community.* Pasadena, CA: William Carey Library, 2009.

Ward, Maisie, and Henri Godin. *France Pagan? The Mission of Abbe Godin.* New York: Sheed and Ward, 1949.

Warner, R. Stephen. *A Church of Our Own: Disestablishment and Diversity in American Religion.* New Brunswick, NJ: Rutgers University Press, 2005.

Warner, R. Stephen, and Judith G. Wittner. *Gatherings in Diaspora: Religious Communities and the New Immigration.* Philadelphia: Temple University Press, 1998.

White, Landeg. *Magomero: Portrait of an African Village.* New York: Cambridge University Press, 1987.

William, C. Peter. *The Ideal of the Self-Governing Church: A Study in Victorian Missionary Strategy.* Leiden: Brill, 1990.

Wilson, George Herbert. *The History of the Universities' Mission to Central Africa.* Freeport, NY: Books for Libraries Press, 1971.

Winter, Gibson. *The Suburban Captivity of the Churches: An Analysis of Protestant Responsibility in the Expanding Metropolis.* Garden City, NY: Doubleday, 1961.

World Council of Churches. "CWME Meeting, Mexico City, Mexico, 1963." In *WCC Archives.* http://archives.oikoumene.org.

World Trumpet Mission. "A Brief History of World Trumpet Mission." Kampala, Uganda.

Zeleza, Tiyambe Paul. "Contemporary African Migrations in a Global Context." *African Issues* 30, no. 1 (2002).

Index

African Christianity's
  influence on, 51
declining, 5–6
dichotomies in, 28, 59–60
diversity in, 81, 134
evangelization in, 166
mainline denominations
  in, and immigrants'
  spiritual needs, 122
as minority, 134
missionary crisis in, 67
superiority complex of,
  202–3
theology of, beginning as
  African theology, 39
Western civilization, prosperity
  of, linked to the gospel, 8
white supremacy, 138
Who Is Afraid of the Holy Ghost?
  (Adogame), 113
Williams, Prince, 76–77

Winter, Gibson, 172
Wooldridge, Adrian, 89
*Word Made Global: Stories of
  African Christianity in
  New York City* (Gornik),
  94, 99, 100
world Christianity, 75, 136–37,
  182
  effect of, 133
  reinvigorating Western
  Christianity, 19
world theologies, 10, 156, 159
World War I, effect of, on
  mission, 8
worship
  communal nature of, 164–65
  length of services, 114, 151

Zambia, 21, 24
Zimbabwe, 24
Zulu, Shaka, 160

PREVIOUSLY PUBLISHED IN THE AMERICAN SOCIETY OF MISSIOLOGY SERIES

The American Society of Missiology Series, published in collaboration with Orbis Books, seeks to publish scholarly works of high merit and wide interest on numerous aspects of missiology—the study of Christian mission in its historical, social, and theological dimensions. Able presentations on new and creative approaches to the practice and understanding of mission will receive close attention from the ASM Series Committee.

1. *Protestant Pioneers in Korea*, Everett Nichols Hunt Jr.
2. *Catholic Politics in China and Korea*, Eric O. Hanson
3. *From the Rising of the Sun*, James M. Phillips
4. *Meaning Across Cultures*, Eugene A. Nida and William D. Reyburn
5. *The Island Churches of the Pacific*, Charles W. Forman
6. *Henry Venn: Missionary Statesman*, Wilbert R. Shenk
7. *No Other Name?* Paul F. Knitter
8. *Toward a New Age in Christian Theology*, Richard Henry Drummond
9. *The Expectation of the Poor*, Guillermo Cook
10. *Eastern Orthodox Mission Theology Today*, James J. Stamoolis
11. *Confucius, the Buddha, and Christ*, Ralph R. Covell
12. *The Church and Cultures*, Louis J. Luzbetak, SVD
13. *Translating the Message: The Missionary Impact on Culture*, Lamin Sanneh
14. *An African Tree of Life*, Thomas G. Christensen
15. *Missions and Money* (second edition), Jonathan J. Bonk
16. *Transforming Mission*, David J. Bosch
17. *Bread for the Journey*, Anthony J. Gittins, C.S.Sp.
18. *New Face of the Church in Latin America*, edited by Guillermo Cook
19. *Mission Legacies*, edited by Gerald H. Anderson, Robert T. Coote, Norman A. Horner, and James M. Phillips
20. *Classic Texts in Mission and World Christianity*, edited by Norman E. Thomas
21. *Christian Mission: A Case Study Approach*, Alan Neely
22. *Understanding Spiritual Power*, Marguerite G. Kraft
23. *Missiological Education for the 21st Century: The Book, the Circle, and the Sandals*, edited by J. Dudley Woodberry, Charles Van Engen, and Edgar J. Elliston

24. *Dictionary of Mission: Theology, History, Perspectives*, edited by Karl Müller, SVD, Theo Sundermeier, Stephen B. Bevans, SVD, and Richard H. Bliese
25. *Earthen Vessels and Transcendent Power: American Presbyterians in China, 1837–1952*, G. Thompson Brown
26. *The Missionary Movement in American Catholic History*, Angelyn Dries, OSF
27. *Mission in the New Testament: An Evangelical Approach*, edited by William J. Larkin Jr. and Joel W. Williams
28. *Changing Frontiers of Mission*, Wilbert R. Shenk
29. *In the Light of the Word: Divine Word Missionaries of North America*, Ernest Brandewie
30. *Constants in Context: A Theology of Mission for Today*, Stephen B. Bevans, SVD, and Roger P. Schroeder, SVD
31. *Changing Tides: Latin America and World Mission Today*, Samuel Escobar
32. *Gospel Bearers, Gender Barriers: Missionary Women in the Twentieth Century*, edited by Dana L. Robert
33. *Church: Community for the Kingdom*, John Fuellenbach, SVD
34. *Mission in Acts: Ancient Narratives in Contemporary Context*, edited by Robert L. Gallagher and Paul Hertig
35. *A History of Christianity in Asia: Volume I, Beginnings to 1500*, Samuel Hugh Moffett
36. *A History of Christianity in Asia: Volume II, 1500–1900*, Samuel Hugh Moffett
37. *A Reader's Guide to Transforming Mission*, Stan Nussbaum
38. *The Evangelization of Slaves and Catholic Origins in Eastern Africa*, Paul V. Kollman, CSC
39. *Israel and the Nations: A Mission Theology of the Old Testament*, James Chukwuma Okoye, C.S.Sp.
40. *Women in Mission: From the New Testament to Today*, Susan E. Smith
41. *Reconstructing Christianity in China: K. H. Ting and the Chinese Church*, Philip L. Wickeri
42. *Translating the Message: The Missionary Impact on Culture* (second edition), Lamin Sanneh
43. *Landmark Essays in Mission and World Christianity*, edited by Robert L. Gallagher and Paul Hertig
44. *World Mission in the Wesleyan Spirit*, Darrell L. Whiteman and Gerald H. Anderson (published by Province House, Franklin, TN)
45. *Miracles, Missions, & American Pentecostalism*, Gary B. McGee
46. *The Gospel among the Nations: A Documentary History of Inculturation*, Robert A. Hunt
47. *Missions and Unity: Lessons from History, 1792–2010*, Norman E. Thomas (published by Wipf and Stock, Eugene, OR)
48. *Mission and Culture: The Louis J. Luzbetak Lectures*, edited by Stephen B. Bevans
49. *Comprehending Mission: The Questions, Methods, Themes, Problems, and Prospects of Missiology*, Stanley H. Skreslet
50. *Christian Mission among the Peoples of Asia*, Jonathan Y. Tan